The Tragedy of Vietnam, Again

"Through the Eyes of a Medic"

By Christopher Noble
(Army Medical Service Corps, 1967-68)

Copyright © 2008 Chris Noble
All rights reserved.

ISBN: 1-4196-5463-2
ISBN-13: 9781419654633

Visit www.booksurge.com to order additional copies.
Visit www.lewisstreetbooks.com for book information.

In Memory of:

Kimmy Hobbs, Medic, Killed in action, 1968

George Coppage, Medic, Killed in action, 1968

Walter Powell, Medic, Killed in action, 1968

Steven Nussbaumer, Medic, Killed in action, 1968

May they rest in peace

Alpha Bandaid, 1968

Contributions:

Winny and Tyler Blether, Bob Jones, Rick Laine, Lincoln Musto, Connor Nyhart, Jay Pateakos, David King, Robert Johnston – for your memory and the use of your Alpha Troop photos, and my wife for all the valuable input, encouragement and advice you all gave me.

Contents

i	Foreword
1	Going to Vietnam
	- The First Leg
7	- The Second Leg
12	Map of Vietnam
15	- The Third Leg
17	- The Fourth and Last Leg
23	My First and Only Guard Duty
31	Building an Aid Station
32	Sketch of Aid Station area
59	The Battle of the Pink Ville
85	Changing of the Guard
95	Trade Bait and To Save a Life
123	Getting in Trouble
141	Someone Looked Out For Me
151	An Unexpected Reward
191	Overnight Visitors
199	Surprise, Surprise
211	Battle of Tam Ky
247	Fear
261	Quang Naig
303	Conscientious Objector
313	The Court-Martial
337	How Some People Got Killed & Drug

345	Press
353	The Politician
355	The Tragedy of Vietnam
359	Politicians & Press – Vietnam
367	Politicians & Press – Iraq
381	Appendix 1 – A Chronology of Events
395	Appendix 2 – Definition of Terms
406	Appendix 3 – 1/1 Armor Cavalry's Battle Map
408	Appendix 4 – Sketch of Hawk Hill

Foreword

I was at my brother's condo where a pleasant looking young man came up to me and asked, "I understand that you were a medic in Vietnam; what was it like to be a medic?"

"Being a medic was terribly boring in the ho-hum routine of everyday life, which was interjected, on occasion, with sheer terror," I answered.

"What type of terror are you talking about?" this young man asked.

My mind wandered back forty years, as I visualized the gravel road of Highway One, as Band-Aid rumbled along. "A tank was no more than thirty feet ahead of us, minding its own business. From out of the underbrush, along the side of the road were two flash points as both RPGs (Rocket Propelled Grenade) simultaneously slammed into the thick steel hull of this tank. The tank swerved off the road and came to an abrupt stop at the road's edge."

"My gut tightened up into a tight ball, as my trembling thumb keyed the radio switch on my helmet as I report, "Alpha Six, this is Band-Aid the tank right in from of us has just taken two RPG rounds."

The Tragedy of Vietnam, Again

"Roger, Band-Aid," Alpha Six answers, as all vehicles come to a defensive stop.

"I saw the tank's driver slid out of the driver's compartment, he was in great pain; it looked like his hand had been hit. The Tank's commander slid out of the turret, leaving a bright red streak of blood, marking his decent down the tank's side. There was no sign of the loader; he was still inside the tank."

"I went immediately to the driver and quickly placed a large soft gauze pad in his hand and then wrapped it with an ACE bandage, which was so mangled by the force of one of the rocket's blast; his little finger was where his thumb used to be, and his thumb was no longer part of his body."

The young man, who asked the question, looked at me in horror and dismay at what had been said, so I asked, "Is there a lesson to be learned in this?"

The young man shook his head, not understanding my question.

"One lesson is our politicians and government leaders had better be honest with their intelligence and the analysis of that intelligence, because there are very serious consequences to each and every action our government officials make. When our government sends our youth off to fight on foreign soil, they do so to defend and protect our nation, here in North America, nothing else is acceptable!"

"Are you talking about Vietnam or Iraq?" the young man asks.

Foreword

"I'm talking about both, because Iraq is nothing more than Vietnam all over again!"

This book is not only an attempt to tell the true story about this medical platoon during the period of 1967-1968 and how the platoon operated in the field—through the eyes of one of its members—but also how the Vietnam experience affected me, a young, immature person, my reflection on the world, war, and values about life and camaraderie.

What I did not know at the time was that governments don't tell their people the truth all the time and it's been that way for centuries. Governments have been deceiving people in order to justify ill-gotten gains. Vietnam and Iraq are no exceptions. One lie our government spun during the Vietnam War was that North and South Vietnam were two different countries, and the North had invaded South Vietnam. The truth of the matter was that North and South Vietnam had been one entity for approximately two thousand years, but was divided after World War II, when France split Vietnam into two separate countries.

Another fact I did not realize was that the media is a business with its own agenda and often the media does not report the truth. I did not realize this fact while I was in Vietnam, because we never saw any news while in the country.

Some events in this book were described in broad details; other, less significant events have been compacted into other events to keep the story fluid so that the reader can experience the events and places described. For example, I was assigned to Fifty-Fifth Medical Group Headquarters for approximately seven weeks before I was sent to the 1/1 Cav. I was the I Corp, II Corp medical regulator, and was in charge of the movement of all Army wounded personnel for the northern half of South Vietnam. I was the lowest-ranking officer at headquarters and every higher-ranking officer (two full colonels, three lieutenant colonels, two majors and one captain) all told me how I should do my job, yet none of these people could give me consistent orders and they often contradicted each other. As a result I requested a transfer. The chapter "Trade Bate" describes Quin Nhon and a medical evacuation that took place while I was at Fifty-Fifth Medical Group Headquarters.

I have used expressions that belong to my family, such as the expression about a skunk; it was a saying my grandfather used to use. I have used the real names of individuals; if I didn't remember the individuals involved, I substituted the names of medics who did an outstanding job. I also used the names of medics and friends of the medics who were killed in Vietnam. This is an attempt to memorialize these people and let them continue to live through this book. I made up names of people who were involved in discredited events, or Vietnamese who might get into trouble if the Vietnamese government today should hear my story. This is a story about the pride and honor of my fel-

Foreword

low soldiers and is not intended to humiliate anyone. If there is any similarity to anyone's name, this is totally unintentional.

It is important to understand the attitudes of many high school and college students during the early and mid 1960s, the most formative years of the future Vietnam veteran. A great deal of worldwide headline-making news was constantly being thrown at us. The future Vietnam vet also had a lot on his mind besides current events, such as concerns about passing his next English or math exam, who'd he go out with the following weekend, and, of course, who was in love with whom.

Most teenagers had heard about Vietnam, but had no clue where this place was in relationship to the United States. Vietnam was somewhere over there, they said, gesturing toward the westerly sky. For all practical purposes, we knew more about the moon than we did about Southeast Asia; at least we had seen the moon and thus it had more significance.

There was no real reason for the youth of America to fear Vietnam, because in 1964 Lyndon Johnson ran for the presidency as a peace candidate. He has been quoted as saying, "I won't send American boys to do the fighting for Asian troops." The American government said nothing to the American public about their forthcoming plans.

There were protesters who got a lot of press coverage, as they tried to disrupt almost any type of govern-

The Tragedy of Vietnam, Again

ment function in order to get their message across. We heard reports of pacifists laying down in front of troop trains in California; antiwar leaflets being mailed to troops fighting in Vietnam; and widows of men killed in Vietnam receiving ugly telephone calls in the middle of the night. There were people who set themselves afire and burned to death, and those who burned their draft cards and the American flag. My friends and I knew not one of those people, and we looked down upon them. We felt that each antiwar protester was not only a disgrace to our country, but, more importantly, they were cowards and were trying to avoid military service. Traditionally, young men were taught it was their duty to defend and protect our country when called upon to do so. When that time came it was a matter of stepping forward and serving one's country, not to question whether this action was right or wrong.

I was amazed that so many of my contemporaries forty years ago had no idea about Vietnam and about the events that prompted the war. I've put together a chronology of some of the more significant events leading up to my and my friend's departure for Vietnam. This list impressively shows what went on in our world, and what effects the war had upon the United States and the rest of the world. Many of the major news events were not only significant, but overshadowed all other news, especially the Vietnam news, sometimes for weeks or even months. (See Appendix #1 – A Chronology of Events.)

Going To Vietnam – The First Leg

My generation grew up hearing the honorable stories of the victories of our parents in World War II, and while at college, most of us heard about the United States military; for the most part, they were all bad stories about the military. We heard about boot camp, drill instructors, about people who couldn't handle the pressure, and about those who were eaten up by the military machine and unceremoniously discarded. I had hoped to join the Air Force or the Navy to become a pilot, but both services were jammed full of applicants from the service academies, ROTC, and/or OCS; my college had no ROTC or military associations, which made officer enlisting more difficult. I joined the US military, trying not to get drafted by the Army or Marines, because in my opinion, that was an excellent way to get killed. I had only one opportunity to obtain a commission and that was to become a medic with the Army Medical Service Corps.

After a lengthy acceptance process and having to go in a roundabout way, I finally received orders to join the Army Medical Service Corps at Fort Sam Houston, in San Antonio, Texas. I went off blindly to fulfill my

The Tragedy of Vietnam, Again

military service. I had no idea about what was in store for me, but I was convinced that I had been called to serve my country, the same way my dad and uncles were called to serve in World War II; my grandfather in World War I; my great-grandfather in the Civil War; his ever-so-great-grandfather in the Revolutionary War; and generations back to the French and Indian Wars before that. It was my turn to do my part and I was proud to be in the military and believed in what I was doing. After all, I believed the United States government was the most powerful and most respected government in the entire world, bar none.

I completed basic officer training and was terribly disappointed, for I felt that Boy Scout Camp was much more difficult, physically. My first assignment was in Washington, D.C., at Walter Reed Field Activities Unit. I became part of a tri-service study team, and our task was to develop a glossary of common medical terms and definitions for all of the medical services. This was a precursor to computerizing through one computer system all medical records of the Army, Navy, Air Force, and Marine Corps.

The advantage to this tri-service medical computer program was that doctors from one branch of service could access any patient's medical file and treat that patient anywhere. That doctor could also upgrade the patient's file immediately, thus greatly improving the level of medical care.

Going to Vietnam – First Leg

I was told many years later, by the registrar of Walter Reed General Hospital, "In my opinion, that study group is the only tri-service group to produce anything of any value." He also told me, "A sitting board of admirals and generals guard the work your group produced and any and all changes to this work has to be approved by this sitting board of senior officers."

All single officers living and working in the Washington, D.C., area have a very lively life, intertwined with the pomp and flair of the military. It was as if we lived in a grand parade. When there was any downtime, a doctor friend of mine taught me some of the finer points about emergency first aid, but only as time permitted. I appreciated these tutorials, because I had a strong feeling I would get orders to go to Vietnam.

After a year of high living, the study team's work was complete. I got my orders for Vietnam. I felt well prepared to go; I had friends from basic training who were already in Vietnam. Some had written me letters and patients from the hospital gave me free advice, as well as a clear picture of what to expect once I arrived in the country. They told me what I should bring and what not to bring, even though many contradicted what the Army said we should take with us. I was told about the climate, heard many war stories about the VC, the NVA, the heat and the rain, the bugs and snakes. They also told me about R&R (Rest and Relaxation), where

The Tragedy of Vietnam, Again

to go and where not to go, all the good stuff and all the bad points concerning this tropical paradise I was about to enter.

Finally, my report date loomed before me, after a two-week leave at home in mid-November. Per orders, I dressed in my summer khaki uniform, and my mom drove me to the airport. It was a cold, rainy November day, three days before Thanksgiving. I felt bad to leave her, because my dad had died a short while before. She cried as we waved good-bye; crying is out of character for my mother, because she was a very strong person.

I hope all will go well for her this coming year, flashed through my mind as I walked to the plane, as a naive, patriotic citizen, doing my duty to protect this fine country of ours.

The flight to San Francisco was uneventful. I sat next to a woman who appeared to be a "flower child," only she was no child. She looked about forty-five, with long, stringy hair. She wore sandals, thus allowing me to see her dirty feet, which really turned me on. I could envision her carrying some sort of protest sign or singing some sort of chanting slogan, thinking she was very smart but being really a total pain in the ass. I could tell she was thrilled about having me sit next to her, in my uniform, so we sat in hostile silence, without uttering one word during the entire trip across the country.

The plane landed at 2:30 p.m. I caught a bus to downtown San Francisco; it was almost twenty-four

Going to Vietnam – First Leg

hours before I had to report to the Oakland Army Terminal. I decided to live it up and go to the Statler Hotel. It was in a convenient location right beside the bus terminal. I struggled with my duffel bag, which weighed seventy-five pounds, and my flight bag and a briefcase. Total weight must had been 110 pounds, most of it unnecessary junk; so much for believing my friends, patients, and the Army.

The clerk at the reservation desk informed me it cost seventeen dollars per night for the cheapest room. I laughed but really wanted to cry. If I paid seventeen dollars for the room, then I wouldn't have enough for a good supper or money left over in the event of an emergency. The hotel obviously had other military people with the same problem, because the clerk suggested a less expensive hotel four blocks away, so off I started.

Once outside the hotel's main door, a porter asked, "Excuse me, are you looking for a cheaper hotel?" I nodded my head yes, and the porter grabbed the lightest of the bags and ran across the street to the Hotel Don. It had a great façade, almost as impressive as the Statler's. The price was right so I took a room. Once off the lift, I suddenly knew why the Hotel Don was so much cheaper. The building hadn't had anything done to it since the beginning of the Korean War. The Don was one tired place, but what really mattered was that there were no bugs in the bed. I didn't need any bites, lice, or any other type of vermin. This was the first leg of my journey toward Vietnam.

The Second Leg

That night, I did not dare to eat anything at the Hotel Don, for fear of what the kitchen might look like. I didn't care if the price was right, I wasn't going to get myself sick. Since this was my last night in the "Good Old U S of A," for maybe a very long time, I decided to find one of the best restaurants on Fisherman's Wharf. I don't remember its name, but I did have a great meal. I also had fun riding the trolley cars and seeing San Francisco for the first time.

The next morning I said good-bye to the Hotel Don, free of bug bites, and caught a bus to the Oakland Army Terminal. There was a large group of people carrying protest signs at the main gate, all being kept under control by a number of uniformed police officers with paddy wagons just off to one side, if needed. I looked for the lady on my plane, but didn't see her, as the bus plowed through the crowd and stopped in front of the place where I was to report.

I entered the building without any concerns about being ready for Vietnam. Walter Reed had done an excellent job; I had already received all the shots I needed and all my paperwork was in order. I was ready to go!

The Tragedy of Vietnam, Again

Wrong, or at least one specialist fourth class enlisted man didn't think so. He made me get three more shots and take a huge malaria pill. After that ordeal, for the first time I was issued some Army clothes that actually fit; it was hard not to wear jungle fatigues that did not fit. I squeezed this new gear into my overstuffed duffel bag.

For the next three hours, I filled out forms, had my teeth mapped, fingerprints taken; most everything done was to identify me in the event that I got myself killed. All in-processing personnel were briefed about Vietnam, the do's and don'ts once we got there, and every person I spoke to wanted at least ten copies of my orders. I was finally told to cross the street and register at the officers' guest house and to return the next day at 10:00 a.m. for flight information.

At the guest house, which was on a par with the Hotel Don, I was assigned a room. My roommate was a warrant officer who was a helicopter pilot. He had four children and was just thrilled about having to go back for his second tour of duty. He wasn't happy and wasn't very good company, but as a good career officer he did as he'd been ordered. We spent the rest of the day and part of the night in the officers' club, not doing very much.

The next morning, we all met at the prescribed time and place, and were informed that the buses would depart at 11:30 p.m. for Travis Air Force Base, and our plane would depart at 2:00 a.m. Our first stop would

The Second Leg

be Hawaii and there would be a forty-five-minute layover to refuel the plane. The second stop would be Okinawa, Japan, and again there would be another forty-five-minute refueling layover. The third and last stop would be Vietnam; total flight time was approximately twenty-three hours in the air. Surprisingly enough, everything ran smoothly, but then I guessed the Army had had enough practice by that time to work out any glitches.

My emotions really worked overtime, and I guessed that all 180 passengers more or less had the exact same feelings as I; I was scared of the unknown that lay ahead of me. What unit would I be assigned to? What would my duties be? Would I get hurt? More importantly, would I get killed? Not that I'd know much about that, if it should happen.

I was angry at the people who were ducking the draft; I had little respect for the people who ran off to Canada or some other country. For all I cared, they could stay there and never return to the United States. The people who were 4-F or 1-Y I didn't mind; they took their chances with the military and came up the big winners, by being medically unfit for military service.

Inside me there was an urge for adventure that said, *go for it!* There was also a family tradition that I must live up to; I had friends in Vietnam and none of them had been hurt. The chances of me getting hurt were slim at best! I didn't know about all these other people

The Tragedy of Vietnam, Again

in this group; I reassured myself by thinking that they might all get killed, but I would be all right.

As the plane was loaded, I looked around to see if there were military police lurking in the shadows ready to arrest anyone who decided, at the last moment, to take an acute right turn and not board the plane. I saw nobody who would force anyone on board; we all navigated our own bodies across the runway, up the stairs, and into the aircraft.

The flight to Vietnam was a terribly long trip, and TWA's flight crew fed us at least four full-blown meals. We missed Thanksgiving totally due to crossing the International Date Line. The closer we got to Vietnam, the greater the tension grew within the cabin in relation to our proximity to our destination; there was a deathly quiet, only the vibration of the engines and the air-conditioning made noise. I was sure that the return trip of this plane would have a very different environment.

The intercom broke the silence as a cheerful voice stated, "Off to our right you can see the Republic of Vietnam." The passengers all became unsettled; there was a murmur throughout the plane, as people tried to peek out windows on the right side. The noise level inside the cabin rose with a lot of nervous talk.

The plane was flying at approximately 15,000 feet, as we approached Ben Hoa Air Base. The TWA pilot suddenly cranked the DC-9 over on about a forty-five- to fifty- degree angle, making three very tight turns,

The Second Leg

and brought us in on a "Ba, Ba Black Sheep" type landing. The intercom said, "Sorry about that landing, men, but I didn't think we should give anyone on the ground a good clear shot at us. Welcome to Vietnam and good luck," We taxied to a stop in front of a medium sized wooden building with a large group of GIs cheering in front of it, all screaming and shouting, "Hey, you're my replacement, good luck, sucker."

The Tragedy of Vietnam, Again

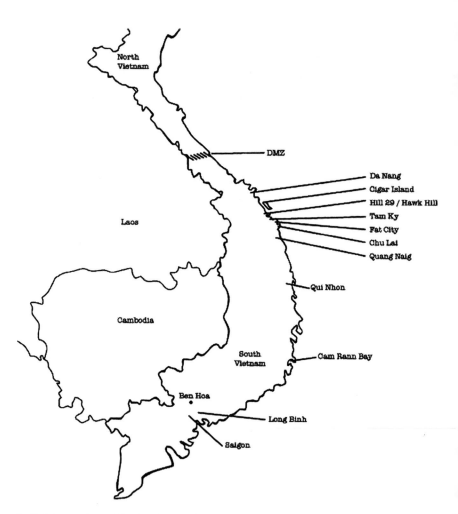

South Vietnam and most of the places mentioned in this book.

The Third Leg

It was about 4:00 p.m. local time on the 25th of November 1967. The drive from Ben Hoa Air Base to the replacement depot gave us our first close look at Vietnam. Vietnam was a dump by our standards; the buildings were shacks. The streets were infested with trucks, jeeps, motorbikes, little motor scooter trucks, bicycles, men, women, children, some—but not many—dogs (the Vietnamese like to eat dogs and cats, as I found out later), water buffalo, and chickens. You name it; it was there in the streets. Heavy metal screens covered all the open windows on our bus to prevent any hand grenades from coming inside the bus; this was a very comforting thought. Every single Vietnamese person I saw was automatically one of the enemy and I was on constant alert.

I spent two nights at the Ninetieth Replacement Depot, called "repo-depot." It reminded me of the television program, "Combat." During my first night, I saw Army equipment I'd never seen before, as I counted fifteen tracked vehicles, three or four tanks, four convoys of about fifty trucks each, and many other types of military vehicles, as they passed our barracks. We

The Tragedy of Vietnam, Again

were all told that if we heard a siren to run immediately—if need be, naked—to the nearest bunker or to jump into a ditch and stay there until we were told to come out.

The next day I was told by the surgeon general's office that I had been assigned to the Americal Division, in the I Corps, for further assignment. My route took me from Ton Son Nuit, to Cam Rhan Bay, to Qui Non, to Chu Lai. This trip took longer than the entire trip to Vietnam; it was thirty-five hours and a lot of waiting.

I was exhausted as the large C-130 cargo plane landed on a metal runway, in the middle of a rice paddy, in Chu Lai. The back ramp dropped and all the departing passengers had to lug their own bags down the ramp and over to a shack at one side of the runway. "Welcome to Chu Lai," was painted over the only door. There was a notice posted on the inside wall, "All AMED (Army Medical) Personnel call this number to arrange for transportation", I called.

I could see that Chu Lai was just being built, as the jeep that came for me sped over a rise and the wheels almost came off the ground. I could see a multitude of activities like an ant colony busy at work. Bulldozers were whacking down trees and leveling off the ground, survey crews were shooting angles and making notation of all information in field books. The Army Corps of Engineers were erecting tropical buildings not only in all directions, but all in neat rows, as if they were soldiers standing at attention.

The Third Leg

There were helipads and parking lots, roads, drainage ditches, a chapel, two major hospitals; an entire town was being built, all at the same time. The Americal Division was brand new in the country, and they had a lot of work to do in order to become established.

I reported to Lieutenant Colonel Anderson, the Division surgeon general. He reminded me of Robert Young, the actor, a very low-key person.

"Welcome to Chu Lai, Lieutenant Noble," he said as he crossed the room and shook my hand. "Please excuse this mess, we're just moving in. We're lucky to be one of the very first buildings to be finished. Would you like some coffee?"

"Yes, sir, I'd love a cup," I replied, wanting not to offend my very much superior officer.

A few minutes later, a Sergeant Major brought in the coffee and it looked plain disgusting. The coffee was blacker than black and it had an oil slick floating on top. It reminded me of a cup of creosote, so I did not drink it for health reasons.

As LTC Anderson shuffled through some papers he said, "Chris, I'm assigning you to the First Squadron of the First Armored Cavalry; it's called the First of the First Cav, and it's a really good unit. This unit is the Americal's power and muscle, because of its fire power, maneuverability, and speed. The 1/1 Cav is also an important historical unit, in the United States Army. It was the very first cavalry unit in the United

The Tragedy of Vietnam, Again

States Army, and it's the most battle-honored unit in the United States Army to date; believe me, this is a very good unit."

I could tell Colonel Anderson liked this unit, as he continued talking about the unit's activities, as if he were a tour guide. I kind of understood what a "track" was, but I could not visualize what it looked like. I knew nothing about army warfare; it had not been part of my Medical Service Corps training. I decided it was best to keep my mouth shut, and keep my eyes and ears wide-open, because in a short time, many of my questions would be answered.

"Sergeant Major," LTC Anderson called out, "We have to get Lieutenant Noble over to Division Personnel so he can sign in, and then get him over to the helipad. We need to hurry in order for him to catch the First of the First's evening chopper."

"Yes, sir, I'll take care of it," The sergeant major replied.

Colonel Anderson wished me well, patted me on the back and said, "If I can be of help to you in any way, you get in touch with me, and that's an order."

I thanked the colonel and promised that I'd be in touch, thus ending the third leg of my journey.

The Fourth and Last Leg

As the helicopter took off, I was crammed in between the helicopter's roof and on top of huge mail bags that filled the entire cabin of the unarmed Huey helicopter. Large block letters stenciled on the sides of the bags indicated what bag went to which troop; Fat City, Alpha Troop, Bravo Troop, Charlie Troop, and Headquarters Troop. Surprisingly enough, the mail bags were quite comfortable to lie on, and I had an excellent view since there were no doors on the helicopter.

The rotor blades turned faster and faster, as a high-pitched whine developed within the engine. The chopper started to skittle about and then slowly rose up into the air, about thirty feet. Then, suddenly, the pilot dropped the nose of the aircraft and Chu Lai's compound started racing past the opening where a door once was installed; this was fantastic, it was my first helicopter ride.

We sped around, barely clearing the treetops and huts, and small boats zipped by. Then the helicopter suddenly shot straight up into the sky, like a fast-mov-

The Tragedy of Vietnam, Again

ing elevator on an express run, and my stomach was left at ground level. The land fell far below; what a beautiful place Vietnam was.

Some say Southeast Asia would become a resort area. Looking out the open doorway, the sky was a light blue with light puffy clouds floating high overhead. The sea was a dark, rich, greenish-blue that ran along one of the most beautiful beaches I'd ever seen. We certainly didn't have beaches like that back in New England. The sand was bright and the beach was the width of about a football field, and it ran all the way around the huge crescent bay, as far as the eye could see, and stuck way out into the South China Sea.

We followed a light brown ribbon off to our left that cut through the rice paddies. The ground looked like a giant green quilt. The light brown ribbon was Highway One, starting in Saigon and ending in Hanoi. The other side of Highway One, about two miles away to the west, was a mountain range. It appeared to rise about 1,500 to 2,000 feet above sea level. It had very steep slopes and the tops of the hills appeared to be extremely acute.

The whole sky beyond the mountains started turning orange as the sun got ready to set. On the other side of these mountains was the beginning of the Central Highlands that ran into Laos.

The Fourth and Last Leg

A sign "FAT CITY" came into view far below, painted on the roof of a tropical hut in a compound right next to Highway One. The helicopter made a wide circle and then dropped quickly out of the sky. Once the helicopter landed, I observed a large white sign in front of a tropical hut that read, "FAT CITY GENERAL," and had a large red cross below it. I dragged my gear out of the plane, while a door gunner removed the large FAT CITY mail bag, dropped it off to one side of the helipad, and then got back on board the helicopter.

I noticed a lieutenant quickly walking down the main street yelling over the sound of the chopper, "Are you Lieutenant Noble?"

"Yes," I yelled back. He introduced himself as Don Venn, the executive officer of Headquarters Troop. He knew I was on my way, because Division had called the unit.

"Let's get your gear over to the aid station and then grab some supper. We eat early around here, because after the sun sets, we're totally blacked out."

He helped me with my bags and introduced me to sergeant Klem, my NCOIC (noncommissioned officer in charge), of the medical platoon. "Where is Captain Davis?" I asked, knowing that he was the squadron's physician, and my immediate boss.

The Tragedy of Vietnam, Again

"Oh, Doc's up at Hill 29," Klem answered in a slow, heavy Southern accent. It was so strong I had to listen extremely carefully, or I might not understand him. Sergeant Klem was an older, graying black man, who was slowing down as his military career was coming to a close.

"You, Sergeant Klem and two other medics are here in Fat City," Don Venn explained. "We'll all be here for about three more weeks, or when the Eighty-Second Airborne arrives in country. They're going to take over Fat City as their base camp. Let's get some chow before it's too late." I was guided across the dirt road, with white painted rocks that lined the edges, and we went into the chow hall.

"The major is waiting to meet you, he's over there," Lt. Venn informed me, as he nodded his head when we entered the building. We picked up our dinner trays and went through the serving line. Don Venn led the way to a table that had the only major sitting proudly at it.

"Sir, may we join you?" Venn asked. "Lt. Noble just arrived on the mail chopper, sir."

"Oh, yes, yes, sit down, and welcome to the unit, Lieutenant," The major stated, somewhat confused, as if he weren't expecting me.

We had disrupted all the small talk going on between tables, about what card game was going to be played that evening and what the stakes should be. I sat down and the three of us ate our meal over the usual

The Fourth and Last Leg

small talk of where were you from, how was your trip, where did you go to college, etc.

I took an immediate dislike to Major Bangstrom. My inner feelings told me, *He's not a nice person.* He was very proud of the fact that the medics not only built their own perimeter bunker, but they manned the bunker every night. I knew this was against Army regulations, because medics can't be tied to one spot, like on guard duty, under these conditions. I tried to question the major about this, but backed off immediately. The long and the short regarding FAT CITY—it was five very long weeks; a lot of this had to do with my predecessor's early departure.

Aid Station, TOC at top of hill, background

The Tragedy of Vietnam, Again

Rice drying just out side of Fat City at 2,000 feet

Main street in Fat City

My First and Only Guard Duty

Major Bangstrom was an asshole. People write books and make movies about his type of person. The hard-drinking, card-playing career officer who's in love with himself, while he breaks his own rules, making life miserable for everyone else, and manipulates the system so he can generate fake awards for himself and his buddies. These egotistical SOBs love to see their names in print; they dislike all noncombat arms personnel, enlisted people, and anyone who gets in their way.

Major Bangstrom insisted that I pull AOD (administrative officer of the day; this was officers' nighttime guard duty.) I objected but it made no difference and Captain Prothero, who was the headquarter troop's commanding officer, quietly advised me, "Don't get in a pissing contest with a skunk, because you can't out-piss a skunk! When your turn comes, I'll help you."

So, I took his advice and kept my mouth shut; when my turn came, the captain assigned Master Sergeant Powell to help me with guard duty, since this was my very first time pulling AOD. I was instructed by

The Tragedy of Vietnam, Again

Captain Prothero, "If you need any help, you're to call me on the direct phone to my bunk."

This made me feel better, knowing I had a fallback.

Fat City was terribly understaffed: there were twenty-two, three-man bunker positions and there were just enough men to fill them, with a total of twelve people left to act as a reactionary force, if needed.

Sergeant Powell and I drove the bunker line, checking that all people were where they belonged, had ammo, weapons, passwords, and to check that each radio was fully functional.

Sarge finally drove the jeep up a rutted road that climbed, at an angle of approximately forty degrees, all the way to the very top of this dollop of a hill that sat in the center of our compound. At the very top of the hill sat a large sandbag bunker and a broken-down tank, in an area about an eighth of the size of a football field. The tank couldn't be repaired; it couldn't move forward or backward, but the turret could rotate and its main cannon went up and down just fine; that tank also had a 180 degree range of clear fire.

Once at the top of the hill, we entered the TOC and settled down for the night. I had a book, Sarge and two enlisted men played cards, while a third enlisted man was on watch, sitting at the radio. At six thirty, "Sparks," the radio operator started to talk into the radio, "Bunker One, report," and he continued until all twenty-two bunkers had reported in. Each bunker had to report every thirty minutes, in the correct order with no prompting from the TOC. If anyone fell asleep and missed his radio report, it led to serious trouble, because sarge and I would pay them a visit and put them on report.

It was so very boring in the still of the night. The night just dragged on and on and one wondered, *Will dawn ever come?* From out of the intense stillness came a loud, clear, authoritarian voice that startled everyone: "Fat City, calling Fat City." "Fat City, this is Raven 5, this is a Red Alert, repeat, RED ALERT. Your location is about to be attacked by elements of the Second NVA regiment. Present location of enemy is one klick northwest of your location; enemy strength is 250 NVA regulars. Weapons counted 14 RPG-7s, 3 sixty millimeter mortars, approximately 230 SKS carbines; uniform color is gray, attack is imminent. This has a reliable level of seven; did you read, over?"

"Holy shit," one of the enlisted men exclaimed.

"What did he just say?" I asked.

"Sparks, have them repeat that message," Sarge ordered with anxiety in his voice.

"Raven 5, this is Fat City, please repeat your last transmission, over."

The radio transmission started all over, word for word. We looked at the map on the bunker wall, and found the coordinates. It was less than an eighth of a mile away. A slight rise in the ground lay between them and us, making it impossible for us to see them.

The Tragedy of Vietnam, Again

"Sarge, what do you suggest we do?" I asked.

"I'm not sure, a LRRP (sounds like "lerp"—long range reconnaissance patrol) team up in the hills must have spotted them," Sarge stated. "I think a mad minute is in order, right now," he answered, with confidence in his voice, but I could tell he was scared.

"I know what a mad minute is; I heard an officer say he felt it's better to have two bursts of thirty seconds each, with a lull of thirty seconds between the two blasts," I blurted out.

"You heard the lieutenant, pass the order," Sarge ordered. "Boy, this is going to wake everyone up in a real hurry."

My heart was pounding, as the radio operator in a very clear, almost a surreal voice, passed the instructions to the bunker line. All positions were told to hold their fire until the order was given and the first burst was to last only thirty seconds. The radio operator finished and looked at me for the fire order.

Sergeant Powell held up his hands and said, "Wait, sir, let all the bunkers get ready; wait another ten seconds...all right, sir, now, they've had enough time."

As soon as I said, "Fire," the radio operator repeated calmly, "fire" and the stillness of the drab night was shattered as twenty-two .60-caliber machine guns burst into action. The men in each bunker strafed the ground as close to the front of each bunker as they could, and then quickly worked their way up in an overlapping

My First and Only Guard Duty

zigzag pattern to a level position, and continued back and forth, up and down as quickly as possible for thirty seconds. This first thirty-second blast of bullets hopefully would catch many of the enemy out in the open and kill or wound many of them. It also told the NVA, *We know you're there and we're waiting to give you some of your own medicine, if you're so inclined.*

Within the first ten seconds of opening fire the field phone rang. I picked it up and Capt. Prothero yelled into my ear, "What in hell do you think you're doing?"

I had completely forgotten about him. "Sir, we just received a RED ALERT radio message from Division, that's a code 7. We're about to be attacked by two hundred and fifty NVA regulars. They were one click from our back wire at the time of the message, sir."

There was stone silence on the other end of the phone. I heard, "I'll be right there," and the phone went dead.

Literally within two minutes Captain Prothero stomped into the TOC, wearing his boots, underpants, 45 pistol, flak jacket and steel pot. He glowered fiercely at Sergeant Powell demanding, "What the hell is this all this about?"

We showed him the radio message that Sparks had written down as transmitted. Then Sergeant Powell showed the captain on the map exactly where the enemy position was at the time of the radio message.

"Good, maybe we got a few of them with that first blast."

"Well, we sure screwed up their surprise. It was the lieutenant's idea to use two short bursts," Sergeant Powell answered cautiously.

"Chris, you've done well tonight, and thank you; now I want you and Sergeant Powell to go down to the bottom of the hill and get ready to take casualties. Sarge, get Captain Kaiser and tell him to set up a reactionary force immediately."

"Should I wake the major...?"

"No, forget him, the last we saw of him he was passed out with his local friend," Captain Prothero interrupted.

I went down to the bottom of the hill and Sergeant Klem and I set up for the wounded. We waited, and then waited some more. The more we waited the more our minds started to work. I finally understood the meaning of what FDR said regarding World War II, "The only thing we have to fear, is fear itself." I can honestly say I'd never been as scared in my life as I was while waiting for those 250 NVA regulars to attack.

Early the next morning a patrol was sent out, to scout the area for any dead NVA. The patrol returned to say they found no NVA, but the other side of the rise was littered with bloody bandages.

Three months later, Major Bangstrom received a Bronze Star medal for valor, as he led his men from bunker to bunker. What really happened was that he was passed out with his Vietnamese whore and he

My First and Only Guard Duty

never knew what had happened until he sobered up the next morning.

Building an Aid Station

I had been to Hill 29 once before to meet Phil Davis. Doc was of a medium build, about thirty-five years old, and was capable of getting upset if events didn't run smoothly. He didn't smoke, curse, or drink; he was a good Mormon from Salt Lake City. Doc was a happy man, because, as the saying went in Vietnam, *He's short!* Doc had only forty-five days left in Vietnam and then back to the United States and a discharge. *Oh, my lord, that's a long way off for me, it seems like a lifetime,* I thought.

I daydreamed as the helicopter followed Highway One north. Hawk Hill came in view, while the chopper started to circle in order to land at the helipad. I realized that Hill 29 was in fact two hills, one on top of the other with two low rises, one at either end. All vegetation had been stripped off to deny the enemy any type of cover to sneak around in. Also, it helped to keep snakes and other cute, but deadly things out of the camp area. Multiple barbed wire obstacles were being laid out beyond the bunker line, all the way around the entire hill.

The Tragedy of Vietnam, Again

All tents were surrounded by three-foot sandbagged walls. Tanks and armored personnel carriers (tracks) dotted the hills. On top of the largest hill stood a lookout tower, about fifty feet tall, that the helicopter flew around. We flew over some armored personnel carriers, adding one more layer of dust and dirt to everything, as we barely passed just over their heads; the occupants, looking up, did not look very happy.

The original aid station set up – Mobile Aid Station is between the two tents.

I walked over to the spot where Doc had set up his operations. It was about a hundred yards from the helipad and consisted of one command personnel carrier, called the Mobile Aid Station. The only difference between it and a regular track was that a person who was six feet five inches tall could stand up in-

Building an Aid Station

side a command track, while in a regular track, a person who was five foot six inches had to crawl about in a crouched position. Other than that, they were basically the same. Doc had also set up two GP small tents; one was the aid station and the other was for sleeping.

I entered the tent and Doc exclaimed, "Where are all the others?"

"They're driving up, there's no extra room, so I hooked a ride with a helicopter. They're bringing up all the junk from Fat City, plus another GP small tent."

"Good, that other tent will provide accommodations for everyone; one for the aid station, one for the enlisted personnel, and the other for you and me," Doc replied.

"Hey, sir, welcome to The Hill," Specialist Fourth Class David Hanes yelled.

"Hi, Hanes, how are you doing?" I liked Hanes; he was a lot of fun. Dave came from some small town in Indiana. He was about five feet ten inches tall and weighed about a hundred and fifty pounds. He had blondish hair, and his fatigues were sun bleached to a very light olive-drab color. His jungle boots no longer had any black on the toes or heels, because the dust had stripped off not only the polish, but also all the dye. Hanes had been in Bravo Troop for about nine and a half months, and his tour was almost over, so Doc pulled him out of the field.

"Hey, sir, what do you think of this?" Hanes asked as he pulled out a centerfold from a Playboy.

The Tragedy of Vietnam, Again

"It looks very nice, Hanes," I replied.

"You see, Doc, there's nothing wrong with this," Hanes said, holding the picture for Doc to see.

Doc shut his eyes and turned away. Doc's Mormon training did not approve of such material. Hanes had a lot of fun giving Doc a hard time about girls, and girly pictures, but Hanes knew there was a limit to what he could get away with. Doc was also good about allowing Hanes some freedom in having his fun.

"Chris, how would you like to get some lunch?" Doc asked, as he looked at his watch. "If you would like, I can show you a little of the unit as we walk over to Alpha Troop's chow hall. Hanes, you look after the aid station while we're gone," Doc ordered.

"Don't worry Doc; I've got everything under control. Also, lunch sucks, sir," Hanes answered as he dug out another Playboy magazine.

"Hanes seems to be a good guy," I stated for the lack of anything else to say, once we were out of ear short.

"I pulled Dave out of the field about a week ago," Doc explained. "He had done an outstanding job in Bravo Troop, and had been in the thick of things for the entire time he'd been in the unit. Dave never had any regard for his own life; everything he did was for his troop. He had come very close to being killed many times, or better, he should have been killed. The good Lord has been looking after Mr. Hanes, for he never even received a scratch; not even a sprain. Bullets passed between his legs, under his arms, under his chin, and next to his ears. Bravo Troop pressured me to pull him out of the field, because they felt he had used up all his good luck. They were afraid that his first scratch just might be his last. As soon as a new medic came in, I pulled Hanes; I needed the help back here anyway.

Doc and I walked up to the top of Hill 29 between rows of vehicles, tanks, and tracks being worked on. One tank had one of its tracks laid out in front of it on the ground, while a group of GIs cut something off with a torch. Metal sparks showered the ground where the group was standing.

"This is Alpha Troop's maintenance area," Doc explained. "That tank hit a mine early yesterday and it took most of the day to drag it back."

"Was anyone hurt?" I asked.

"No, not badly; it's the platoon sergeant's tank and he was the only person hurt with a sprained wrist. They were lucky, it was only a small mine that got them. The maintenance crew will work on that tank all night if need be, but that tank will be back in the field tomorrow, as good as new,"

Doc seemed to know a lot about how the squadron worked. It would be hard not to know, because at the officers' club every night, the day's activities were discussed over a few drinks.

"The squadron has a policy," Doc rambled on. "You don't take care of yourself until your vehicle had been

The Tragedy of Vietnam, Again

taken care of. It's a throwback to when the Cav ran on horses."

We passed three armored personnel carriers, all with their front hatches reaching for the sky, while the crews checked to make sure the oil levels were correct and the radiators were full of water. At the end of the line of downed vehicles was a maintenance tent; it looked like a huge canvas Quonset hut.

"It's too hot to work in the tent, so during the day it's outside. If night work is required, then they will drag the work into the tent so the enemy can't see the light. It's a farce, because that tent is full of holes from all the mortar attacks. The Dinks have fun trying to shoot them up."

"I have a silly question, but just what is a Dink? I know it's an oriental, but which one?"

"The Dink," Doc started off in a professorial tone, "is the enemy. The North Vietnamese are called 'Super Dinks,' the VC are called 'Dinks' and the regular South Vietnamese are called 'The Little People,' but around here every oriental is called a 'Dink.'"

"What happened to 'Charlie'?"

"One word of advice; never use the word 'Charlie;' that's John Wayne stuff. We just watched the movie *The Green Beret*. It was a lot of fun watching the men critique Hollywood's best and made fun of every mistake. I advise you, don't use those terms, because the troops will only make fun of you behind your back."

Doc led me all the way through the maintenance area and as we started to head down the back side of the hill, Doc spotted the squadron's commanding officer.

"Have you met Colonel Cousland yet?"

"No, I have not."

"Well, you're just about to," Doc replied. "Good day, Colonel Cousland; this is Lieutenant Noble, my new medical platoon leader. He's just arrived from Fat City, sir."

"I heard that you had some help on the way. Colonel Anderson gave me a call awhile back, and Major Bangstrom told me you had reported into Fat City. Welcome to the squadron, Lieutenant; are you going to get some lunch, gentlemen?"

"Yes, sir, that's where we were headed," Doc answered.

"How would you gentlemen like to join me?" the CO asked.

"We would like that very much, sir," Doc replied, and the three of us continued down the hill to the chow hall.

I was totally impressed with LTC Cousland. Here we were in a very dusty environment and the temperature was in the high eighties or maybe low nineties, and the colonel stood as if ready for inspection; in his creased fatigue pants and shirt, he was spotless.

The topic of conversation over lunch was all about Blue Ghost shooting a faulty rocket from one of its gunships that slammed into one of Alpha Troop's tanks. Someone complained to Doc about how it wasn't fair for those who were injured not to get a Purple Heart.

Colonel Cousland explained loudly for all to hear, "It has to be a hostile rocket in order to get a Purple Heart, and the rocket that hit that tank was a friendly rocket."

I kept my eyes and ears open trying to make sense of all the slang, abbreviations, and local lingo being spoken; it sounded like a foreign language. (Please see appendix #2 in the back of this book.)

Later that afternoon the rest of the aid station from Fat City arrived, looking like a gypsy wagon. The two-and-a-half-ton truck, called the "Deuce and a Half," arrived with truck and trailer crammed full of the contents from the Fat City aid station, plus all the personnel gear. There was a refrigerator, folding chairs, one large floor fan capable of blowing a gale-force breeze, about twenty litters, litter stands, and many chests full of medical supplies.

Sergeant Klem, Doc, Hanes, and I spent the rest of the afternoon pitching the new GP small tent to replace the present tent that had many holes. We didn't need an extra one, because Doc reassigned one of the Fat City medics to Bravo Troop and the other to Charlie Troop.

This new tent was being erected next to the mobile aid station and would be the new living quarters for Doc and me. Sergeant Klem chose to sleep inside the

Building an Aid Station

mobile aid station, which was being used as the administrative office, medical records room, as well as the medical supply area for the medical platoon. Hanes was instructed to move in with Doc and me.

Doc was very happy to have us up on The Hill, because Sergeant Klem was an excellent medic with many years of experience. Doc was also happy that I was there, because he had been running the whole show by himself. There were a lot of administrative duties he just hated doing. Taking care of enlisted people's problems, trying to get new medics, figuring out which medic would be allowed to go on R&R, inspecting chow halls, reordering supplies, managing rodent control, following up on where patients had been transferred after they were sent to the large Division evacuation hospitals was all part of my job. Doc was the squadron's physician and was responsible for the health of the troops twenty-four hours a day, seven days a week, week in and week out, until he left Vietnam.

It was a dark night January 31st of 1968 when we all settled in the best we could to our new accommodations, sleeping on litters. Doc, Hanes, and I slept in the new tent, and Sergeant Klem was snug inside the mobile aid station. The cloudless night was cold, as a wind blew from the west. About one in the morning, I awoke to a gut-wrenching whamp. The noise was tremendously loud, but what really bothered me the most was that my entire insides were jolted due to the concussion from the explosion. Then there was a

The Tragedy of Vietnam, Again

consecutive whump, whamp, whump, blam, whump, blam, blam, wham that lasted about a half hour.

"Everyone, stay down and don't move," Hanes yelled. "You hear me, Sergeant Klem, don't move."

"I ain't going no place, I'm staying put right here, but I sure would like the back ramp to be up," Sarge yelled back in his heavy Southern drawl.

"Stay down, Sarge that sandbag wall across the rear of the track will protect you," Doc yelled back.

The entire time this was going on, a high-pitched "whishing" sound was heard, as if a giant chain were being whirled violently about, just above our heads. This was the shrapnel flying by, as well as passing through our tents. I could see stars shining through the roof of the new tent. It was terrifying to lay in the dark waiting for an explosion to materialize, and blow you to smithereens.

Hanes was cool; he kept up his chitter-chatter about how this was nothing compared to LZ Ross, or being out in a good firefight like in the Que Son Valley. Doc was concerned about wounded and how we'd get them to the aid station.

"Don't worry, Doc, if someone is hurt, the line medics will bring them here in Band-Aid. Each line troop had one APC (armored personnel carrier) that belonged to the aid station and was for the line troop medics' use. "There's nothing we can do until they get here," Hanes said to reassure Doc.

Building an Aid Station

"I hope nobody is hurt badly, because we can't turn on the lantern. Canvas is not meant to stop shrapnel," Doc complained.

"Hey, Doc, we can work on the floor. Let Lieutenant Noble hold a muffled flashlight and I can assist you," Hanes volunteered.

Hanes was great; he knew this was my very first encounter with mortars and rockets. Doc had witnessed two such attacks, but never as up close and personal as this attack. Hanes was doing a great job keeping everyone calm.

The attack lasted for forty-five minutes and the squadron was very lucky. No direct hits, many flat tires, many punctured radiators, almost every tent received multiple new holes, but most importantly, after approximately eighty to ninety mortar rounds, nobody was hurt. We learned later that this was North Vietnam's way of saying Happy Tet—1968, as they broke their own truce.

Hanes counted forty-three holes in our new tent and we had to replace approximately fifty sandbags due to shrapnel damage. Doc's jeep needed a new tire; one of the frontline ambulances (FLA) needed two new tires; and the Deuce and a Half (two-and-a-half-ton truck) needed to have its radiator fixed.

The next day, Lieutenant Colonel Cousland ordered that bunkers had to be built as soon as possible for safety reasons: tents would no longer be allowed. The line troops had the personnel and some heavy equipment

The Tragedy of Vietnam, Again

to help with the heavy framing material. Within two days, bunkers started appearing all over Hill 29. To the outside of the six-by-six framing, half-inch plywood was nailed all over to create walls and a roof. Then thousands of sandbags were each filled approximately two-thirds full. Then each bag was tied off and stacked carefully, then molded into the surrounding bags. The sandbagged walls were two to three bags thick and were about seven feet tall. The floor was a raised platform of plywood so the occupants weren't living in the dirt.

Doc and I planned how we wanted the aid station laid out. Doc wanted to finish this project before Sergeant Klem and he left Vietnam. We also wanted to pull four medics out of the field to help in the aid station.

We had only one major problem: we had no personnel to build anything. I inspected most all of the bunkers being built, and it didn't make much sense to me to build a huge hulk standing tall on the side of a hill. It was an open invitation for everyone to try to hit it.

My concerns proved correct about two weeks later as one bunker, next to the aid station, took a direct hit, collapsing the entire back end. Nobody was hurt because that troop was out in the field with a downed vehicle.

Building an Aid Station

Doc Davis standing in a rocket crater made near the aid station

I wanted to build an aid station into the ground. When I mentioned this to Hanes, he almost went nuts. "What, did I hear you correctly, sir? Where did you want this aid station?" Hanes demanded. (As long as "sir" is put at the end of a statement, the enlisted man can't really get in trouble for disrespect.)

"In the ground over there," I pointed. Doc was listening with much amusement off to one side.

"Why do you want it there, Lieutenant?" Hanes asked.

"Because it will be in a slight hollow and the enemy can't get a direct shot on this spot," I replied with confidence.

"Sir, with all due respect, how are we going to dig a hole big enough to build an aid station in?" Hanes didn't like what he thought would be the answer.

"Well, there are always shovels."

"Oh, come on, Doc, we can't dig that dirt; it's like cement," Hanes complained.

Doc laughed as he went along with my plan. Doc had waited a long time to get even with Hanes and he wasn't about to let this opportunity pass. The only thing about my plan was that I wasn't joking; I really did want the aid station in the ground. I had no idea as to how we were going to build it, but my goal was firm in my mind.

That night, unknown to us, our new aid station started to became a reality. The 1/1 Cav was the northernmost US Army unit in all of South Vietnam at that point in time. We were in Marine country and a Marine engineering company occupied part of the back side of Hill 29. This Marine unit was responsible for keeping Highway One open and to repair any and all bridges as fast as they got blown up in our AO (Area of Operation).

The Marines had only one Navy corpsman attached to them. In order for the Marines to see a doctor, they had to travel approximately thirty miles up the road, or come see us. Doc had told the corpsman that if he could be of any help, to bring any Marine patients over and he'd be happy to help out.

One fact we discovered about these Marines—they were total animals. These men inflicted far more casualties on each other than the enemy could ever hope to do. That night, Hanes tried to wake Doc quietly.

Building an Aid Station

"What time is it?" Doc demanded.

"Its 1:45, Doc," Hanes whispered.

"What? Why can't the Marines beat each other up at a convenient hour?" Doc demanded.

"I don't know, Doc," Hanes whispered. "I'm in the Army."

"You guys need any help?" I asked, waking up.

"That's fine, if you want to see a bunch of animals, I'm sure we can find something for you to do," Doc said, as he slipped into a pair of pants and a shirt.

When I approached the aid station tent, I heard Doc giving the Marines holy hell about trying to destroy each other, and to please not do it so late in the night the next time.

I walked into the tent as dark shadows hung in the background, not saying a word, trying not to get in the way. Hanes was holding the ophthalmoscope while Doc surveyed the damage. A young marine lay on the litter and his left ear had been almost torn off. His ear lobe and a small part of his ear were still attached to his head, but most of his ear was flapping in the breeze. Doc was pissed!

"Chris, take over for Hanes. Hanes get me..." Doc rattled off a list of supplies we'd need. Doc turned to the Navy corpsman, Scotty, and said, "You're going to assist me." All total, it took about an hour to sew the ear back in place, and Doc did a great job.

We tried to find out what happened, but all the Marines told the same story, including the patient—"He

The Tragedy of Vietnam, Again

fell down." Scotty hated the Marines, but was stuck in this unit of animals. He told us later he wasn't sure whether the patient was hit over the head with a shovel or a rifle; he wasn't there when it happened. One thing he did know; everyone in that bunker was drunk at the time of the accident.

Late in the morning the next day, a jeep drove up to the aid station and behind the wheel was a Marine sergeant. I don't know what his rank was, but he had a lot of stripes and his men called him Gunny.

"Sir, may I have a word with you?"

I thought he was conducting an investigation about what happened last night, so I was willing to supply any information he might need.

"What can I do for you?"

"Sir, with all due respect, I want to thank you and your people for helping us out last night. You have helped our corpsmen out many times, and the Marines feel it's beneath their dignity to have your doc sew our men up using that flashlight you shove up people's noses."

Before I could explode, this sergeant said, "Sir, we would like to build you a proper aid station; would that be all right, sir?"

I was in shock; he caught me completely off guard, and I stammered, "Yes why yes, that will be just fine."

"You tell us where you want it and we'll do the rest," the sergeant replied.

Building an Aid Station

I showed the jeep full of Marines what Doc's and my plans were. After some small talk among the Marines and a few measurements were taken they were ready to go. The sergeant turned the jeep around and said, "We'll see you in a few days, sir. We have to scrounge up the material, and thank you for taking care of us." He slipped the jeep in gear and drove off.

"Hey, Doc, all your bitching last night just paid off." I told him what the Marines had offered; Doc was elated with the news.

"What's all the commotion about?" Hanes asked as he walked into the aid tent.

"Well, Hanes, I think you have just been saved by the US Marine Corps. Some sergeant from the engineer unit just said they will build two bunkers, dug into the ground for us. One is for a barracks for medics and the other is the aid station with a room for Doc and me in the back."

"You know, Doc, maybe I should live a more pure life, like you."

"Well, those Marines should, after all we've done for them. They're still all animals! If it weren't for us there would be a lot of strange looking Marines running around. When are they going to start work?" Doc asked.

"I don't know, they said they have to gather some material and they will be back in a couple of days."

"Don't hold your breath. I wouldn't trust those pecker heads at all, sir," Hanes chimed in.

The Tragedy of Vietnam, Again

"I don't know; it would be wonderful if they do follow through," Doc said.

Three days passed and there was no sign of the Marines. I wondered if this offer was some sort of sick joke. Neither Doc nor I said one word about the Marines offer; we were afraid that "Rank had its privilege." We wanted this aid station, and not to have it become Major Bangstrom's bunker, or even the colonel's bunker. We were only following orders, after all; the CO did say we all had to build a bunker, as quickly as possible.

The next day, about 10:00 a.m., I heard a sound that made a lot of rumbling and clanking. I turned to see what was making this terrible clatter and there came the largest bulldozer I'd ever seen. The blade must have been at least fourteen feet wide and a good eight feet high. I ran around to meet it and was shocked at how high up the driver sat; he was a good seven to eight feet off the ground.

The operator cut the motor and asked, "Where you want me to make a pass, sir?"

I showed him what I had shown the Marines; two bunkers, one at right angles to the other with a roadway between the two.

The operator said, "The other people should be over in a little while."

He then restarted his machine. The bulldozer spun around and within fifteen minutes had dug a trench approximately fifty-five feet long by twenty-six feet wide,

Building an Aid Station

and about six feet deep; at the far end was a mountain of dirt.

The dozer operator then turned his machine and cut another pit for the EM bunker and finished this off in about ten minutes; the entire amount of time spent, on the job, was under thirty minutes.

That afternoon we waited for the Marines to show up, but they didn't come. We did receive some unexpected company. Major Bangstrom came over to see what was going on and to give me some encouragement. His greeting was, "Lieutenant," in as demeaning a tone as he could possibly muster. "What the hell are you and Doc doing, digging swimming pools?" he chided.

"No, sir," I answered as positive and upbeat as possible. "This is the new aid station and that will be the living barracks for the enlisted personnel, sir."

"Lieutenant, don't you know it rains here? Matter of fact it rains very hard. How long do you think it will take to fill these pits up, Lieutenant?" the major contemptibly spat out.

I just hate this man; he's so disgusting, how did he ever make the rank of major? I thought.

"Sir, I have taken that into account. These bunkers are on a hill and if a trench is dug around the bunker on the uphill side and left open on the downhill side, all the water will be channeled around the bunker." I didn't tell him that I had learned that in Boy Scouts when pitching a tent, and was shocked that he would have even asked the question.

"We'll see," and then he wheeled about and walked off in his usual arrogant Nazi-style swagger.

The Marines came the next day, about eight of them in four overloaded five-ton trucks. The first two trucks were loaded with twelve-by-twelve beams, used to build bridges. The Marines worked in teams and got the beams out. Using chain saws they notched the twelve-by-twelve beams to fit snugly. The floor joists were notched together so nothing could move in any direction, and were placed two feet off the ground. Everything was notched and secured by huge spikes into the twelve-by-twelve support beams. By having the floor raised by two feet, in case we did spring a leak, we could accommodate quite a lot of water beneath the flooring.

By three that afternoon, both bunkers were all framed up and plywood flooring installed. It was almost quitting time, and the five-ton trucks returned and off- loaded thin metal roofing material, enough to cover all outside walls. Old portable metal airport runway strips were dumped off to one side to be used to hold the roof in place. The runway strips were a lot stronger than the thin roofing metal; they had to be in order to carry the extreme pressure of aircraft landing upon them, and they were perfect to carry the load of the sandbags on the roof.

Building an Aid Station

The Marine sergeant came over at quitting time and told me, "Sorry, Lieutenant, but you'll have to finish the job; two bridges have been blown up and the rebuilding of them takes priority. Here are some gifts from us to you. We scrounged a sink we thought you could use. And so Doc doesn't have to use that flashlight, here's a proper light to sew people up by." He got out of his jeep and took out a spotlight about eighteen inches across with US Navy neatly printed on the side, and a nice medium-sized stainless steel sink with a faucet, and a stainless steel side counter attached.

"Sarge, Doc and I don't know how to thank you."

"Look, sir, you take care of us and we'll take care of you, OK?"

"All right, but where did you get all this stuff?"

"Look, Lieutenant, there are some questions you just don't ask, and that is one. Let's say the Navy doesn't know their ass from a hole in the ground, so we just took advantage of it. I'll see you around, Lieutenant." And I never saw him again.

We did see the Marines on many occasions, usually between midnight and three in the morning, but for some reason, Doc didn't seem to mind quite so much.

The Tragedy of Vietnam, Again

The TOC area top left, Alpha Maintenance area top right, aid station in foreground with Medic's Bunker directly behind.

Building Aid Station, Doc's area rear right, C. Noble's area rear left, sink foreground left, medical records area right foreground.

Building an Aid Station

Doc Davis supervising Medic Haines and Freeman with wing tank installation for water to sink.

EM Bunker being built, Medic shower directly behind, and Alpha Troop's maintenance area in right rear.

The Tragedy of Vietnam, Again

The next morning LTC Cousland stopped by to see what was going on, for there was a lot of noise coming from the aid station area. What he saw was every line medic left in base camp, plus all their buddies from all three line units who had nothing better to do, all working like mad. Some nailed the thin metal roofing to the side supports to create the bunker's walls. Others were making shelving out of old ammo crates; two others made a long counter, where patients could check in and where the medical paperwork could be done. On top of all the banging, shouting, and laughing a portable radio played Armed Forces Radio at full volume. This, the men felt, was important, because it set the tempo that all work was to be performed at— they had to show progress in order to earn their beers at the end of the day.

LTC Cousland came over to where I was and asked, "What's going on?"

"We're building a bunker, sir," I answered.

"How do you know if this is safe?"

"Well, sir, I guess I don't, except that the Marine engineers made all the framing. It's all notched and it's held in place with twelve-inch spikes driven in with sledge hammers, sir."

The colonel watched for about two or three minutes and then said, "I don't want anyone to move into these bunkers until the Army Corps of Engineers has checked them out, all right?"

Building an Aid Station

"Yes, sir," I replied, and then saluted the colonel; he returned my salute and left.

I knew we had nothing to worry about, because I saw how the Marines cut and locked all the fittings into place. The work progress went very well; all we needed to do by the end of the day was to fill the sandbags to cover the aid station, and to backfill the narrow void around the outside of the bunker with dirt. This had to be done by hand for fear that a heavy machine would cave in the bunker's thin metal walls. We all took turns in the evenings doing the necessary grunt work of hauling dirt in five-gallon pails.

Unfortunately, we were mortared that night and shrapnel flew through some of the uncovered side metal. Dirt could trickle into the aid station through the holes. Larry Gaydon, the senior medic for Alpha Troop came up with the best solution to solve the problem. We cut up some leftover metal siding into smaller squares but larger than the holes and then taped each patch over a hole with medical tape. Once the dirt had been all backfilled, the dirt would hold the patches in place. For the very small holes, we just put four or five layers of medical tape over those holes and that would hold the dirt in place; it really didn't matter, because we would have already departed Vietnam by the time that tape gave out.

The aid station was finally finished. We had a total of eight layers of sandbags on the roof, with two layers of metal runway strips at different levels between the

The Tragedy of Vietnam, Again

sandbags. There were two layers of sandbags between the metal strips and the plywood roof. We felt that the first metal layer would explode the rocket and the second layer would take most of the force from the blast. In order to make the roof waterproof, we spread a large, heavy-duty plastic sheet over the top and then added another layer of sandbags to hold it in place and to give the plastic some protection from mortar rounds.

When the Army Corps of Engineers came to inspect our bunker, LTC Cousland and our friend Major Bangstrom were both on hand, along with half the officer corps of the First of the First. According to the engineering major, the aid station was one of the best-constructed bunkers he had seen in all of Vietnam, and it was strong enough to have an armored personnel carrier drive over the roof, but not a tank.

The colonel then went inside and was truly impressed. The medics and friends had really outdone themselves. We found old crates in Chu Lai that hospital mattresses had come in. We carefully broke these crates apart and used the thin plywood for paneling. We *acquired* some unused aircraft napalm tanks from the Air Force, and Headquarters' Troop maintenance cut a hole in the top of one, and affixed a fitting on the bottom, so a hose could run from the tank to the faucet on the sink. We now had running water inside the aid station.

Building an Aid Station

That evening, new orders were issued to all members of the 1/1 Cav, "All new bunkers were to be built in ground, along the lines of the aid station."

Major Bangstrom turned his bunker over to the squadron's command sergeant major who did not believe living underground was morally correct. The major had a new bunker built that was completely underground.

Our aid station was used on occasion by Division and Saigon's military medical brass, to show what can be done in the field with nothing.

Sketch of Aid Station area

Top left generators, stockade, Lt Venn and SSG Deljudice's bunker, medics shower, medic's EM bunker, latrine, jeep's garage, mobile aid-station and the Aid Station.

The Battle of the Pink Ville

It was a gray February day as Miller and Kline were cleaning out the mobile aid station. Miller had removed all the gear from inside, taken up the floorboards and was checking the bilge pump. Bravo-Band-Aid had crossed a stream about a week ago and water sloshed around inside for two days, because the bilge pump was plugged with a lot of grime, dirt, and crude.

Specialist Stewart was washing Doc's jeep and then the two FLAs. The trick in creating the illusion that these vehicles looked almost like new, but for a very short amount of time, like for an inspection, was to wipe them down with a light coat of diesel oil. The diesel soaked into the paint and gave a luster as if the paint were new. This illusion lasted only as long as no dust or dirt got on the paint; otherwise, it stuck and made more of a mess than before.

I surveyed the medics from my vantage point and thought, *we're very lucky to have such a good group of people working for us. They are not only good professionally, but they're fun to have around. They enjoy each other, as well as helping other people.* Needless to say, each and every one of these medics had proven

The Tragedy of Vietnam, Again

himself way beyond a shadow of a doubt in the field, and they had earned the respect and admiration of all the line troops.

The sun was starting to set, "Hey, Hale," I shouted. "Why don't you start the shower?"

"We need some more diesel fuel, sir," Hale yelled.

"Well, take the jeep and get some," I yelled back.

The shower was a very basic affair. A fifty-five-gallon drum full of water with a pipe, a valve and a showerhead affixed to the bottom; the drum stood on top of a twelve-foot semi-enclosed frame. A large metal artillery round casing, about five feet long and eight inches wide, was immersed into the water with its top sticking up toward the stars. Stuck inside the first canister was a chimney-canister with both of its ends cut off. This was a thinner artillery casing about four and a half inches in diameter and about five feet long. The chimney stuck above the larger canister by five to six inches, thanks to a chunk of brick dropped down the larger tube to ensure the chimney was at the correct height to ventilate properly.

The Battle of the Pink Ville

Johnston testing shower's heating unit.

All one had to do was carefully pour two full canteen cups of diesel fuel down the chimney, followed up by a half cup of gasoline starter, being careful not to spill any fuel into the water. The lucky person who got to light the shower had to light a match, then duck down and drop it down either tube. After using about a half box of matches, the canisters roared into action and in about twenty minutes the water in the fifty-five-gallon drum was almost boiling.

By the time supper was over, the water had cooled off, in the evening air, to just the correct temperature for a shower. Up to ten people could shower, providing everyone was water conservative.

The Tragedy of Vietnam, Again

We had our nightly ritual in the aid station and then went to sleep early. I liked to sleep on a litter on top of the aid station. It was beautiful looking at the stars in total blackout conditions. At first, the heavens were two dimensional, but after staring at them for about thirty seconds or so the heavens suddenly became three dimensional. I almost felt as if I could reach up and touch the moon, it seemed so close. I was also fascinated by looking at the Southern Cross off in the distant southern sky, and was amazed that people had been looking at the same group of stars as I was for many thousands of years.

I liked playing games to try to locate a patch of sky that was devoid of stars. Since there was perfect blackout condition, there was nothing to spoil one's night vision; I always found stars, even in the darkest of voids. All you had to do was stare at a dark space for a short while and then shift your eyes just off to one side of the hole, and then small pin-prick specks of light appeared ever so faintly. I realized the heavens were completely covered by trillions upon trillions of stars.

The next morning, right after breakfast, Specialist Gaydon came to the aid station to get supplies. He acted as though he was going to the local supermarket with his shopping list. He needed six bottles of Ringers, seven three-inch ACE bandages, ten rolls of two-inch ACE bandages, one fifty-capsule bottle of Darvon (the Army's Vietnam aspirin), three syrettes of morphine, two bottles of hydrogen peroxide, one

The Battle of the Pink Ville

package of cotton-tipped applicators, eight packages of gauze pads—3 inch squares—and the list went on. Gaydon was not only resupplying Band-Aid, but all three platoon medics as well.

Gaydon was about five feet ten inches tall and had dirty blond hair. He was as strong as an ox, strength he had developed through hard work on his father's farm just outside of Fairfield, Iowa.

That day, I was going out with Alpha Troop for my orientation trip to the field. Also, as it turned out, they were short one medic, who was on R&R.

After Gaydon had picked up his supplies from the aid station and discussed two medical problem patients with Doc, he turned and said, "Are you ready to go to the field, Lieutenant?"

"I've got all my stuff and I'm ordering you to tell me what I have to do; forget that I'm an officer."

Gaydon grinned and said, "Thank you, sir, let's go," and walked out of the aid station with his cardboard box full of medical supplies.

Kline yelled out the door, "Keep your ass down and don't get it shot off, sir!" and he then howled with laughter.

We walked over to Alpha Troop by cutting through their motor pool. Alpha-Band-Aid was being checked over very carefully by a motor pool mechanic. Engine oil, hydraulic oil, and water level were all being gone over, as well as the condition of the tracks and sprocket wheels that guided the track.

The Tragedy of Vietnam, Again

Larry Gaydon walked about fifty feet past the motor pool and then ducked into Alpha medics' bunker. Specialist Charles Peeples, a fun-loving practical jokester from Detroit City, was going through the contents of his aid bag, as he sat on his bunk. He was making an inventory of all his missing medical supplies.

"Hey, are you going out with us today, sir?" Peeples asked, grinning from ear to ear, already knowing the answer.

"Yes, I am, why?"

"Man, that's dumb, I mean, really dumb, sir!"

"Why's it so dumb, Peeples?"

"You've got it made back here—you get to drink beer all day long. You can even work on your suntan. Hell, if I had a choice, you wouldn't catch me out there."

"Well, Peeples, I have to go out to check up on you, to make sure you're not goofing off."

"Me goof off, sir? I may have a good time, but I never goof off, sir," Peeples stated.

"Oh, bullshit, Peeples," Gaydon exclaimed. "You don't have to work on your suntan, it's all built in; now get off your ass and restock Band-Aid's supply box."

"There, did you see that, sir? That's the way it goes, good looks, shining personality and all they do is piss all over you." Peeples laughed as he went about the task of restocking the supply box.

Another medic, Dale Sacher entered the bunker, as Gaydon was directing Peeples. Sacher was one of the .60-caliber machine gunners on Band-Aid when his medical skills were not needed.

"Hi, sir, I've got your .60 all set up."

"How is the ammo supply?" I asked.

"Sir, I hope we don't have to ford any deep water, because we will sink for sure. We have two levels of ammo boxes, completely covering the floor of the track, both .50- and .60-caliber, each placed under their respective weapons."

Band-Aid had finished their readiness inspection and had passed. Peeples and Sacher were stowing the last-minute items inside Band-Aid. The big supply box was located directly under Gaydon's place, so he could stand upon it as he directed the track and fired the .50-cal machine gun. If the box weren't there, a ten-foot tall track commander would have been needed in order to function properly.

Litters were stowed on the floor along one side of the track. Small personal gear was stowed on a shelf just after where the radio sat. A blood box, made out of Styrofoam, had approximately three inches thick walls, and had a Styrofoam lid that fit almost air tight. It rested snuggly in a heavy-duty plastic-covered cardboard box. The blood box made an excellent ice chest to keep beer, Coke, and Orange Crush cool. Ice stayed frozen up to four to five days in one of those boxes. We were encouraged to drink beer and pop while in the

The Tragedy of Vietnam, Again

field—beer in moderation. The reason was that the interior of those tanks and tracks could get very hot, and keeping one's body hydrated helped to assist in keeping one's core body temperature down, thus helping to prevent heat exhaustion.

Gaydon yelled, "All right, you guys, let's get going; everyone get their helmet and flak jacket on, it's fifty dollars every time the CO (the troop's commanding officer) sees you without them. Peeples, let's roll out."

The APC roared to life, belching out a great cloud of black oily diesel smoke. Band-Aid moved slowly around the slope, in front of Alpha Troop medics' bunker, onto the dirt road that wound its way around to the staging area. APCs were being fired up all over Alpha Troop; they were like bugs all running out of their holes to see what was going on.

A column was being formed, three large tanks were in the lead, with the rest of the First Platoon falling in behind. Alpha One-Six was the First Platoon leader's radio call sign. Alpha-Six, Alpha Troop's commander, and his "Green Element" were right behind the First Platoon leader's APC. We, Alpha-Band-Aid fell in behind the troop commander's track; behind us was Zippo, the flame-throwing track, plus two mortar tracks, and then Alpha Two-Six's platoon, consisting of three tanks and nine tracks, fell in line. Alpha Three-Six's platoon was left behind to pull guard duty and make repairs to their vehicles.

The Battle of the Pink Ville

Alpha Troop moved out at about seven o'clock in the morning. The road was a horrible dirt road where many mines were still buried, which had yet to explode. Much to my surprise the APCs took these roads in stride and produced a very comfortable ride. It was like riding in a rocking chair, or like on a kid's rocking horse. It was not at all like trying to ride in a jeep where one had to hang on for dear life. The column moved down the road at about twenty miles per hour, in a great cloud of dust and diesel exhaust.

We went through two small villages along the way. As we rumbled by, children ran to the side of the road waving, laughing, jumping up and down, and all screaming, "Chop-Chop." Most of the men in Alpha Troop recognized many of the villagers, due to the many encounters they had had in and around the local area. Every time they rolled past this village, the troops tossed out all the food items the GIs refused to eat at the eagerly waving arms.

"Hey, sir," Sacher said, "Can you reach those cans of chopped eggs and ham? Man, that stuff is nothing more than pure monkey puke." With that said, the cans were heaved over the side and a little girl with nearly no clothes on came up the proud new owner of these three cans. Tropical bars, the Army's high-energy candy bar, were another favorite to heave overboard. All they had ever had done for the GIs was give them a good case of the runs.

The Tragedy of Vietnam, Again

As Band-Aid rolled through the second village, Peeples slammed on the brakes and brought Band-Aid to a skidding stop before we smashed into the rear of the track directly in front of us. The entire column came to the same graceful stop, like one you'd see in a Charlie Chaplin movie.

Our objective was off to the right, about three miles away. Highway one was approximately ten feet above the rice paddy levels, on either side. All the vehicles played a very important game of follow-the-leader, as they carefully slid down the steep embankment and went out into the rice paddy. In terms of the trade, this was called "tracking"; the three lead tanks blazed a trail, one right after the other. If any mines were planted in a paddy where we went, hopefully one of the tanks would drive over it first and set it off. A tank could absorb the force of a mine much better than an ACP, the reason being a tank weighed about forty-eight tons, while a track weighed only twelve tons.

It was fantastic seeing so much power and destruction on the move to make a surprise attack. Our mission was to flatten a fair-sized village, which the Viet Cong and the North Vietnamese army used as a staging area. We were to capture as many prisoners and gain as much information as possible from the area.

The vehicles ploughed through the rice paddies, worming their way across the countryside, at fifteen miles per hour. Water and clods of mud the size of softballs were tossed up into the air; the rice plants

The Battle of the Pink Ville

under the tracks disappeared, never to be seen again. After about twenty-five minutes of follow-the-leader, we reached our objective.

The battle of the "Pink Ville" was just about to start. "Alpha One-Six, this is Alpha-Six, let's hold up here for a moment, out."

"Roger, Alpha-Six," Alpha One-six replied. On a different radio frequency, the First Platoon leader gave his orders to halt the lead tanks. Within seconds, all vehicles had stopped in their tracks.

"Alpha One-Six, your unit goes on line to my left; Alpha Two-Six, have your unit go on line to my right; Green Element will take up the middle. I want two tanks from each platoon to move out now to the far side of the village, to close the back door. Keep your eyes open for anyone trying to escape out the back door; if you see anyone blast away."

The two lead tanks from the First Platoon moved forward and moved quickly off to the left of the village. The other two tanks from the Second Platoon raced around the right side of the village, to act as a blocking force.

"Band-Aid, I want you right next to me; Zippo, I want you the other side of me. Have half the men on each track dismount and walk ten feet ahead of your vehicle. The speed of attack will be at idle speed; we'll recon by fire."

The Tragedy of Vietnam, Again

Band-Aid needed all medics to be available, so Sacher and I stayed on Band-Aid. Peeples made Band-Aid do a right face, so we were staring right at the center of the village. All of a sudden, there was a sickening exploding sound off to our left, from within the village.

"What the hell was that?" Alpha-Six demanded.

"One of my tanks took an RPG round. No serious damage, only a fender got blown off; nobody is hurt," Alpha One-Six responded.

"All right, everyone keep your cool and stay on line; Alpha Troop, move out and recon by fire!"

The noise was deafening, all forty plus .60-caliber machine guns opened fire. Also, approximately twenty-five .50-caliber machine guns opened fire. Red tracers cut their way across the open gap between us and the village, clearing the heads of those on the ground by a few feet.

"Over there," Sacher yelled as he pushed me off to one side and opened fire with my .60-cal; He strafed the brush near our track.

"Band-Aid, what the hell are you shooting at?" Alpha-Six, demanded over the radio.

"Hey, Sacher, knock it off," Gaydon relayed over the intercom.

There was more weapon fire from the other side of the thick brush.

"Chalk me up for two," Sacher exclaimed into his microphone.

The Battle of the Pink Ville

"Alpha-Six, I think Band-Aid got two KIAs," (killed in action) Gaydon replied.

"Band-Aid; get verification," Alpha-Six ordered.

"Alpha-Six, this is Alpha Two-Fiver; what Band-Aid didn't get we finished off. Chalk Band-Aid up, two Victor Charlies; both KIA."

"Roger, Alpha Two-Five," Alpha-Six responded.

Back at base camp; the entire battle was being monitored and a log was kept of everything said over the radio.

The smell of cordite (burnt gun powder) had destroyed my sense of smell and taste. We worked our way about a third of the way through the village when we came out into a large open area that had been carefully cultivated in neat rows, mounded up about two feet high. It looked as though vegetables had been planted and the plants were just popping above the ground. One of the GIs wanted to dig up some fresh food to bring back to base camp. Purely by chance, in doing so he uncovered a piece of plastic. When he pulled the plastic, out came a neat bundle of greased AK-47s. Alpha-Six ordered all gardens in the village to be dug up. The quickest way to tear up the sandy mounds was to drive the APCs across the rows and waggle the tracks back and forth as it moved. Within twenty minutes, thirty-five bundles of AK47s were found, for a total of one hundred and forty weapons, along with twenty RPG launchers, twelve M-16s and twenty-two mortar tubes. This had been a major weapon cache. By this time it was almost twelve thirty and orders were given to halt for "lunch" and to regroup.

Band-Aid was still located next to Alpha-Six's track. Gaydon ducked down inside Band-Aid, and then came up the back hatch with a box of C rations. Sacher grabbed a large pot and pulled out a broken track wheel. He put the wheel on top of the back deck and lit a chunk of C-4, which burned white hot. In less than a minute, we had a gallon of boiling water.

It was extremely depressing to eat food that was prepared twenty-four years earlier; on all the ration boxes was stenciled "C rations—1944." The peanut butter, like the cheese crackers, was dried out. Most of the crackers were broken and the canned meals were very greasy.

Rifle fire was heard off and on during lunch. Everyone was very edgy and mindful as to what was going on around them; all weapons were very close at hand.

"Band-Aid, this is Alpha Two-Six, we have some wounded Dinks for you; do you want to come over and get them, over?"

Alpha Troop's commander broke in, "Band-Aid, move out!"

"Roger Alpha-Six," Gaydon replied. Peeples jumped up on top of the track and then dropped down into the driver's compartment. Sacher dumped the hot water over the side, along with all the trash.

Peeples revved up the engine and made a right face and charged up a small dike and through the thick hedge, as if it were made out of papier-mâché. We went through two more hedgerows and came upon a small group of Vietnamese. They were either very old or very young, nothing in between. An old woman had a slight bullet wound on her left arm.

It was a wonder that any survived our entrance into the village. Gaydon jumped down, leaving Peeples in the driver's seat and Sacher behind his .60-cal. Gaydon estimated Momma-son's injury as very minor, so he cleaned it, put some ointment over it, and then wrapped it in a gauze bandage. He checked the others for any wounds and found none. One little boy had a bad cold, so Gaydon gave him a shot in his hip with penicillin and made him swallow a cold tablet. With that, we were on our way back to our position, on the line. Alpha-Six was not there; he had moved off to his left to be with the First Platoon.

"Band-Aid, get over here, there's some more business for you," the radio blared.

"On our way," Gaydon replied into his mike.

This time Peeples turned Band-Aid to the left and it was easy to follow Alpha-Six's tracks. About four minutes later, we pulled up next to three APCs. On the ground, beside one of the tracks was the second platoon's medic, Edmonds, with one of the line troops. (Edmonds was our youngest medic, he was only seventeen.)

"What's the matter?" Gaydon yelled down.

"Not much, just a sprained ankle, can he ride with you?" Edmonds asked.

"Sacher, pop the back hatch," Gaydon ordered.

Sacher ducked under the back deck and swung open the rear door.

Alpha-Six and a group of GIs were on the ground examining a dark hole that led into the ground. From out of this hole suddenly popped the head of one of our tunnel-rats. He passed out an NVA uniform, an M-16 rifle and a large pile of papers; the tunnel rat then ducked back down the hole and disappeared.

One of the interpreters went over the papers and became very excited. Evidently, these papers were worth the effort spent on this mission. These papers contained the names and locations of all the local VC higher-ups. They gave the location of ammunition and food caches, and they outlined in detail planned events that had yet to happen.

Alpha-Six got on the radio and called our squadron's commander, telling him about the papers. Before Hawk-Six could answer; a voice broke in with, "Alpha-Six, this is Saber-Six. I'm sending my chopper to your location to retrieve those papers and any other material you may have picked up."

"Roger your transmission, Saber-Six," Alpha-Six replied.

"Hey, how about that, sir," Sacher exclaimed, hitting me in the ribs. "The big boy himself, Major

The Battle of the Pink Ville

General Koster, listens in on our own little war." MG Koster was the commanding general of the Americal Division, in Chu Lai

"It's probably the only action going on and he's bored," Peeples chimed in over the intercom from the driver's compartment.

"Alpha-Six, Alpha Two-Six," the radio blared, "We have found another ammo cache, approximately two thousand AK-47 rounds, ninety-seven hand grenades, five RPG launchers with twenty-three RPG rounds, and six mortar tubes with thirty mortar rounds." This message was relayed to Alpha-Six, who was still on the ground.

"Roger Two-Six, this is Alpha-Six's track. Alpha-Six says to bring the weapons with you, but blow the ammo."

"Roger!"

Sacher turned to me and explained, "They're going to dig a couple holes about three feet deep and three feet across, and then pack the ammo with a bunch of C-4 sticks in and around the ammo. As we drive out of this area, we'll blow the C-4. You saw what a little piece can do to some cold water; well, you're about to hear what four or five bricks will do to some ammo.

Alpha-Six got on board his track; the tunnel rat, completely covered with dirt, had finished exploring the tunnel and was climbing on board another APC. There was a muffled sound as a CS (tear gas crystals)

The Tragedy of Vietnam, Again

grenade exploded and a cloud of white smoke belched out of the hole in the ground.

"Well, that tunnel is not going to be used for a while," Gaydon announced.

From off to the right came a gut-jarring explosion that was clearly extremely violent. The enemy's ammo was no longer in a usable format; it had just been spread all over "hell's half acre."

The APCs moved deeper into the village; still there were no village people to be seen. This was strange because all the huts gave clues that many people were there, but left in a great hurry. Food was still on the cooking fires, overturned furniture was scattered about in most huts, and Blue Ghost (our helicopter unit), looking down, could see military-aged males running from one location to another.

Sure enough, as we kept pressing on, I heard the sharp crack of M-16s being fired off to one side, and then an explosion, as a grenade went off, then an AK-47 fired. The sound from the AK-47 was different from that of a .45 or M-16; each weapon had its own particular sound.

"Band-Aid, get over here, we took one of Blue Ghost's rockets," Alpha One-Six reported.

Peeples gunned the engine on the word "Band-Aid," and since he recognized the voice, he knew in which direction to turn. We slammed through a couple of hedgerows and then came upon two APCs close together. One was obviously standing guard over a stricken friend. On the ground lay two soldiers while a third was propped up against the track. Sacher and Gaydon were off Band-Aid before Peeples had come to a full stop. I told our passenger with the sprained ankle to take Gaydon's seat behind the .50-cal and to keep a lookout. I then jumped over the side to assist in any way I could. Peeples remained with Band-Aid, in case Band-Aid had to move quickly.

Sacher worked on one of the men lying on the ground. Gaydon fit a splint over a shattered arm of the soldier propped up against the track. The third soldier was dead. After Gaydon got the splint on, he said, "Sir, give him a shot of morphine, I'm going to give Sacher a hand."

Sacher continued treating the patient, Gaydon checked very closely for other wounds. The patient had multiple wounds to his left side, but he had a strong pulse, and not much bleeding. It was obvious the patient was going into shock.

What saved this person's life was the fact that he was wearing his flak jacket. An IV solution was plugged into his arm. By this time Sacher had patched his patient up so most wounds were covered.

I finished giving the other patient his shot and went over to the dead soldier. He was killed instantly; he had a gaping hole in his head, and there was nothing anyone could do for him. I took down his line number, his name, and serial number. I also removed his wallet and put it in a waterproof bag and placed it around

The Tragedy of Vietnam, Again

his neck. This was to keep it from getting soaked in blood. Part of my job, being the medical platoon leader, was to oversee the identification of the deceased, to inventory all personal effects, and to ship all off to the proper authority for forwarding through official channels back to the next of kin.

Peeples retrieved a body bag and tossed it down to us. Gaydon helped me put the dead soldier in the bag and zip it up. Some extra hands appeared to help lift the body up onto Band-Aid, and we cradled him between the open surfboard and the front of Band-Aid. (The dead could not be carried via medical transportation, they had to use nonmedical means, and thus the body came with us and not Dust-Off.)

"Dust-Off is on its way," Peeples yelled to us, "ETA (estimated time of arrival) about five minutes."

Gaydon and Sacher attended to their patients and put both on litters. While they did that, I cleared an area so nothing would be blown away when Dust-Off came in to land. After about three minutes' time, Peeples threw a canister of violet smoke. In no time, a helicopter burst overhead and proceeded to live up to its name. We were completely blasted by the prop wash and pelted with dust, dirt, sticks, rice stalks, and anything else free to go flying about.

The Dust-Off helicopter set down about twenty feet from the wounded. Gaydon and Sacher grabbed the closest litter and moved out toward the helicopter, keeping their heads low. No sooner had they loaded this litter than they turned and helped load the second litter, which was being carried by some friends of the wounded man. As soon as the two litters were loaded, Dust-Off took off.

The sun was just beginning to set. Alpha-Six was waiting for the wounded to be medevacuated out of the area, before giving the order for all vehicles to pull out. Gaydon told our patient with the ankle sprain to ride the track that had lost three of its crew and to help them get back to base camp. Once in base camp he was to report to the aid station.

On the way back to Hawk Hill, Gaydon called in the line numbers of all the wounded and the dead soldier, so the necessary paperwork could be started. Every soldier in Vietnam was given a number that was unique only to him. This allowed personal information to be sent over the radio, but was useless to any unauthorized listener, especially the enemy. (For example my line number was 317 and if I were to be injured the radio message would have gone something like, "Headquarters Troop, line number 317, Mike Foxtrot Whiskey right leg." Translation, Christopher Noble, Headquarters Troop, name of next of kin, home town address, etc, had multiple fragmentation wounds of his right leg.")

It was after five o'clock when the order to pull out was given. The sun had just ducked down behind the mountain ridge to the west. The day's tally was twelve NVA soldiers killed, three prisoners taken, a bunch of papers had been sent to Division, and a major weapons cache had been found and destroyed. We had one killed and two wounded, but not due to the enemy; it was due to "friendly fire," which in fact was not very friendly.

I never really saw any "live action" during the entire time. That was the way it was much of the time when fighting in Vietnam. The underbrush and hedgerows were too high and dense to see through; if you were on one side and the action was only three feet away, you'd see nothing but hear a great deal.

I did not go out with Alpha Troop the next day, because I had to take care of the soldier killed the day before. Alpha Troop went back to the same village, but from a different direction. That day ended up in a huge shoot-em-up, with the enemy losing sixty-five soldiers KIA, and twenty prisoners captured; Alpha Troop had no causalities.

Because of the papers the tunnel rat discovered that first day, our unit later uncovered five tons of rice, which we gave back to the villages whose rice paddies had been destroyed by our vehicles going through their fields. Also, on those papers were the names of all the local VC members in the area, including some who were members of the local government military forces. Needless to say, those individuals were rounded up very quickly by the local forces.

The Battle of the Pink Ville

Tank busting through some "wool".

The garden with weapons hidden in it.

The Tragedy of Vietnam, Again

Tunnel entrance

Medic Charles Peeples

Treating a patient in the field.

The Battle of the Pink Ville

In the field and concealment.

Searching the enemy area

The Tragedy of Vietnam, Again

Treating the wounded in the field.

Medic Dale Sacher left and Larry Gaydon to right.

Changing of the Guard

Well, Doc Davis was so short; this was the day we all look forward to. He'd gone to the helipad to catch the helicopter to Chu Lai so he could out-process. The only problem was that the medical platoon had not received Doc's replacement.

What we did receive was a very upset interim doctor. This creature arrived in the aid station and everyone knew immediately that someone was doing all of us a big favor. "I'm Captain Goldberg, and I'm not pleased at all being here. I don't know why I'm here or why that asshole in Chu Lai sent me up here!"

This was Doc's interim replacement's exact greeting to all of us, word for word. I think, *I have a good idea as to why we got him. Maybe the person in Chu Lai is not the ass, maybe it's you Captain Goldberg,* I thought.

"Hi, I'm Chris Noble," I said, holding out my hand.

"I don't care who you are, I'm here for one week and then I'll never have to see any of you ever again."

The Tragedy of Vietnam, Again

Holy smokes, I thought. *What the hell are we to do with this guy?* All the medics left the aid station as if it were afire; it was just Captain Goldberg and me.

Maybe if I tried all over again we could get off to a better start. "Welcome to the First of the First," I stated. "Let me show you where you can stow your gear."

"I already found it, thank you, Lieutenant."

"Look Captain, I don't know what your problem is, but we're trying to make you feel welcome. If you have a problem then I suggest you take it up with the Division Surgeon General; don't take it out on us, all right, sir?" I then turned and left the aid station before he could answer.

Once outside I thought, *"Oh my Lord, what do we have on our hands?"*

"Psst...Lieutenant, come here," I heard and looked over toward the medics' bunker. Nathan Snow, one of the medics that Doc and I pulled out of the field, was waving for me to come over.

I walked over as if nothing was wrong and went down into the bunker. All the medics who had come to say good-bye to Doc Davis were there, and it showed on their faces; they were just as concerned about Captain Goldberg as I was. I said to myself, *be positive and don't shoot him down, at least not too badly.*

"What's the matter, guys?" I asked. *What a stupid thing to say; I knew darn well what the matter was.*

"What do we do, sir? How are we going to work for this guy?" Dan Miller asked.

"Lieutenant, this Captain Goldberg can go back to Chu Lai for all we care," Gary Lambdin added.

"This guy is a shithead and he can go to hell. I won't do anything he tells me to do," Reed stated.

"Wait a minute, I don't like what I see so far, but we have a job and we'll do our job just as Doc has trained us. Now, as I understand, this Captain Goldberg will be with us for only one week. We can all suffer for that long. Just think about boot camp and that DI (drill instructor) you just hated. We're all going to do just as Captain Goldberg says, just as if Doc Davis had ordered it. If any of you feel you have a personnel complaint, then you come to me and I'll see what I can do, but we have to continue regardless of any problems that Captain Goldberg might have, all right? Do any of you have any questions?"

"I don't like him, not at all," Stewart stated.

"You don't have to like this guy, but at least be polite. Don't do anything where he can get you in trouble."

There was general agreement that the motions would be gone through, but no one was going to go out of his way for our uninvited guest.

"Why don't you people bust up and get some chow? Then do the morning chores. You all know what each is required to do."

I left the enlisted men alone. They were good people and they would do the correct thing.

I went over to the aid station and found Captain Goldberg looking the place over.

"I apologize for our last conversation," I said.

"No, I apologize. Look, I don't want to be here. Those idiots in Chu Lai stuck me up here, because they don't like me; it's not your fault."

"Well, as I told you before, my name is Chris." I held out my hand.

"My name is David," he replied as we shook hands. "Where are all the medics hiding?"

"Over at the EM bunker or they're off eating breakfast; are you hungry?"

"What's the food like here?"

"You really want to know? It sucks! The food is good until the cooks get hold of it, but then something happens and it's not for the best. Once in a while we get a good meal, but the medics prefer to eat LRRP meals over the chow hall food. You want to go to breakfast? They can't screw up dried cereal," I suggested.

David Goldberg sighed. "Why not, let's go."

I gave him basically the same tour as Doc Davis gave me the first time when we went to lunch. In the chow hall David Goldberg did a wonderful job impressing the other officers. He let it be known that he was doing the 1/1 Cav a big favor. All I could do was roll my eyes and hope any and all flak that came our way landed all over our new captain and not on the rest of the platoon.

David Goldberg was a piece of work. He came from New York City and was very proud of the place. He had the same attitude toward New York as Texans have about Texas. He managed to make everybody's life absolutely miserable. Our only salvation was that our new Doc, Captain Albers, was due to arrive within six days. I knew that David Goldberg would never last in this unit, because the CO would throw him right out. You can't have a person in a responsible position with as big a chip on his shoulder as this guy had.

On the last night Captain Goldberg was with us, about an hour after sunset, Charlie Troop was showered with mortars. The attack lasted for no more than a minute.

At the first sound of an explosion, all the medics quickly went to the end of the bunker toward the incoming rounds and sat on the floor with their backs against the wall.

About ten minutes later, we heard an APC approaching the aid station at a high rate of speed, so we sprang into action to receive any injured. I ran outside to make sure no lights were showing through any cracks of the bunker's blackout curtains hanging over the ends of the windows.

The mortar rounds caught a group of Charlie Troop maintenance people out in the open. There were two

The Tragedy of Vietnam, Again

killed and eight wounded. The Charlie Troop medics quickly moved the wounded into the aid station; the dead were left outside, out of the way.

David Goldberg was so scared, he couldn't move. Dan Miller said, "Hey, Doc, come on, we have wounded to take care of." All David Goldberg could do was huddle in the corner and shake.

"Come on you guys, get to work," I ordered. "Lambdin, you help Kelly." Kelly was a 91-Charlie, (our super-trained medic, and was classified the same as a practical nurse.) "Kelly, you take the most seriously wounded. Kline and Miller, you take the next, and Stewart, Reed, each of you take someone; I'll take care of the med-evac." That was all the pep talk the medics needed; Doc Davis had trained the unit well.

Kelly and Lambdin cut off the clothing of their patient and revealed approximately thirty fragmentation wounds to the back of his legs and butt. All appeared to be flesh wounds as there was no severe bleeding.

Kimmy Hobbs, Charlie Troop senior medic, quickly checked all the wounded and came up with a preliminary diagnosis for our wounded. One broken arm, one patient who showed no signs of wounds, but kept saying, "I'm dying, I'm dying." All the rest had multiple fragmentation wounds.

I had most of the paperwork done and called the TOC, where LTC Cousland answered the field phone. I gave him my report on the wounded, the line numbers

Changing of the Guard

of the dead, and told him we needed to Dust-Off eight patients immediately.

When I finished talking with the colonel, Captain Goldberg stood up and walked very calmly to where Kelly and Lambdin were working. Everyone in the aid station had completely forgotten about him. Captain Goldberg said quietly, "I'll take over," and went to work. There wasn't enough room for three people to work, so Lambdin came over to help me with the Dust-Off.

David Goldberg was very concerned about the patient who kept crying that he's dying. He went over to the patient and questioned him. "Why do you say you're dying? Where are you hurt?" he asked.

"I don't know, but I'm dying; I just know it," the patient said quietly.

"Set him up with an IV and make sure he's on the first Dust-Off," Captain Goldberg ordered.

The field phone rang and it was the TOC telling us that Dust-Off was bringing up a Chinook helicopter and all patients would be taken at the same time. We were to have all patients at the helipad within ten minutes.

"Hobbs, you take all ambulatory patients up in Charlie-Band-Aid. What do we do with the two litter patients?"

"No, you have three litters," David Goldberg ordered. "I want him to go on a litter," as he pointed to the patient who thought he was dying.

The Tragedy of Vietnam, Again

"Three it is, we'll take them up in the FLA," I stated. "Let's get going!"

We set up two jeeps about one hundred feet apart and they were positioned so that when the headlights were turned on, the light beams intersected over the helipad where the helicopter was to land. We kept everything in total darkness, and when needed we quickly turn on the lights to guide the helicopter in. The lights were to be cut off as soon the aircraft touched down; we didn't want to help the enemy; they had already done enough damage for one night.

After the patients were on their way, we then had the grim task of taking care of the men who had been killed. We did what we had to do and what wasn't urgent could wait until the next morning. When I finally got back to the aid station, David Goldberg got up and walked to the center of the room to speak.

"Men, I have something to say. I owe you all an apology. I have never witnessed such coolness, such professionalism in my life. I have been way out of line and I'm very sorry for that. You stand head and shoulders above your counterparts in the hospitals in Chu Lai. I'm proud to have had the privilege of knowing you; I'm sorry for my actions." David Goldberg then went to his room. The Charlie Troop medics returned to their bunker, and the aid station medics went back to their bunker, all except Snow, for he had the duty, and had the pleasure of cleaning up the aid station.

Changing of the Guard

The next day, Dick Albers, our new doc, arrived and much to our relief he wasn't at all like our interim doc. Dick Albers came from Illinois, was about thirty-nine years old and was one hell of a good doc. He knew his stuff, and fit in very quickly; everyone liked him.

Unfortunately, the patient we dusted-off who thought he was dying, died before the helicopter reached Chu Lai. We never did find out what was wrong with him. Doc Albers said, "When a patient tells you he's dying, listen to him, because usually he's right."

Alpha medic's bunker and rear of Alpha Bandaid.

The Tragedy of Vietnam, Again

Standing in Headquarters Troop, Bravo Troop far right, Charlie Troop far left

The back side of the mountain to our west.

Trade Bait and To Save A Life

A comparatively long time had gone by without any of our platoons sighting the enemy. Doc Albers and I felt that this would be a good time to scrounge various items for our unit, to provide better service to our troops.

The colonel wanted to convert one of our slick (unarmed) helicopters into an impromptu medevac helicopter, because we had been having problems with our local Dust-Off unit. Basically this unit was chicken and they didn't like picking up wounded if the enemy was still in the area firing their weapons—neither did we, but we still did what we had been trained to do.

There was an unfortunate experience when we had to wait for the action to clear before Dust Off would pick up the wounded. In doing so, one of our patients died after waiting for approximately an hour to be evacuated out to one of the nearby hospitals.

If we could obtain some litter straps, then with these straps we could carry up to three litter patients, plus four or five ambulatory patients, all at the same time. The litter patients could be carried one stacked above the other. I was on a quest and was going to Quin Nhon, ironically on a Dust-Off helicopter.

The Tragedy of Vietnam, Again

As I looked out the helicopter's open side, I watched the green patchwork countryside slip under the aircraft, in a slow methodical manner, as we worked our way south toward Quin Nhon. The rice paddies reminded me of a green velvet skirt lying on a floor, where a child or puppy had run over and given it a mighty kick, so that the material no longer lay flat but was badly mussed. In between the wrinkles, thin, light coffee-colored ribbons wound their way around the ridges and moved extremely slowly toward the dark blue South China Sea, which, at that moment, had white caps throughout.

The helicopter followed Highway One, and a Red Ball Express, or truck convoy, was pounding its way north with great clouds of dust bellowing up after each truck. It was agreed upon by all transportation people that there was no good position in any convoy. The lead vehicle did not have to contend with the heavy curtain of dust, so long as you didn't end up behind another convoy. All vehicles behind the first truck had the pleasure of hitting any mines the first truck missed, or whenever a VC decided to push the button to detonate his planted mine. They also had to eat and breathe the thick curtain of powdery dust for the entire trip; the dust was so thick you couldn't see anything more than thirty feet in front of you. The only saving grace was when it rained, but then everyone had to drive on a dirt road that was slick.

Trade Bait and To Save A Life

It didn't seem as if we were flying very fast, for we were flying at twenty-one hundred feet, and at that altitude, the aircraft is out of small-arms range, which was a comforting thought. Also, the temperature was cool compared to the hot, humid, steam-bath environment at ground level. Highway One ran parallel to the South China Sea and at times almost ran out onto the broad white beach itself. The scene reminded me of a travel poster for Hawaii. The wide beaches lined with palm trees and little bamboo huts tucked along the beach, far enough up the beach so the big surf could not reach them. The only thing missing were the hula girls and their grass skirts. Someone, someday, will make a fortune by selling off South Vietnam and turning it into a cheap tourist attraction that will cost a fortune: "The last tropical paradise on earth."

It was amazing, as I looked down at the rice paddies and the sun's rays shone through the clouds, they played upon the fields, as if they were spotlights on a grand stage. As I studied these lit-up areas, a flight of snow-white doves flew in formation, and flashed their brilliance off and on as all the birds turned in unison. The striking contrast between the snow-white and the dark green background was inspiring, almost as if the doves were a message sent from high above this war-torn land.

The pilot received an urgent call to pick up some wounded; it was along our way. As we approached our targeted landing zone (LZ), I was brought quickly back

The Tragedy of Vietnam, Again

to reality. Vietnam was not and probably would not be for a long time, a favorite watering hole for the rich and famous international jet set.

Cobra gunships were working an area hard to the southwest of our location. These helicopters looked as if they belonged to a hive of bees that had just been robbed of their honey. There were five or six aircraft flying around in a circle formation, trying never to cover the same ground twice. It was like watching a silent movie; you could see what was happening, but you heard nothing except the whamp, whamp, whamp of our aircraft's rotors.

All of a sudden, a Cobra gunship would break away and quickly dart off at an angle. Slowly from the trees, a small cloud of smoke rose. This action was repeated time and again, as we drew closer and closer. This was the Vietnam War, as a bird saw it.

The earphone that was part of my flight helmet burst into action as the pilot told the copilot, "Call Angry Beaver and have him pop smoke. I think that's him over where the action is."

"Roger," the copilot replied and turned some knobs on the radio to the ground forces' radio frequency, which Dust-Off control had given the crew.

"Angry Beaver, this is Dust-Off Four-Three."

"Dust-Off Four-Three, Angry Beaver One-Niner, you're to our east, it's all right to come in. Our gunships will escort you; we'll give you cover fire, over."

Trade Bait and To Save A Life

"Angry Beaver One-Niner, pop smoke, I'll identify color, out."

"Roger, Dust-Off."

I thought, *those infantry grunts have better be telling the truth about the east being free of enemy fire.* It's no fun going into a hot LZ in an unarmed aircraft. All we had on board in the way of self-protection were two M-16s, and one M-79 automatic; this was like fighting a duel with a BB gun against a 12-gauge shotgun. I could understand our Dust-Off unit's reluctance to come into a hot LZ, but it was their job to retrieve the wounded and get them back to a hospital as quickly as possible. That was what they had been trained to do; just like the 1/1 Cav had to stand up and fight the enemy on the ground, eyeball to eyeball.

Violet smoke drifted skyward from a small clearing about a mile and a half away. The pilot keyed the mic. "Angry Beaver, this is Dust-Off, I see violet smoke."

"Dust-Off, that's a Roger, out," the radio barked back.

Dust-Off suddenly broke to the left and fell out of the sky, dropping approximately eighteen hundred feet before pulling out at treetop level, about a mile from the violet smoke. This maneuver was so that Dust-Off did not tip off the enemy any sooner than necessary as to what their exact course of flight would be.

Two helicopter gunships had already come over to where they'd intercept us and give covering fire as we made our approach at fifty to sixty knots toward the

The Tragedy of Vietnam, Again

makeshift landing zone. Each gunship took up a station in front of Dust-Off, one on each side, both firing their mini guns. Between these two gunships, thousands of rounds of ammo were being fired every minute to keep any enemy well hidden, thus preventing them from shooting at us as we flew overhead.

The Dust-Off pilot tried to keep the aircraft as close to the ground as possible, making the craft as hard a target as he could. The trees whipped past the open side, while the flight crew played the trees like a game of chicken.

All of a sudden there was a small clearing full of violet smoke in front of us. The pilot cranked the helicopter on its side and pulled maximum g's (gravitational force) in the opposite direction. The end result was very dramatic, as I sat upon the floor looking out the doorway; all I saw was ground, but my brain's ability to think clearly was slowed down and refused to register what was going on around me. My eyes felt as if they just fell back into my head, and my stomach felt as if it was nowhere near the helicopter; the next thing I knew we were on the ground. How those pilots could function under those g-forces, I'll never understand.

I grabbed hold of a litter lying on the cabin's floor and slid it out onto the ground to replace the litter we were about to receive. Just as the litter hit the ground, two ambulatory patients jumped on board. One of the crew's medics pushed these wounded soldiers off to one side, to make room for the litter patient.

Trade Bait and To Save A Life

The pilot looked over his shoulder to where I was; he cut in over the intercom. "Where's the litter patient?"

I shouted to one of the ambulatory patients, "Where is the litter patient?"

"He's coming, he's coming," the bewildered soldier replied, and pointed off to the right.

Off to the right side a group of GIs made their way toward Dust-Off, trying to stay as close to the ground as possible. When the procession was about ten feet away from the aircraft, there was a dreaded sound of, clunk, then clunk-clunk.

"For Christ's sake, can't those grunts see we're taking fire," blasted in my ears. Two handles of the litter appeared in the doorway and with one mighty pull from the crew chief, the litter, patient and all were jerked in one motion into the helicopter. As the litter was grabbed, the pilot gunned the throttle. Before the litter was entirely inside, the aircraft was ten feet off the ground and making fast tracks out, the same way we came in.

I observed the wounded soldier on the litter, as one of the Dust-Off medics locked the litter into the straps and then adjusted his bandages; making the patient as comfortable as possible. A bottle of dextrose solution rested next to the patient's head, connected to the patient's right arm, by a thin plastic tube. The clear fluid in the bottle was supplementing lost body fluids, thus keeping his blood pressure up.

The Tragedy of Vietnam, Again

The helicopter climbed back to two thousand feet by the time I switched my attention to the two ambulatory patients. One had a flesh wound on his upper left arm. The medic checked his field medical tag and asked if he would like something for his pain. The patient looked as pale as a ghost, nodded his head yes, so the medic took out a quarter-grain Syrette of morphine and gave the patient the injection. The Syrette looked like a baby-sized tube of toothpaste with a darning needle attached to the tube. Most patients agreed that the needle was a second cousin to an ice pick, and did more damage and produced more pain than the bullet or frag (shrapnel) that wounded them. Quickly, the medic made a note of the medication on the field medical card and the time it was given.

The third patient had a minor fragmentation wound on his right arm and was talking to his buddy on the litter, telling him he was going to be all right.

The pilot called Quin Nhon Control for instructions, "Quin Nhon Control, this is Dust-Off Four-Three, over."

"Dust-Off Four-Three, this is Quin Nhon Control, over," the radio replied.

"Control, I have one Uniform Sierra (American) litter, sucking chest (a puncture wound to the lung); two Uniform Sierra ambulatories, one Mike Foxtrot Whisky (multiple fragmentation wounds) left arm, the

Trade Bait and To Save A Life

other Mike Foxtrot Whiskey right arm, where do you want us to go, over?"

There was a pause before the voice on the other end of the radio answered, "Roger Dust-Off Four-Three, 67 Evac Hospital, over!"

The pilot answered, "Roger Quin Nhon Control, 67 Evac Hospital it is, out."

The copilot entered the necessary adjustments to the aircraft's autopilot to bring us to the intended destination. The wounded passengers were very quiet and showed signs of being terribly scared about what lay ahead. The litter patient was talking to himself and to God, convincing himself that he'd make it. After approximately twelve minutes of flight time, the material yards of Quin Nhon came into view and, at the same time, the aircraft started to lose altitude. The material yard was piled high with boxes of all sizes and shapes. Navy landing craft were transferring the supplies from the ships at anchor in the harbor and running them onto the beach. Men without shirts were driving huge forklifts around piling the material in neat rows, only to be moved again by some other crew. As the helicopter lost altitude to about one hundred feet, it was more or less like walking into a sauna bath, as hot humid air replaced the cooler thin air.

Dust-Off had to be careful to follow flight plans or else it might end up being run over by a large, four-engine cargo plane or a high-performance jet fighter taking off or landing at the airport.

The Tragedy of Vietnam, Again

The Sixty-Seventh Evac Hospital came into view next to the airfield, all gleaming white with huge red crosses painted on its roof. There were four or five soldiers in neatly creased fatigues waiting at the helipad and they kept a close eye on our Dust-Off. The pilot brought the plane down in the center of the runway, about ten feet off the ground and carefully worked his way over to the waiting reception committee.

As soon as we touched down, the ground crew started moving toward the craft. The litter patient was ready to go, all clamps had been released. Two hands grabbed hold of the litter and pulled it out while other hands grabbed hold of the other end, and then the patient was on his way up a ramp that led directly into the hospital's emergency room.

The two ambulatory patients followed the procession, each with an attendant by his side, ready to give assistance if needed.

"Hey, Lieutenant Noble," the pilot yelled, "They want you at Group Headquarters."

I shrugged my shoulders with a questioning look, as to ask, "What's up?"

The pilot shook his head and yelled back, "It just came over the radio; they want you, that's all."

I gathered my box full of junk and headed up the ramp to the hospital's emergency room to locate a phone. My trip so far had been fairly successful, but I still needed a set of litter straps. I tried Dust-Off in

Chu Lai, but that was an abrupt dead end. I turned to observe my surroundings before I entered the hospital. I saw the Dust-Off crew looking over the aircraft's tail carefully. They estimated the bullet damage made while our patients were being picked up. One of the medics gave the OK sign to another enlisted man, and pointed to the Red Cross painted on the tail boom with three fingers held high. I guessed that meant all three rounds hit the red cross and there was no great damage done. The airport was dead; nothing was going on, except for the small group around Dust-Off.

55Th Medical Headquarters

The Tragedy of Vietnam, Again

Unloading the wounded at the 67th Evac

67th Evac Hospital's ER

Trade Bait and To Save A Life

The back view from C. Noble's quarters - One six foot wire fence and some mosquito screening was our security defense

I walked into the emergency room where a doctor, nurse, and two corpsmen worked on the litter patient. All his clothes had been cut off and lay in a heap under the litter. He lay as naked as the day he was born, while a nurse cleaned dried blood mixed with mud off his body, trying to get him ready for surgery. The IV bottle had been removed and replaced with whole blood; an oxygen mask was clamped over his face. The doctor had a metal probe and was sticking it into the various wounds.

In a corner, another nurse and two corpsmen were working on the ambulatory patients. They had removed their shirts, and the painstaking task of debriding and cleaning the wounds had started. One patient com-

The Tragedy of Vietnam, Again

plained that the nurse was as gentle as a Mack truck. I checked her out closely and observed she was almost as big as a Mack truck.

I picked up a telephone on a desk next to the door and called 55 Medical Group Headquarters to ask for a jeep to come pick me up. The voice on the other end assured me someone would be dispatched right away. This meant maybe sometime within an hour or so. I put the phone down and took in the rest of the emergency room.

Other than the patients we had brought in and the medical personnel working on them, the emergency room was empty. The room was set up to simultaneously handle thirty to forty litter patients and an equal number of ambulatory patients. All along the far wall were litter stands, which were nothing more than metal sawhorses without any litter. Each litter stand had a fresh IV ready to be used. Oxygen bottles were allocated to every other stand. Medical cabinets lined the walls at the foot of every space. A slop bucket was halfway between the front stand and the rear stand. The lighting was excellent, four rows of large neon lights went across the room, plus the building was of a tropical type. Tropical buildings had walls that went only halfway up, while screening made up the upper half of the side walls, to keep the bugs out. The roof had a long overhang, which prevented any water from coming in, but let light and air pass through freely.

Trade Bait and To Save A Life

By this time, the litter patient was on his way to X-ray, along with one of the ambulatory patients. The other ambulatory patient was being treated as he was, in the emergency room, and would be released back to his unit for duty.

I walked outside but found the jeep had not arrived to take me to Headquarters. As I sat upon a wall I thought, *what does Headquarters Group want with me? They don't even know that I'm here. All my trades have been fair; nobody's been screwed too badly, so it can't be that. Maybe the motor pool guy is upset, I traded four new inner tubes for one AK-47 that had been run over by one of our tanks and the barrel is slightly bent. No, it can't be that, because that Sergeant seemed pleased with that trade.*

My thoughts were rescued as a cloud of dust came to a screeching halt in front of me, with a large sign painted across the lower part of the front windshield that read, "MEDICAL REGULATOR."

"Are you looking for a ride to the Fifty-Fifth Medical Group, sir?" a youthful private asked, grinning from ear to ear. "Sarge sent me, sir."

I dumped my gear in the back of the jeep and climbed onto the passenger seat. The driver did a U-turn and quickly drove through Quin Nhon. The ride took all of five minutes and ended up in front of a bluish, pea-green double-story tropical building right next to the Eighty-Fifth Evacuation Hospital.

The Tragedy of Vietnam, Again

I jumped over an irrigation ditch and entered the Medical Regulator's office. This was a room with eight large blackboards taking up two walls. Each blackboard represented a large evacuation or surgical hospital under the control of Fifty-Fifth Medical Group Headquarters, to include all of the I Corps and II Corps areas, or the northern half of South Vietnam.

Each hospital's specialty was listed by the number of beds and how many beds were currently available. It also listed whether or not that specialty was available, and the status of the doctors at each hospital. If a doctor was sick or was on R&R, it was noted and patients requiring that specialty would not be sent to that particular hospital. The most critical patient, whether American or not and where the nearest specialty was available, dictated where Dust-Off went.

The Medical Regulator was the nerve center as far as the movement of all Army wounded personnel for the northern half of South Vietnam. This was the voice on the other end of all Dust-Off's radio, "Quin Nhon Control"

There were seven or eight radios along a third wall with long lists of unit call signs and radio frequencies. The radio Sergeant looked up at my name tag; he then turned and rummaged through a pile of papers and said, "Here you are, sir" as he handed me a note.

Printed in very neat handwriting were the words, "Lieutenant Noble, return to 'The Hill' as soon as possible, forget your mission, Doc."

Trade Bait and To Save A Life

"This came down for you on our Chu Lai radio, sir," the radioman stated. "I'm afraid there aren't many aircraft leaving at the moment."

"How about the Air Force?" I asked.

"I'm not sure, but I'll check with Sarge, at the field," the radioman answered. He turned to one of the radios, flipped a switch and spoke into the microphone, "Lazy Gopher, this is Quin Nhon Control, over."

"Yeah, Tex, whatcha want?" the radio barked back.

The Sergeant adjusted the volume and answered, "I have a person at my location that needs a ride to Chu Lai; what are his chances, over?"

"Tex, you tell him to get his ass down here pronto, for I've got a special going out in about twenty minutes. You had better have him check in with me, or else he ain't going to get on board, OK?"

"Lazy Gopher, this Quin Nhon Control, thanks a million; he's on his way right now."

The grinning private who had driven the jeep, had just entered the radio room and sat in a corner awaiting fresh orders, like driving the lieutenant back to the airfield. To the private's surprise, an E-5 Sergeant, who had POW Regulator on his desk, volunteered to drive me. He didn't seem very busy and this looked like a good excuse to get out of the office legitimately. I picked up my box, and followed the sergeant out the door, over the ditch and then headed for some jeeps.

The Tragedy of Vietnam, Again

We climbed into a typical, nondescript Army jeep, and we retraced the route I took before, through the crowed streets, dodging hordes of people, motorbikes, bicycles, and all sorts of military equipment, all crammed into a tight two-lane road.

We passed the Sixty-Seventh Evac Hospital; past a large aircraft hanger, where Bob Hope gave his Christmas show and where an aircraft was being repaired. We continued toward the airport control tower. The sergeant stopped the jeep in front of a small tropical building and jumped out with me in hot pursuit. We walked through a side door and entered where hopefully my ticket to Chu Lai lay.

There was an Air Force sergeant sitting behind a desk talking on the telephone. "Yeah, yeah, I'll see what I can do, but you're asking for a lot. It's going to cost you too…Yeah, yeah, OK; well somebody just came into my shop. Yeah, I'll see ya," the sergeant said as he hung up the phone.

"Hey, Joe, how's it going, how short are you now-a-days?"

My driver exclaimed, "One-oh-six, and getting shorter, how about you?"

"I'm down to 32 days and a wake-up. I'm so short I have to jump the cracks. Hell, 106 days, I'd slit my throat. Man, you're going to be here forever," the sergeant stated with disgust.

As for me, I didn't want to even think as to how many days I had left; it was well over two hundred.

Trade Bait and To Save A Life

"This is Lieutenant Noble; he's the one who needs a ride to Chu Lai. What can you do for him?"

"Nice to meet you, lieutenant, how about a beer?" the sergeant asked as he opened a small refrigerator and took out three cans of Miller. He handed one to me and tossed the other to my E-5 Sargeant.

"Look, I've got this bird coming into the Sixty-Seventh Evac to pick up a special patient and it's due in about twenty minutes. There's no problem in getting a ride, because there's only four people going up in that C-130; we'll go over once they've loaded up."

I put my "trade bait" box down beside the sergeant's desk and took the chair next to it. I drank my beer and listened to the Air Force sergeant dominate the conversation with what he was going to do once he got back home from Vietnam. Slowly, the sergeant became interested in the pile of junk I had in my box and asked, "What you got, lieutenant?"

"Oh, just some trade bait."

"You got any good stuff there?"

"That depends upon what you're looking for."

"Well, let's have a look, maybe we can do some business."

I put the box on his desk and the sergeant picked over it very carefully. "Where did you get this stuff?"

"My medics brought it in from the field."

"Hell, most of this stuff you couldn't give away," the NCO exclaimed.

The Tragedy of Vietnam, Again

He picked up a North Vietnamese army helmet, which was made out of pressed cardboard and it had a bullet hole going in one side and out the other; the insides were covered with dried blood.

"Man, I'm glad I wasn't wearing this when these holes were made," the sergeant exclaimed, pointing to the holes. He put the helmet down on his desk. The next item taken out was a belt buckle that had a five-pointed star stamped on the front. The sergeant flipped the belt buckle over two or three times and then put it down beside the helmet.

"You got any weapons, sir?"

"No, not anymore. I had some but they were all traded."

"What do you want for these?" the sergeant asked pointing to the helmet and the belt buckle.

"I need a set of litter straps that will fit a Huey helicopter."

The sergeant waited for a bit, and then said, "Boy, you don't want much, do you, sir? I think that's too rich for this junk, I don't know though."

"I'll tell you what I'll do, Sarge, I'll throw in an NVA cigarette lighter that works." I reached into my pocket and tossed the lighter on his desk.

He picked up the cheaply stamped aluminum lighter and he spun the wheel. There was a shower of sparks that covered the back of his hand, and the top of the lighter; the wick burst into flame. I didn't tell him the lighter was totally useless if there was any wind.

Sarge was still not content, so the last item of any value I had were some North Vietnamese coins with the head of Ho Chi Minh stamped upon them. I put these on the bargaining table and this seemed to seal the negotiations.

"OK, it's a deal." The sergeant got up and led the way out of his office to a large metal storage container, in back of the building. The sarge pulled out a key and unlocked the door. Inside, shelves had been built and boxes were neatly stacked. The sarge went inside and picked up a box and tossed it to me. "Complements of the US Air Force, sir; I hope this is what you're looking for."

I opened the lid and much to my delight, inside was exactly what we needed. "Thank you, Sarge; thank you very much." (This was not stealing government property; this was called, "The unauthorized reallocation of government assets.")

There was a sharp increase in the noise level outside the storage shed. The Air Force sergeant walked me around the container and much to my surprise, a huge C-130, four-engine plane, taxied right up to where the Dust-Off helicopter had stood, right next to the emergency room entrance, at the 67 Evac Hospital.

"I think the plane is here," I shouted.

"Yeah, we had better get a move on," Sarge yelled back. "Dump your gear into my jeep, we'll take a shortcut. Hey, Joe, I'll see you later, OK?"

The Tragedy of Vietnam, Again

The POW Regulator, who had been quiet during all these high negotiations departed with, "I'll see you later, at the club."

The sergeant climbed into his jeep as I scrambled onto the passenger seat with all my belongings and off we went. We didn't go out on to the road, but up and over a sidewalk, down a ditch and then up a low embankment and out onto the runway.

"I don't believe in roads, they take too long," Sarge exclaimed proudly. It took us all of about a minute and a half to reach that plane. As we approached we were blasted by the prop wash.

The patient was being carried on a litter up the back ramp of the plane. He had a blanket wrapped around him and over his face, to keep the dirt and dust from covering him. I shook hands with the Air Force NCO and thank him for his help. I then followed the patient up the ramp and staked out my claim in an unoccupied corner, out of the way.

Much to my surprise, there was really nothing inside the aircraft but crew and some medical equipment; the medical team consisted of one doctor, two medics and the patient. The inside of the plane reminded me of the inside of a huge empty tin can.

A suction machine was being checked out by one of the medics as the doctor adjusted the oxygen mask on the face of the patient. Everybody else fumbled with his seat belt, including myself, as the back ramp closed halfway.

Trade Bait and To Save A Life

The plane started moving away from the Sixty-Seventh Evac, heading down the taxi strip for take-off. I was glad to be leaving Quin Nhon, because I didn't feel very safe there; too many local Vietnamese lived way to close to the US troops. Also, there were no American field troops nearby. The whole place was nothing but rear echelon people called REMFs, who barely knew which end of a rifle the bullet came out of. This was what I liked about the 1/1 Cav, many of their officers were West Point graduates, and I felt safe with them; at least they were supposed to know what was going on.

The plane gave a bump here and a lurch there. Occasionally, I was forced back into my seat, a canvas contraption that ran along the side of the aircraft; it was tremendously uncomfortable. It became hot inside the cabin, even with the tail ramp halfway open. The air-conditioning pipe ran along the cabin's ceiling and gave off what looked like a cloud of smoke, as it fought the humidity and heat. The plane moaned and groaned, it writhed and shook; none of which put me at ease. The worst part of the trip was there were no windows in the plane so I couldn't see where we were going.

The back ramp was raised all the way up and locked into position. After what seemed like an eternity, the engines increased their RPMs and the plane made its run down the runway. I felt sorry for the patient in one way; he was being bounced around as

The Tragedy of Vietnam, Again

the plane lurched along. On the other hand, he didn't know what was going on, because he was under heavy medication.

The flight to Chu Lai was very uneventful; the patient slept the whole trip. I found out from one of the medics that the patient had been shot five times and had developed a serious blood clot in one of his lungs. What he needed was a special operation that required a heart-lung machine. Incredibly, the only heart-lung machine in all of Vietnam was on board the Navy Hospital Ship, the *USS Repose*, which was presently heading at flank speed south to Chu Lai from Da Nang.

Once the plane landed in Chu Lai, the patient would be removed and loaded onto a waiting Dust-Off helicopter. The Dust-Off would then fly the patient out to the hospital ship. The flight took about one hour. After the plane landed, it pulled up beside a waiting helicopter at the end of the back ramp of our large aircraft.

I jumped off and went directly over to the Dust-Off pilot, whom I recognized and asked, "Can I hook a ride back to Hill 29 with you after this run?"

The pilot shrugged his shoulders and replied, "Wait, we have to see if there will be any room; if there is, no problem."

Nearby was the Chu Lai Arrival/Departures building, which had been dramatically improved since my arrival three months before. Troops waited for flights to all points within Vietnam. We were the entertainment for about thirty GIs, as the patient was carried slowly down the ramp by the aircraft's crew. The Army medics carried all the special equipment and lined it up beside the helicopter. This would all be loaded after the patient was on board.

One end of the litter was passed to the Dust-Off crew inside the helicopter and the litter was clamped into place. Next, the suction machine and the oxygen were to be loaded. The suction machine couldn't be used, as there was no electrical hookup in this particular aircraft. The doc and the medics climbed on board. The medics and doctor hooked up oxygen; the doc checked all vital signs and some more tubes were connected to the patient.

The outside audience was extremely interested in what was going on. They all had a look saying, *I hope the guy isn't too badly messed up, but it's better him than me!*

The pilot gave me the OK sign so I climbed on board and squeezed in just behind the pilot and copilot's seats. The doctor sat on the floor beside the patient's head, and the two medics sat on the floor near the patient's feet.

The helicopter skidded about for a second or two as the pilot lifted off gently, higher and higher, straight up, then dropped the nose slightly. We were heading off on the home stretch for the heart-lung machine.

The Tragedy of Vietnam, Again

The airport streamed beneath us as the helicopter gained speed. We passed tropical buildings lined up in neat rows. The Second Surgical Hospital streaked by, and then the port of Chu Lai with its water's edge piled high with war supplies. Out in the harbor, it looked like a Navy squadron of ships was at anchor.

There were LSTs, cargo ships of all sizes, and many other types, all painted the same color, except for one. The *USS Repose* was not battleship gray; it was a gleaming white ship with huge red crosses painted on her sides and deck. There was a helipad on her stern, which looked smaller than a postage stamp from our present location.

The pilot headed straight for the stern of the ship. The South China Sea was flat calm and the wind was slight. This made the landing process easy, and as soon as the pilot cut power to the engine, the waiting Navy crew came forward and removed the patient. The doctor and medics grabbed all their medical gear and jumped out of the aircraft. The last we saw of them, they were following the patient onto the ship.

The pilot gunned the engine and we took off again. The time to unload was approximately two minutes. One of the Dust-Off crew tapped me on my shoulder and shouted in my ear, "Where do you want to go?"

"Hill 29; follow Highway One north; it's just past Tam Ky. I'll show you when we get there," I yelled back.

Trade Bait and To Save A Life

The crewman relayed this to the pilot, who gave the OK sign. My mission had been successful. What I had just witnessed made me very proud of the US military, about how they took care of their own when the chips were down. Here was a young private, in the Army, who'd never know how the military had gone the extra mile to take care of him. Three branches of military services had to pull together so that all the pieces could get to the correct place, at the right time. This joint operation had required orders from one Navy admiral, one Air Force general, and two or three Army full colonels to work. Also, it was amazing that the Air Force unloaded this C-130 plane, full of combat troops waiting to take off on a mission; then the plane flew two hundred miles empty to Quin Nhon, in order to pick up one critically wounded Army private. The Navy admiral had to give the orders for the *USS Repose* to pull anchor and steam at flank speed to Chu Lai, to meet an Army Dust-Off helicopter.

A lot of armies would have let that private just die. I was so proud to be able to witness this incredible show of support for one boy. That unconscious patient probably felt, "The f-ing Army screwed me up; look at me now!" I was the Medical Regulator for the Fifty-Fifth Medical Group when this medical evacuation took place.

Getting in Trouble

The day was beautiful, not a cloud in the sky. The temperature was just right, a very pleasant seventy degrees. The First of the First had not fired a round in anger for nearly three weeks. It was as if the North Vietnamese had packed up and gone home. Maybe the last encounter hurt the enemy more than we had anticipated. A physical body count had revealed that 167 North Vietnamese army regular soldiers had been killed. The question remained how many wounded. A rice paddy due west of the battle scene, beyond a low hill was littered, like a convention floor after a big victory party, but this field was littered with bloody gauze bandages. We found this evidence two days after the battle and the enemy had long since left the area.

Doc and I estimated, by the amount of debris laying on the ground and the damage done to the rice crop that somewhere between two to three hundred people had been treated in that area.

All the units of the 1/1 Cav were in base camp with the exception of one platoon from each line troop who went out looking for the enemy. All other units were required to do the necessary maintenance work on their equipment and repairing bunkers. Some of the troops got into trouble, because there wasn't enough to keep them busy. The first sergeants were not happy, because they had to earn their pay by keeping the units running smoothly; they didn't like troublemakers.

I had no worries, because my medics were a good group and very rarely did they get into any trouble. The field phone rang in the aid station, so I picked it up. "Aid Station, Lieutenant Noble speaking, may I help you?" I'd been programmed to say.

"Sir," exploded in my ear. "You get this son of a bitch out of my unit now! I'm going to court-martial him, there's no way he's going to get out of it; I have had it with him!"

I figured the voice belonged to the master sergeant Grant from Bravo Troop, nicknamed "the Bear." He got the name because he was as cuddly as a mother bear when defending her young cubs; he was also as hairy as a bear.

"All right, sergeant," I answered, "but who are you going to court-martial?"

"Radford, that's who, I got him this time and there's nothing anybody can do to save his ass!"

"All right, I'm coming over." I hung up the phone. I'd had some problems with Specialist Radford in the past. I knew what the problem was before going over to Bravo Troop; Radford got drunk and then opened his fat mouth. That was what had always gotten him into trouble before; Radford couldn't hold his booze.

Getting in Trouble

I got in the jeep and drove slowly over to Bravo Troop. I was not in a hurry to see my problem, or to listen to the Bear. Radford was sitting in front of Bravo Troop's Orderly Room, on top of his duffel bag, looking very forlorn as I drove up.

I pulled the jeep up in front of the building and looked as stern as I could possibly muster. "Put your junk in the jeep and wait for me."

I got out of the jeep, before Radford could say a word, marched up the steps, and entered the tropical building.

Master Sergeant Grant was sitting at his desk going through the Uniform Code of Military Justice. He looked up at me as I walked in and stated with total venom, "I've got him and I'm going to hang his ASS!"

"Can you tell me one thing, what did he do?"

The sergeant rose from his desk with the look of a mad man and screamed, "He punched out one of my E-7 platoon sergeants. That medic of yours broke my sergeant's jaw, and knocked out three teeth! That's what your medic has done, sir!" Sarge was really mad; the veins on the sides of his neck were sticking way out.

Oh, Christ, Radford, you have done it now, I thought.

"OK, Sergeant, I'll get him out of here; he'll be back at the aid station, if and when you need him."

The Tragedy of Vietnam, Again

As I walked out the door, the first sergeant yelled after me, "And I don't want to ever see him in Bravo Troop again." The door slammed shut; I walked slowly to the jeep.

Once in the jeep and heading back to the aid station, I stated, "Well, you've really done it now! What the hell did you think you were doing?"

Radford was visibly shaken up. All he could say was, "I'm sorry, sir. I didn't mean to screw up, I'm really sorry."

I thought he was about to burst out crying, which I did not need, so I stopped the jeep. "I would like to ask you only one question, why did you punch the guy?"

Radford looked right at me and said, "Because Sarge was cheating at cards, sir!"

"What? Come on, you've got to be kidding!"

"No, sir, I'm telling you the truth, so help me God, sir."

"Then you tell me everything from the very beginning."

"Well, sir, there was nothing going on, and me and some of the other guys were in the bunker."

"What other guys?"

"The other medics, sir. Well, Sarge comes over to the bunker, looking for a game of poker and we had nothing to do, so we said OK."

"Were you gambling?"

"Yes sir."

"Who suggested playing for money?"

"Sarge did."

"OK, continue."

"Well, we all had some booze and were playing. Everyone was enjoying themselves. Well, after a few rounds and everything was going real smooth, I would say maybe an hour after we had started, I noticed Sarge started winning all the big pots. Well, I'd had more than I should have to drink, but I see that Sarge is cheating. He was cheating, sir!" Radford pleaded, looking right at me.

Go on, what happened?"

"Well, I accused him of cheating and he just sat there looking at me, dumb like. I reach over and grab his hand to uncover the cards he's hiding. He knocks my hand away, so I punched him. I only hit him once, so help me, sir."

I started up the jeep and drove back to the aid station, not saying a word. I had to weave my way around some APC lined up at the fuel rack. When we reached the aid station, I brought the jeep to a stop and said, "Radford, you're in a world of hurt right now, and you have gotten yourself into a hell of a lot of trouble. I told you the last time if you screwed me over one more time, I'd screw you five times as bad. Do you remember that?"

"Yes, sir, I remember and I'm sorry I messed up."

"How many witnesses were there when you punched the sergeant, and who are they?"

The Tragedy of Vietnam, Again

"Five or six, all the medics in the bunker and a couple of others," he answered, as he dragged his duffel bag into the aid station.

"You stay here and do not leave the aid station," I yelled after him. I turned the jeep around and headed back to Bravo Troop's medics' bunker.

The trip was short and not much action was going on in Bravo Troop. I walked into the bunker and it looked like a wake. All the medics were sitting around, not saying very much. To add to the gloom, the bunker had no windows; the only light came in through the open door.

"OK, Clancy, I've listened to Radford, now you tell me what happened."

"Have a beer, sir?" he asked.

"Yes, I would love to have a beer, thank you; now what happened?"

Clancy was my senior medic, in Bravo Troop, and he was older than all of the medics; he was in his mid thirties, or possibly early forties, it was hard to tell. He handed me a beer saying, "Well, Sarge comes over looking for a card game. We were all agreeable, so we set up right here at this table. Well, Sarge has had quite a bit to drink, as had Radford, and you know how well Radford can hold his booze. Well, we're playing along for a while and all of a sudden Radford accuses sarge of cheating. He grabs Sarge's hand and sure enough there are extra cards in it. Radford then goes wild and he hits Sarge only once with a really good shot and,

Getting in Trouble

man, did he mess Sarge up. We all jumped Radford, and Sarge bolts out of here like a shot. We haven't seen him since; you know the rest, sir."

"All right, are you sure that Sarge was cheating?"

"There is no question about it, Lieutenant; he was cheating."

"Would you be willing to testify at a court-martial as to what you just told me?"

"Yes, sir, I will. I don't really care for Radford and he was wrong to punch the platoon sargeant, but he shouldn't be court-martialed for what he did.

I left the medics' bunker and headed for the Orderly Room in Headquarters Troop to do some homework. The master sergeant for Headquarters Troop reminded me, every time I saw him that he would make a wonderful grandfather to a small child.

As I walked into the Orderly Room, I said, "How's it going, Sergeant Williams?"

"Oh, paperwork and more paperwork, that's what this Army seems to run on. I just never seem to get out from under it," he complained.

"Sergeant Williams, I've got a couple of questions for you."

"All right, fire away," he answered with a smile.

"Is it against Army regulations for personnel to gamble?"

"Yes, it's against regulations to gamble."

"Then it's against regulations for noncommissioned officers to gamble with, let's say spec fours or fives is that correct?"

"That's correct. May I ask why you're asking these questions?"

"Well, one of my medics was gambling with a platoon sergeant and my medic caught the sarge cheating. There was money involved and the short of the story is he punched the NCO. Now Bravo Troop is going to court-martial my medic for striking the sergeant. If they want to get my medic, that's all right with me, but this sergeant, I feel needs to answer for his actions."

"Well, sir, it looks to me as if you might want to countercharge this NCO with, let me see…definitely conduct unbecoming of an NCO. You can also get him for gambling with a lower-ranking enlisted man. With what you say, they will not have much of a chance."

"Thank you, Sarge, thank you very much. I'll be giving you a present shortly."

I left the Orderly Room and drove back to the aid station, to find Radford stowing his gear in a footlocker at the end of an unoccupied cot in the Aid Station's enlisted men's bunker.

"Radford, come over to the aid station."

I had him come into my office area and informed him, "You're going to countercharge the platoon sergeant with conduct unbecoming and also gambling with lower-ranking enlisted men, all right?"

Getting in Trouble

Radford went into shock; he sucked in air and held his breath for a few seconds and then let it out saying, "Do I have to, sir? I'm just going to get in more trouble."

"Yes, you have to, and you won't get in any more trouble; you're already in enough trouble."

Resigned to the fact that he was as good as in jail for a while, Radford sighed, "All right, whatever you think is best, sir."

I typed out a note to the first sergeant in Bravo Troop, informing him of Radford's desire to counter-charge the platoon sergeant and had Radford sign it. I then drove over to Bravo Troop to hand deliver the bad news to the Bear, but he wasn't in. I left the note on his desk so he couldn't miss it, and then beat a hasty retreat over to the Bravo Troop's medic bunker.

Clancy was getting ready to go to supper, so I told him what we were up to, and asked if he should see the Bear, to tell him I'd left a note on his desk. I was glad the Bear was not around, because I didn't need to get into an argument with him, since I knew I'd lose. The Bear had way too many years of experience, so this was a hit-and-run operation on my part.

On my way back to the aid station I dreamed up various punishments I could dish out for my favorite misfit medic. I hit upon a scheme that I felt was fitting, not only for the crime that had been committed, but that would satisfy me for going to bat for the culprit, as well as help the local community in Headquarters

The Tragedy of Vietnam, Again

Troop. As I pulled up in front of the aid station, I'd worked out most of the details; all that remained was the presentation.

Radford was talking with Dan Miller and Ron Kline, telling and showing them the finer points of the story. I detected that most of the remorse and sorrow he showed to me earlier seemed too have vanished. As I entered the treatment area, I let my presence be known.

"Radford, do you have all your gear settled in the other bunker?"

"Yes, sir," my hero answered in a humbled voice.

"Good, then go outside and police the area around the aid station. You will not function as a medic until further notice, do you understand?"

"Yes, sir," he said, and he almost ran out of the aid station.

"Don't either of you get taken in by Radford; he's in a world of trouble."

I walked back to where Doc and I had our bunks. As I changed my shirt, the aid station's field phone rang and Dan Miller answered it. There was a brief conversation before Dan called, "It's for you, Lieutenant."

I returned to the treatment area and whispered, "Who is it?"

Miller put his arms over his head and whispered, "Master Sergeant Grant, Bravo Troop." He made a face as he handed the phone to me.

"Lieutenant Noble speaking, may I help you?"

Getting in Trouble

"Lieutenant what are you trying to pull?" the Bear growled.

"I'm not trying to pull anything, Sarge. Radford is just pressing charges against the platoon sergeant, that's all."

"You're not going to get Radford off the hook with this. No way, he's going to be court-martialed for what he did!"

"That's fine and I agree with you, but we want that platoon sergeant to be held accountable for his actions, just like Radford is going to be held accountable. Any person who starts a card game and then turns around and cheats..."

"What? Hey, Lieutenant, don't try to pull that on me," the Bear interrupted.

"Sarge, I have five witnesses who'll all testify to what they saw in that bunker as to why Radford hit the platoon sergeant."

"Well, we'll see about that!" the Bear exclaimed and hung up the phone.

Doc returned from Chu Lai, so I filled him in on what had happened. After a few moments, Doc and I left the aid station and went to the chow hall for supper. After an artificial meal, Doc and I then went over to the Officers' Club.

The "O" Club was a very small tropical building that consisted of one long bar, and about five or six large round card tables. All along the bar was displayed the unit's 68 battle streamers, which dated back

The Tragedy of Vietnam, Again

to the Indian Wars, the Civil War, the Mexican War, World War II, the Korean War, and now the Vietnam War. We had not been awarded any battle streamers for Vietnam, but we had surely made ourselves felt. Also, the unit liked to lure high ranking officers up to the hill and have them leave minus their collar, which was then nailed up along with the battle streamers. There was an impressive array of ranks all higher than major and the highest ranking collar had two stars, but "they" were looking for three or even four stars. It was really neat, because I realized that we were part of a sassy unit that had been very much a part of American military history.

Doc and I had a couple of drinks and played a hand or two of rummy before heading back to the aid station. (Doc, Mr. Dunn, and Mr. Werner, our two warrant officers, and I were the regulars at that table and played for no money, no money was allowed to pass at our table; we played only for fun or for who would pay for the next round of drinks. By the end of each month most of the officers ended up at our table and still no money passed hands; the newcomers had no money.)

The medics were all sitting around the treatment room talking, drinking beer and making popcorn. When we entered, there was a good debate going on as to whether we should attack Hanoi and invade the North, or continue as we were. Kline was arguing, "When a patient has skin cancer on his right hand, the doctor doesn't fool around and cut off the left foot; he goes after the cancer at the source, on the right hand, right Doc?"

Right, unless that doctor has really good malpractice insurance," Doc replied.

Miller added to support Kline, "Well, why don't we attack North Vietnam, it's like what Kline just said. You go after the cancer and Hanoi is the cancer; cut off the supply to the south at its source. We can't do it sitting here in the South."

"Yeah, you do that," Johnston interjected, "You'll have Russia, China, and a whole lot more come racing to aid the North, and then we'll have World War III."

"Hey, when you have solved the problem as to how to win the war, go tell General Westmoreland. I'm going to bed, and who has got the duty tonight?" Doc said as he started to move across the treatment room toward his own quarters.

"I have it," Dan Miller answered.

"OK, good night everyone," Doc disappeared.

I wasn't in a very good mood, and I didn't want to have to look at Radford, so I said good night, found my favorite litter, and went on top of the bunker with my poncho liner to gaze at the stars.

The next morning, after breakfast, the phone rang; it was the Bear.

"Lieutenant, this is Master Sergeant Grant." I recognized the Bear's voice.

"Yes, Sergeant, what can I do for you?"

"We've been thinking this matter over, and what we're willing to do is drop all charges against Radford, if you drop the charges against my sergeant. But, I want you to promise me one thing, Lieutenant; don't you let him get off free."

"Sergeant, we have a deal and I can promise you, Radford's troubles have just begun."

"OK, sir, we have a deal." The phone went dead.

Radford was cleaning the aid station's floor, sweeping up the dirt that constantly got tracked in.

"Radford, as soon as you have finished, you're coming with me over to Headquarters Troop."

"I'll be through in a few minutes, sir."

Kline stood in the entrance and yelled, "I'm going down to the Ville, does anybody have any laundry?"

"I do," I yelled back and went to my area. I grabbed my dirty clothes, stuffed them in a laundry bag, and brought it out to the treatment room. Kline collected all the laundry from all the medics, as well as all the surgical drapes. Hale announced that he was also going to help. I had a feeling that both were going down to the Ville to get more than just the laundry washed, by the looks on their faces.

"Radford, are you ready?"

"Yes sir."

"Then get in my jeep."

Radford walked up the ramp, out into the bright sunlight. I followed him up and got into the jeep. Before I started the engine, I looked right into Radford's eyes and said, "Radford, for some reason all charges have been dropped against you."

"Do you mean there's no court-martial?"

"It means no court-martial, but you're in a world of trouble with me, do you understand?"

Radford broke out in a huge smile as tears flooded his eyes. "Thank you, thank you, sir, thank you so very much. I'll do anything for you, anything." He choked, trying not to cry.

"OK," I answered and started up the jeep. "Let's go."

I drove to the Headquarters Troop and pulled up in front of the Orderly Room. Once my jeep had stopped I commanded, "Come with me."

Sergeant Williams was working at his desk and asked with a smile, "Did everything work out with Bravo Troop, Lieutenant?"

I suddenly realized I had some background help, "Yes, it did and I have a present for you Sarge. You know that latrine detail you have?"

"Yes, sir, what about it?"

"Well, I would appreciate it if you would call it off for a while."

"What, but why?"

"Because, I have a man here who has just volunteered, right, Radford?"

"Yes, sir, that's correct, sir."

"You can't do that, it's too much for one man. We have eighteen outhouses, and most have three holes; one man can't burn all that, sir."

"Oh sure, Radford can; he's good at burning crap, aren't you, Radford?"

"Oh sir, I just love burning shit, especially all by myself," Radford chimed in as if we had practiced it, especially the "love."

"Well, all right, but I still don't think he'll be able to do it," Sergeant Williams stated.

"Good, Radford, you'll start right now and you'll stir each and every bucket until there is nothing left in it. You will start as soon as breakfast is over, 0700 hours. You will work until twelve noon and you may have forty-five minutes for lunch. You'll then burn crap until the rest are finished. To help you carry the necessary supplies you may use one of the jeeps. You will then get water for the first sergeant's shower, the CO of Headquarters' shower, as well as the medics' shower. Do you have any questions?"

"No sir."

Sergeant Williams, you're a witness to these orders I have just given Specialist Radford, are you not?"

"Yes, sir, I am, but I have one question. How long is this one-man detail going to last, Lieutenant?"

"I'm not sure; it's up to Radford and his attitude; I don't think you'll need this detail for a while; I'll let you know when Radford will come off, all right?"

"All right, Lieutenant."

As it turned out, Radford tended to the outhouses for five weeks before I needed him back in the field. Radford informed me that he had taken care of

Getting in Trouble

1,575 honey buckets. He felt that it was not fair, because the enemy had gone underground, which meant we couldn't find them. As a result, the troops for the most part stayed back at base camp, which meant for Radford that most of the buckets were jammed full.

Radford worked from seven o'clock in the morning till six at night to complete the latrine detail. Since this was a full day's work, the extra shower duty was given to others who were just as deserving of it.

Alpha Troop's Latrine.

Someone Looked Out For Me

It was time for me to go back out to the field again, to help maintain the morale within the line medics. Three of the medics in Charlie Troop were relatively new to the unit and thus new to going out in harm's way. Also, one medic was sick so Doc wanted to keep him back at The Hill for some rest.

It was a pleasantly cool early March morning, not a cloud in the sky. A gentle breeze blew as Charlie Troop's Second Platoon rolled out of the base camp. I thought as we passed through the back gate, *this is going to be a sightseeing trip. It's out and back and in the meantime I can check out the new men.*

The mission for this platoon was to scout a certain area to see if there were any signs of enemy activity. It had been almost three weeks since we'd had any sight of NVA or VC in the area. We plowed single file through rice paddy after rice paddy. The paddies were not only full of bright green young rice plants that had been transplanted from the various seed beds, but they were flooded, which was necessary to grow the plants, at that time of year.

The Tragedy of Vietnam, Again

It was about noon when the platoon entered a huge rice paddy; it was the largest paddy I'd ever seen. A fair-size village ran across its back and along the left-hand side of the paddy. There's dense "wool" (the brush and small trees) that lined the left side and across the far back separating the village from the paddy. Because of the wool, much of the village was hidden from view.

"This looks like a dry piece of ground to stop and take a break," came over our radio. We'd been bouncing around for approximately four and a half hours and had seen nothing; there was a lot of scenery seen, but not one single person.

As we busted out the C rations, Stewart, the senior medic for Charlie Troop, said, "Boy, this is one hell of a place to have to defend, what with the mountains to the west and that two-hundred-foot nub of hill on our right side. All the enemy has to do is put some mortar tubes on that pimple and there's nothing we can do to defend ourselves."

This thought did not make me feel very comfortable. For the rest of this break I kept telling myself, *The NVA doesn't have time to get their act together to raise hell in our direction, so enjoy the C rations.*

After about thirty minutes of rest, one of the platoon's tanks was ordered to cross a small stream that passed through the middle of the paddy and to stand guard on the other side. Much to all of our regret the tank's driver and tank's commander were not the brightest of individuals. They did not scout to see if there was a fordable place to cross, they just plowed straight in. The stream was about thirty feet across with steep, five-foot banks on either side. The tank slipped right down the first bank, but as it tried to come up the far side, it only churned mud; the far bank was too steep for the tank to pull itself out of the stream. When they tried to back the tank out, the same result happened, but only at the opposite end. They just got about twenty-five feet of solid steel stuck in a thirty-foot stream; there was not enough room to turn the tank around.

We spent the next three hours trying to pull this tank out by hooking cables to the other tanks and personnel carriers in various combinations, all to no avail. It was stuck and stuck very, very well.

The platoon leader, Jarred Smith, called for help and words came from the squadron's TOC that the recovery vehicle (the VTR) could not make it out to our position before nightfall, but it would come out first thing the next morning. We had to spend the night guarding our stuck "hippo," in an area that was totally undefendable.

After about a half hour wait, Jarred headed towards Band-Aid with his platoon sergeant, when we all heard the whap, whap, whap of a helicopter approaching our little group. The helicopter landed about fifty feet away; all the rice plants were plastered down to the ground, in a huge circle surrounding the helicopter.

The Tragedy of Vietnam, Again

Out jumped our squadron's new executive officer, Major Filbert, and Mr. Werner, the chief warrant officer of Headquarters Troop Maintenance and owner of the VTR, to survey the situation. Jarred and his platoon sergeant changed direction to meet the helicopter's passengers halfway.

The major and Mr. Werner weren't very happy, because about two hundred feet upstream was a natural crossing point, low banks and a firm bottom; however, that was much easier to see from a helicopter than from inside a tank. Nevertheless, rank had its privilege and the platoon leader and his platoon sergeant had to stand and take the wrath from above.

The bottom line was the XO was furious, because of stupidity. Now, approximately forty-five men were going to have to risk their lives to defend a stuck tank, which should not be stuck. In situations like that, it did little good to get mad, because there was so much that had to be done, such as deciding how to defend ourselves, and what to do with the stuck tank.

As Major Filbert explained in detail what he wanted done, Mr. Werner went over to the helicopter and took out four starlight scope cases. After a few minutes of talk, the major and Mr. Werner got back in the helicopter and flew off. (Major Filbert was a fantastic improvement over Major Bangstrom; there was no comparison between the two, Major Filbert was a joy to have around.)

Someone Looked Out For Me

Jarred and his platoon sergeant returned to Jarred's track, and called a meeting of all track commanders. I went along with Stewart to see what was going to happen. As I walked up to the command track, Jarred called down, "Hey, Chris, you really know how to pick them when going out to the field; a simple routine mission and now this mess."

"All right, commanders, this is what we're going to do." Jarred explained how we were going to set up our defense for the night; it was very straightforward. The stuck tank was to be locked up so nobody could get inside during the coming night. The tank's crew was to become one of the ambush teams, since they had gotten us into this mess. All vehicles were to form a herringbone defense with about eight feet between each vehicle, and all vehicles were to position themselves so their fire power was to overlap, as well as be able to fire into the stream, if need be. One ambush team would be at the front of the formation and the other would be to the other end, both beside the stream.

It was felt the enemy might try to sabotage the tank sometime during the night and the logical way for anyone to approach undetected would be underwater. Hopefully the ambush teams would be able to detect any activity and give the alarm by firing their weapons and then run like hell to the nearest track.

Jarred very carefully explained that nobody was allowed to open fire until the ambush teams were on board. When the end tracks reported all were on

The Tragedy of Vietnam, Again

board, only then were the rest in the formation allowed to open fire. The platoon sergeant suggested that all vehicles work out their perimeter defense, where each and every vehicle would be positioned, and that we should wait until darkness had set in before moving into these positions. "Why help Chuck by showing him where we are," he stated.

It was about six o'clock and the sun was starting to slide behind the hills in front of our positions. This was a situation where it wasn't if we would be attacked, but when we would be attacked. Everyone was on edge and my stomach was tied up in knots. There was a lot of nervous small talk about what people would do, once we were attacked.

All gunners cleaned their weapons and test fired them into the rice paddy. Why try to keep it a secret that we were there? After all, we'd been only been sitting in plain view for most of the afternoon.

Jarred's voice came over the radio, "This is Two-Six; if anyone wants to eat something hot tonight you have thirty minutes to do so. Once it's dark we'll be in total blackout conditions. Also, set up sleeping arrangements now. I want two people on guard duty at all times. Two-hour shifts all through the night. The rest of the crew can try to sleep. God help anyone who goes to sleep on guard duty!" The radio went dead.

The experienced people on Band-Aid were Steward and me, and I wasn't that experienced. The other men were not only new to Vietnam; they had been in the army for less than six months. The newest man had never spoken to an officer before he reported in to the aid station.

Band-Aid had six litters on board so we kept two and lent the rest out to the other vehicles, so other troops didn't have to sleep on top of the ammo boxes that lined the floor of every vehicle.

Larson broke off a chunk of C-4 and lit it. He then placed a large, open-ended coffee can on top that had holes punch around its sides to let air pass through. Then he carefully balanced a pot of water on top for coffee, tea or hot chocolate. Larson opened some cans of aged rations by cutting the top three quarters around. By bending the lid back it formed a simple handle. Each person took a small amount of C-4 and lit it, being careful not to burn them self or the food. It looked as if we were jigging for fish as our hands bobbed up and down, only to stop for a quick stir with a stolen spoon from the chow hall.

This hand bobbing went on for less than two minutes when Larson announced, "Supper is served on the rear patio." The four of us sat down to eat a lukewarm, greasy meal. That was all we would have to eat for the rest of the night. The peanut butter and cheese crackers were a treat to try to eat; all the moisture had been sucked out and the peanut butter had the consistency of dried clay. The instant coffee was the best part of the meal, even though it was stale. The conversation at meal time was about how terrible the C rations really

The Tragedy of Vietnam, Again

were, and what a shame it would be to have this as your last meal.

"All vehicles are to move into our night position, about fifty yards to our right, within five minutes' time," Jarred ordered over the radio. I was very nervous, we all were. Darkness was upon us and all I could imagine were a bunch of little Orientals, dressed in black pajamas climbing up the hills with their mortar tubes, while other enemy troops were doing the same low crawl toward our position from all sides. I figured if I were the enemy's commander officer, I would mortar our position heavily, hoping to wound or kill as many people as possible, but more importantly force us to keep our heads down. During the mortar attack I would advance the ground troops close enough so that when the mortars stopped, these ground troops would be able to rush each track and drop hand grenades or a satchel charge down the hatches, killing or wounding all inside.

"Hey, Chris," Jarred called across.

"It's a nice dark night, isn't it?" I called back.

"Come over, I have something for you," Jarred answered.

I crawled out the back hatch of Band-Aid and crossed the fifteen feet to the rear of Jarred's track and slipped inside. The power light on the radio gave off a faint red glow that allowed me to see inside the track.

"I'm sorry to get you in this mess."

Someone Looked Out For Me

"Well, it's not as if you drove the tank into the stream, but thanks anyway," I replied.

"I wish the colonel felt the same way." Jarred sighed as he leaned around one of his crew and grabbed a case with one of the starlight scopes in it. "I want Band-Aid to use this tonight," Jarred continued. "Stewart is a good shot and he has used this before. I want you to concentrate on the area in front of Band-Aid and off to each side up to about sixty degrees; be careful of the track in front of you. If you see anything, don't fire; call me on the radio first, OK?' Jarred said, looking right into my eyes.

"I understand," I answered, taking the case out of his hands.

"Make sure your crew has their flak jackets on, all night long, and don't let anyone wander about outside for any reason. I'll give the order nobody is allowed out of their vehicles except the ambush teams; they should be set up by now. Just be careful, tell the guys on Band-Aid." Jarred was scared that his men were about to get hurt, because of the stuck tank.

I was halfway out the rear hatch when Jarred's track radio announced, "Charlie Two-Six, this is Hawk-Six."

"What the hell does he want now?" Jarred snarled.

"This is Charlie Two-Six," Jarred answered.

"Two-Six, please pass on to your men that we appreciate the situation you and your men are in. We are

The Tragedy of Vietnam, Again

monitoring your frequencies and will do so all night. I have Blue Ghost on standby, the artillery batteries here at Hawk Hill and at LZ Baldy are at your disposal, and they're also monitoring your radio frequency. Do you read me?" the squadron's commander asked.

"Hawk-Six, I read you and thank you. Are you aware that Headquarters Troop line number…?" Jarred released the mic quickly and asks, "Chris what's your line number?"

"Headquarters 317," I replied.

"…That Headquarters line number 317 is at my location?" Jarred released the mic.

"Two-Six, yes, I am. Tell him to keep his head low; he has a habit of attracting our little friends. Tell your men that they may be there, but we're ready to help at a moment's notice, out."

The colonel was poking fun my way. My nickname in the Officers' Club was 'Magnet Ass,' because every time I'd gone to the field, that unit had gotten into a firefight with the enemy.

I brought the starlight scope to Stewart and explained to him what Jarred and the colonel said.

Stewart attached the scope to his M-16, made some adjustments by the red light from Band-Aid's radio, and then slipped out the back hatch to get permission to test fire his weapon to check the accuracy of the scope's alignment.

A few minutes later there was a single rifle shot that echoed across the rice paddy, and then there was total silence. As Steward slipped back through the rear hatch he stated, "Be careful with this rifle, don't knock the alignment out."

I suggested that Larson and I stand guard duty together, while Stewart and Patten stand the other guard duty. This was not going to be a very nice night.

As the long night drew near to an end, and the eastern sky started to lighten slightly, I heard a high-pitched buzzing sound approaching quickly from the south. I couldn't see the helicopter, but I knew what it was by the sound; it was an LOH (light observation helicopter), or scout helicopter that looked like a flying sperm cell.

"Jesus Christ, we're taking fire!" blared over Band-Aid's radio. Stewart had switched it over to the squadron's frequency. I did not hear any gunfire, because the morning breeze was at our backs and blew the sound away from us.

I looked at the village and watched the small helicopter shoot straight up into the air, as green tracer bullets followed it. The plane then dove off at an angle back to treetop level and shot off a burst of gunfire.

Radios blared as orders from the squadron were passed quickly down; everyone was wide awake. Jarred ordered the Second Platoon to start their engines, and to spread out across the rice paddy on the other side of the stream; the platoon was to act as a holding force.

The Tragedy of Vietnam, Again

As we started to cross the stream, at the correct ford, the high-pitched whine of incoming artillery passed over our heads and exploded in back of the village and off to each side. The artillery fired constantly for about a half hour, then all of a sudden all incoming rounds stopped.

Way up over our heads was a small silver Air Force "push-me/pull-me" propeller-driven observation plane. "The fun is just about to start, sir," Stewart said as he pointed to the small airplane overhead, "The jets are coming."

After about three to four minutes, from out of nowhere, a jet aircraft screamed over our rice paddy about five hundred feet above the ground. As the jet reached our position, it released two five-hundred pound bombs and at the same time pulled up hard, hitting his afterburners, and went into a tight climb. The bombs exploded with a bright flash, and a cloud of white, black, and battleship gray rolled away from the flashpoint. No sooner had the dust started to settle than another jet came screaming in and dropped two more bombs. When all the bombs had been dropped, these two jets, one Air Force and the other a Marine jet, strafed the village area with their twenty-millimeter cannons. I could hear the gunfire from the aircraft, but there was a secondary explosion on the ground that hurt my ears even though we were about two hundred yards away from the village.

Someone Looked Out For Me

As soon as these two jets were out of ammunition, the small Air Force plane flying overhead swooped down to survey the damage. The Air Force pilot was in total control of the battle. He could give Jarred orders to move and we had to follow his commands.

Jarred's voice came over the radio, "Heads up, men, the Air Force says they can see 'Dinks' running all over the place; some more birds (planes) are on their way. We have to hold the enemy here until the rest of the squadron gets here." The radio then went dead.

The high-pitched whine of incoming shells could be heard again, and then a barrage of explosions erupted from behind the village and off to both sides. Those shells were coming from the two artillery batteries, one at LZ Baldy and the other from Hawk Hill.

That should slam the backdoor shut on these NVA troops, I thought.

The artillery batteries kept a steady rain of artillery shells falling upon the village, in no set pattern. Two more pairs of jets arrived to unload their payload on our friends inside the village. This alternated between the jets and artillery. Watching the performance was unreal; it was like watching a 3-D movie that had smell-a-vision. We were far enough away so we all felt safe. We weren't part of the combat, even though we saw everything, we smelled the cordite, and when the bombs exploded we felt the concussion in the pit of our stomach.

The Tragedy of Vietnam, Again

It was incredible seeing so much power and destruction going to work. I'll never forget the feeling inside of me, being part of a truly joint military effort. Back in all base camps everyone was very protective of "their branch of service;" the Army was great and the Navy sucked, or visa versa. On that particular day there was no Army, no Air Force or Marines fighting; we were all Americans, all fighting a common enemy and all working beautifully together, like a well-oiled machine. It made me feel proud to be an American, seeing all our training come together for a common cause.

Jet drops two 500 lbs bombs.

About ten o'clock in the morning the rest of Charlie Troop and Bravo Troop arrived, with approximately sixty armored personnel carriers, about eighteen tanks, and one VTR. We also had available the Blue Ghost's sixteen helicopter gunships and seven or eight slicks (unarmed helicopters) loaded with an infantry company that was going to assist us in clearing the area.

I wasn't sure what happened next, but Jarred was no longer in command, the colonel was in his helicopter overhead giving orders to all the troop commanders, who in turn ordered their platoon leaders, who ordered the individual vehicles.

Captain Prothero, my friend from Fat City, was now the new commander of Charlie Troop; he was getting his combat command time, which was important for his advancement within the Army, being a West Point graduate. For some reason he instructed Stewart to stay put and hold what ended up to be the squadron's left-flank position.

Before Stewart could question our position, the order was given to advance at idle speed and to "recon by fire." All vehicles slowly advanced toward the dense shrub line that lined the edge of the rice paddy in front of us.

I noticed, as we started to move forward, that this paddy had about a half foot of water in it. It had been unnoticeable because all the rice plants hid it. Suddenly we were consumed by the noise of gunfire. Our entire line of attack opened fire. My mind was somewhere else; it was going around in circles. I thought it was mainly due to the lack of sleep over the past twenty-four hours, and my nerves were fairly well shot. I remembered looking over at the water right beside Band-Aid

The Tragedy of Vietnam, Again

and thinking, *boy, look at all those minnows in the paddy.* It took about two seconds to flush that thought from my head to realize that those minnows were very deadly.

Larson was behind his .60-cal submachine gun; he was the left flank for the entire squadron and was firing his weapon into the dense brush on our left side. I was training my .60 in front of Band-Aid, being careful not to shoot the exhaust pipe off, or fire too close to the track next to us on the right.

I glanced over at Larson to see how he was doing and realized he was trying to un-jam his weapon. I kept firing my weapon. There was no way for me to cover the left flank from my side of the track. Larson wasn't making any progress, so I was going to be helpful and started to cuss him out.

Stewart was unaware of what was going on behind him, because he had his radio helmet on listening for orders, and was firing his .50-caliber machine gun off to the left side of the paddy.

In the next few split seconds, everything happened as if all in slow motion. I don't know if this was because I was exhausted, or because of all the commotion surrounding me, or both. I felt something very warm and gently, yet very firmly, push me down so I ended up in a heap on top of Larson. I felt I must have been knocked semiconscious, because I could hear what was going on around me, but I just lay in a dazed heap, as did Larson.

I thought, *a mortar round must have gone off nearby and the concussion knocked me down.*

I remembered hearing in my fog, "Band-Aid is hit! Band-Aid has been hit!"

"Are you all right, Band-Aid? What are your causalities?" I was aware of the chatter over the radio, but whose voice it was, I didn't know.

Then Larson screamed, "I've been hit! I've been hit."

I looked over at Larson, with my messed-up mind and asked, "Where have you been hit?"

Larson pointed to his neck and shoulder. Both he and I had on olive drab T-shirts, along with our flak jackets. My mind cleared considerably; as I saw no blood, I told him, "Shut up, I see no blood. Get that GD weapon un-jammed."

I realized I had a sharp stinging, a burning sensation on the back of my neck and along my right shoulder, as if I had spilled very hot water over myself. During the entire episode my helmet never came off my head. I poked my head up out of the rear hatch, and, much to my surprise, Captain Prothero's concerned face was staring right at me, about four feet away.

"Chris, are you all right?" he asked.

"Yes, I am; I have a burning sensation all over my neck and on my shoulder."

Captain Prothero's left gunner said, "Why don't you take your 'F-ing" helmet off, sir, and take a look."

The Tragedy of Vietnam, Again

I took off my helmet and to my horror, part of the backside of my helmet cover had been torn off and shiny metal was staring at me. I was totally confused as to what had happened.

The left gunner then stated, while looking at Captain Prothero, "Jesus Christ, sir, look at his .60 shield."

I looked at the metal sheet that's meant to protect me. It looked as if some giant had taken a bite out of the very top edge; there was a nice neat crescent-moon piece of metal missing out of the top edge.

"I don't believe how lucky you are, Noble!" Captain Prothero stated. "That bounced off your sixty-shield and was deflected up into the air without exploding. What used to be part of your shield took out the back of your helmet. Why the hell you weren't killed, I don't know! Stewart, bring Band-Aid behind my vehicle and make sure the lieutenant and Larson are all right."

The colonel, for some reason had stopped the war to check on Larson and me, because all vehicles had stopped. Other tracks surrounded our position giving us protection. Stewart quickly dropped down and came to give both Larson and myself a quick going-over. He stated we had first to second degree burns to our necks and shoulders.

It took about a week for the fact to settle in, just how lucky I really was. Events happened so fast in the field, there was no way for people to comprehend what was happening to them at the moment of impact. If I had not been cussing Larson out, I would probably have been blinded by flying fragments, if not killed. If the rocket had been approximately two inches lower, the nose of the rocket would have hit the .60 shield and it would have exploded. The blast would have removed my entire upper body. If the rocket had been two inches higher, it would have cleared the top of the shield and taken my head off.

Yes, I was very lucky that day, and someone was looking after not only me, but Larson as well. We weren't sure of the damage inflicted upon the enemy, because the fight went on all day and into dusk. Contact was broken off with just enough light to find our way back to the base camp. The next morning Bravo Troop returned to the area to see if any enemy was still there. The enemy had all gone, where to, who knew, but by the amount of blood on the ground and the amount of bloody bandages littering the village, there were a lot of NVA soldiers who didn't feel very good.

The stuck tank was pulled out of the stream, in all of ten minutes by the VTR, and fought alongside the rest of the troop on that first day.

An Unexpected Reward

The monsoon season was just beginning, which none of us really looked forward to. It was a miserable time of year, because it looked as if it would rain at any second all the time. Mother Nature seemed to have put us on a schedule for several daily downpours; the first deluge started about ten o'clock in the morning, the second around three o'clock, and the last really big rain around seven to eight o'clock in the evening; we also got one or two that were unscheduled.

When the rain came, it just poured for about a half hour. When I say pour, I mean you could not see an object such as a jeep or a bunker that was only twenty feet away. The raindrops were huge, dense masses of water, which made a large splash when they hit anything. After the downpour the rain then eased off to a drizzle, then faded off into a heavy mist; it was called very high humidity. The conditions stayed like this only to reach another climax where you could see nothing in front of you, while torrents of water cascaded upon you, and then rushed down the slope. I wore my sweater for three months straight, day and night.

It was impossible to stay dry, and you became used to the fact that the back of your neck was going to get

The Tragedy of Vietnam, Again

wet even though you had a poncho on. You became used to the fact that your clothing and your bedding was never really dry and mold was everywhere. Anything made of leather, after a week or two under these conditions was completely covered with green mold; if you allowed it to grow for three weeks or longer, there were two to three inches of mold hanging off the edges of the soles of your good leather shoes, that the Army said I needed to bring to Vietnam, but never wore.

The mold was not as bad as the mud; mud was everywhere! In order to try to keep most of the mud out of the aid station, wire-mesh pallets were placed in front of the ramp leading down into the aid station. These pallets acted somewhat like a boot scraper; up to eighty percent of the mud came off the boots and fell through the six-inch clearance. The plywood ramp leading down into the aid station, even though we had nailed wooden cleats across the ramp, became as slick as greased ice. There was very little we could do to correct the situation, even though the medics were accused of trying to generate new business for themselves.

Specialist Johnston and I were conducting an inventory of all the controlled drugs. This had to be done monthly and careful records were kept as to where each and every pill, Syrette, or injection had gone.

Doc was holding sick call and Specialists Miller and Kline were helping. There were five or six members from various troops sitting on the bench along one side of the treatment room.

Doc was treating a young private, who went to Bangkok on R&R, and bought himself a good dose of VD (venereal disease). Doc pumped his butt full of penicillin. Miller had another patient facedown on a litter in one corner, as he applied heat treatment to a large boil on the back of his leg. Kline was taking the temperature of a sergeant who was complaining he had a cold.

Stewart, who had been brought back to the aid station, was in charge of logging everyone into the register and writing out "excused from duty" slips. He helped in any other way as needed. Every day the medics rotated around the jobs, so no one got stuck being on "the desk." The log desk was considered the "pits" job.

My old buddy from Fat City, Don Venn, entered. He had become the unit's S-5 civil affairs/psychological warfare officer. He claimed he was coming down with a cold and complained about the horrible weather.

"You know, Doc, our bunker sprung a leak last night; it was terrible! Sergeant Deljudice got out of bed last night to visit the 'piss-tube' and when he put his foot on the floor; the water came over his ankles. Man, did he let out a scream; I've never seen a candle lit so fast."

"What did you do?" Kline asked.

"Sarge ran out and got a gas-driven pump and we pumped all night long."

The Tragedy of Vietnam, Again

"Where'd the water come from?" Dan Miller asked.

"Oh, some fool skidded last night and drove through the dike that goes around our bunker, but never told us. As you may remember, it was raining like hell last night. Well, when you have one or two inches of rain coming down all at the same time and a bunker like yours, dug into the ground with no way for the water to get out, well, we could have ended up like that bunker over at Headquarters Troop that completely filled up."

Two of the Headquarters' patients waiting to see Doc filled in the details about how all the wooden furniture floated up and out of the bunker's entrance. The small talk continued among the waiting patients until Doc was ready to see them.

Don Venn came over to where Johnston and I were counting pills, and asked, "Hey, Chris, how about going for a ride with me when you're through."

"What for, it looks crummy outside."

"It won't rain, at least not for a while. I want to check out that village up the road; I hear they have some sick people who need help. We want to get friendly with this village and now's a good time."

"Is this the village up the road about three miles that keeps shooting at us as we drive by?"

"Yes, that's the one, but they haven't been shooting at any vehicles for the past couple of weeks," Don Venn quickly replied.

"Who else is going?"

An Unexpected Reward

"Just you, me, and Sergeant Deljudice," Don stated confidently.

"You mean nobody else, just the three of us. You're out of your mind!"

"I'll go with you, sir," Johnston offered.

It was bad having Johnston volunteering, because then I more or less had to go. It wasn't that I was chicken, but my better judgment told me it wasn't healthy for three or four people to drive into a village that wasn't friendly toward us.

"All right, I'll go and Johnston will go also; when do you want to take off?"

"We'll leave right after lunch, OK?"

"We'll see you then. Johnston and I will take our jeep and we'll follow you."

"See you then; I've got to go dry my things out, can I bring them over here?"

"Hang them up in my room. Chris lives in a hallway," Doc stated.

After Don Venn left the aid station, I quietly said, "Look, Johnston, don't you go around volunteering; it's not healthy; do you understand!"

Johnston looked at me with a smirk on his face and answered, "Well, there's nothing going on around here, and I thought it might be fun."

"Well, make sure you bring along some weapons and plenty of ammo. Also bring an aid bag, in case we need it for ourselves."

"Yes, sir, everything will be taken care of, I'll also check the gas in the jeep," Johnston added.

The Tragedy of Vietnam, Again

We finished the drug inventory and all the drugs checked present and accounted for. I had business to tend to in Charlie Troop. We had received a complaint that rats had been seen around their chow hall. I tried to drive one of the FLAs, but the tires were bald and they only spun around beautifully in the mud. The only way to move about was in a tracked vehicle, so I fired up the Mobile Aid Station. I latched the driver's hatch back carefully, so as not to have it come crashing down on my head. A cloud of diesel smoke poured out of the exhaust stack and filled the driver's compartment. I unlocked the laterals (two steering levers), shoved the transmission into the forward position, and stepped down on the accelerator. The mobile aid station moved forward slowly at first and as soon as it cleared the other vehicles next to the aid station, I goosed the accelerator. The vehicle made even more noise and more black smoke streamed out of its exhaust as the speedometer read ten miles per hour.

Mud flew out behind, as I took the track around Alpha Troop's hill, and then out toward Charlie Troop. The trip took me about ten minutes total. I brought the vehicle to a stop in front of Charlie Troop's chow hall, much to the surprise of everyone inside eating his meal.

Upon entering, my old buddy Captain Prothero asked, "What the hell are you driving that thing around for?"

An Unexpected Reward

"I can't get our jeep to move in this muck; not one inch and this baby needs the exercise, she just loves mud," I replied.

"Yeah, it's a bitch, isn't it? What brings you here?"

"Oh, we got a report of rats in the area and I want to make sure your food supplies are all right."

"Sounds good, here let me go with you. Hey, Sarge, show the lieutenant around, will you?"

"Yes, sir," the mess sergeant answered. "Do you want to see the kitchen or what, Lieutenant?

"Show us everything," Captain Prothero ordered, before I could say a word.

We inspected the kitchen and it was clean, as was the dining area. The next area was the wash rack where the pots and pans were washed. This area also passed inspection. We then went to the small tropical building that stored the mess supplies. Inside, it was stacked high. We climbed over boxes and inspected all corners of the building; no rats.

"I know there are no rats in here, because when we built the building it was lined with metal," the cook stated.

I was ready to quit and start to walk back to my command track when I decided to look under the chow hall, and much to my surprise I found nice neat rows of food particles that lined up with the cracks in the floor above. Captain Prothero took a look, as did the sergeant.

The Tragedy of Vietnam, Again

"Sarge, get a detail to get under the building and remove all those droppings." The captain shook his head, as I climbed back up into my track and charged back to the aid station. I reported my finding to Doc and we both felt that once the food was removed, the rats would have to go elsewhere to find food.

After lunch, Johnston and I packed our jeep. We brought two M-16s and about fourteen clips of ammo, plus two aid bags completely restocked, just to be on the safe side. I instructed the aid station to turn our aid station's base radio to the same frequency as the jeep's radio, with orders not to turn it off. Lieutenant Venn and Sergeant Deljudice came by, all loaded up; they looked like stuffed teddy bears wearing their flak jackets and helmets.

Doc's jeep had fairly new tires, thanks to the last mortar attack that took out three of the old ones. As a result we had fairly good traction, so long as we kept moving.

We slipped and skidded our way out the main entrance all the way to Highway One. We made a left-hand turn, going due north on the highway, which was in fairly good shape and the traction was good.

Johnston drove, following Sergeant Deljudice and Lieutenant Venn's jeep for the three miles. There was virtually no traffic on the road so the trip went by quickly.

Sergeant Deljudice pulled his jeep over to the side of the road, being careful not to put the jeep in the

An Unexpected Reward

ditch. Bob Johnston was careful to follow suit, but left room between the two jeeps.

Don Venn and Sergeant Deljudice were out of their jeep and were approaching a small group of local inhabitants, as we got out of our jeep. Johnston handed me half of the ammo, as I slid out my side. I slung them over one shoulder and carried my M-16 fully loaded and very much ready to use, if need be.

We joined Don Venn and Sergeant Deljudice, but did not understand a word being said. Sergeant Deljudice was talking in Vietnamese with the villagers, telling them that if they liked, the American doctor would come to their village. The villagers agreed they would like that, but the village chief needed to be consulted.

We were led off the road, over a ditch, and into the hamlet. Thatched huts lined the pathway. We walked past many huts and into a common area, where the village well was located. One of the villagers ran ahead and disappeared into a hut. After a few moments the villager returned with an older man.

We were introduced to the village chief, and Sergeant Deljudice explained to the elder that if he would like, we'd send a doctor and his staff to help the village.

The chief wanted to know what we wanted in return for the doctor's services. Sergeant Deljudice gave us a quick translation and then informed the chief, "Nothing!"

The Tragedy of Vietnam, Again

By now quite a group of villagers had gathered to view the enemy. Johnston saw a little boy who had an open sore on his cheek, and was trying to coax the little boy into letting him treat him. When Johnston pulled out a piece of candy, they both got their message across through sign language. If Johnston treated the sore, then the boy got the candy. Timidly, the little boy let himself be had.

Johnston got some water and then took a small cake of soap from his aid bag. He cleaned the infected area carefully and covered it with an ointment. All Vietnamese loved bandages. Johnston put a gauze patch over the ointment to keep it in place.

The little boy made off with his candy and was very proud of his bandage. The next thing we knew from out of nowhere, people were showing up with cuts, colds, sores, pains, lumps, bumps, and birth defects; all wanted to be cured. We tried to do what we could, with what limited supplies and time we had. It was very evident that this village needed a lot of medical help.

By the time our supplies gave out, it was time for us to start getting back to camp. Lieutenant Venn and Sergeant Deljudice promised the village chief that the American doctor would come back in about one week's time, if possible. The village chief agreed and we drove off to return to The Hill before darkness set in completely.

Johnston and I pulled up in front of the aid station just in the nick of time, because the heavens

An Unexpected Reward

opened up just as we parked the jeep. We couldn't have planned it any better if we had tried. We both got wet with about thirty drops of rain each. Our faded fatigue uniforms looked as if they had a mild case of smallpox.

We went down the ramp and entered the treatment room. "Well, how did it go?" Doc asked.

"We have a job ahead of us," I answered.

"How's that, what did you find?" Doc asked.

"Well, to start off with most of the kids are walking around with open sores. Those who don't have sores have colds, and a few have both."

"The same holds true for the adults," Johnston added.

"What's it going to take to get them back on their feet?" Miller asked.

"Oh, about two or three visits about a week apart. It will be just like the Ville at the end of our access road when they needed help," Doc answered.

Just then Sergeant Deljudice and Don Venn burst into the aid station, "Did Chris and Johnston tell you, Doc?"

"They told me there's a village out there that needs help, right?"

"That's correct; when do you think you and your boys can go out?" Don Venn asked.

"Well, that depends upon the enemy. If the unit is not engaged, which does not seem likely, we can go out whenever you would like us to go. Is that good enough for you?" Doc smiled.

"We'll set it up for day after tomorrow," Lieutenant Venn stated. He and Sergeant Deljudice went charging up the ramp, to do whatever "psy-ops" people did to set up a Med-Cap.

The next day I had Johnston and Miller go over the Med-Cap chests to ensure all supplies were fully stocked. We'd carry three large metal trunks that would contain all the material required to treat two hundred patients. Most of the medics were all charged up about going out for a couple of reasons. First, they were tired of being inactive; second, while out on a Med-Cap the medics could really play "Doc," screening and treating patients. Also, it was fun playing with the children and patching them up all at the same time.

Lieutenant Venn sent word over that LTC Lawrence wanted a line platoon with their APCs to go with us, just to be on the safe side. Doc felt it will be wise to see if any of the line medics would like to come along.

"Johnston, you used to be with Alpha Troop, Miller, you were with Bravo, and, Kline, you were with Charlie Troop. Each one of you take a vehicle and go to your old troop to see if your old buddies want to come along. Miller, if Clancy wants to come tell him to bring Bravo-Band-Aid; we won't be able to carry everybody in the jeeps," I instructed.

The three medics took off as if lightning had just hit them, and the aid station became as quiet as a morgue. Stewart had the duty for the night so Doc, Stewart and I sat around catching up on personal matters. I took time to put down on paper what had happened over the past couple of weeks, so I could put together a journal at some point, like my dad did during World War II and my great-grandfather did during the Civil War.

The morning of the Med-Cap, about 07:00 hours, right after breakfast, Clancy brought Bravo-Band-Aid over to the aid station. The track looked like a refugee vehicle with so many bodies hanging all over it. Clancy had taken it upon himself to go to Alpha Troop and picked up four medics, then over to Charlie Troop and acquired another three medics; four from Bravo Troops were all on board. At the aid station, there were three more medics, plus Doc and myself, for a grand total of sixteen medical personnel. All medics remaining in base camp were to treat any problems until we returned.

All medical supplies were lugged out of the aid station and placed inside Bravo-Band-Aid. Johnston took Doc's jeep and filled it with gas. Sergeant Deljudice came over to the aid station and informed us there would be a delay, because the road sweeping crew had not cleared all the mines. This unnerved me, because I surely didn't want to be in the first vehicle to go down that road.

Bravo's third platoon got picked to provide protection for this Med-Cap. The aid station looked and sounded like the pits at some local stock car race track. There were about fourteen vehicles, counting jeeps and tracks, all ready to go as the drivers revved their engines to ensure they would get a good start. Clouds of

The Tragedy of Vietnam, Again

exhaust smoke and noise enveloped the aid station, to the point where it became funny.

The line medics jumped off Band-Aid, all eager to help in any way possible. Vehicles were parked all the way around the aid station, and I was concerned that someone would get run over by a track as drivers jockeyed their vehicles for one reason or another.

After about an hour's wait, Lieutenant Venn received word that the road had been cleared and was open for traffic. I hopped on Bravo-Band-Aid while Doc chose his jeep. The tracked vehicles fell into a column and proceeded out the access road. Lt. Venn and Sergeant Deljudice took up the rear of the column in their jeep.

As we approached the village, at the end of our access road, the Vietnamese hookers were out in front of their little shacks, waving at the column and calling out various friends' names as they passed by. There was a great deal of traffic on the road, much to our relief. We turned and fell in line with the civilian traffic—bikes, motor scooters taxis, and trucks of all shapes, but mostly small in size.

After about twenty minutes of traveling north on the highway the lead track pulled off to the side of the road and cut through a rice paddy. Other tracks went past the village and did the same, but on the far side of the village. In about a minute and a half the village was surrounded by APCs. Bravo-Band-Aid, all twelve tons, pulled up in front of the community well; Doc's jeeps parked beside Band-Aid.

An Unexpected Reward

The day was wonderful for a change; the sun was out and it didn't look like it was going to rain. In and around the thatched huts small groups of people gathered. We eyed them and they eyed us. Doc gave some quick orders; Johnston, Clancy and the rest of Bravo medics organized the people who came for medical treatment. "Kline and Miller, you're in charge of the wash rack, Stewart you work with me."

Within five minutes, we were in full operation. Clancy was ordering the locals around as if he were some sort of general. Johnston was his enforcer, dragging people into lines and chasing off those who were curiosity seekers. Miller and Kline set up a smooth-running operation near the main water well. All children who had a runny nose or oozing sore were stripped naked, boys and girls alike. They then were given a good scrubbing with soap and water; once dried off, ointment was smeared over all open wounds, with a gauze bandage taped over the ointment to keep it in place. The white gauze bandage was the children's white badge of courage, signifying that they had faced the American doctor and survived. The children were so impressed with these gauze bandages, that if one fell off, other children would grab it and stick it on themselves.

Walter Powell, a medic for Alpha Troop was screening the patients before they got to Doc. If their complaints weren't very serious, no internal aches or pains, then he would treat them. Patients who needed a good

The Tragedy of Vietnam, Again

bath went over to Miller and Kline, who by this time were just as wet as the children, except they had their clothes on.

Any patient who had a high fever or internal complaint had to go to Doc for treatment. This way, those who needed to see a real doctor got to see one. Those who were not really sick got to see a medic. Kline and Miller were having fun playing with the children. Some of the kids were bashful and didn't like the idea of undressing in public. However, they knew that in order to get candy they had to take a bath. Slowly their bashfulness was worn down, and sure enough, even the shyest little girls were running around ankle deep in mud, naked as jaybirds, and got a good scrubbing.

Lt. Venn, Sgt. Deljudice and mouth piece ready to go off to a Med Cap.

An Unexpected Reward

Little boy comes to the Med cap on own transportation.

Little boy brings his little brother to Med Cap

The Tragedy of Vietnam, Again

Doc Albers with mouthpiece treating a patient.

Doc checking out a little boy.

An Unexpected Reward

Lt. Venn with civilians all lined up to see Doc

Johnston bringing in a Dust-Off.

The Tragedy of Vietnam, Again

The local elders stood by the sidelines laughing at the children having a good time. The interpreter instructed the parents to wash the children once a day for one week. If the sores didn't go away, then they should bring the child back to the doctor the next time he comes to the village.

An old man stepped out of the spectator crowd and brought a small boy dangling almost lifelessly in his arms to Miller. The old man spoke some Vietnamese, obviously asking for help. Miller took one look and motioned to the old man to follow him.

"Hey, Doc, I've got a case you need to see right away; this kid may be dead."

Doc looked up from the patient he was treating and motioned to the old man to come closer. Doc took the child out of the old man's arms and laid him in his lap. This little boy must have been three to four years old; it was hard for a Westerner to tell the ages of any Vietnamese by looks. Everyone looked much younger than they really were, until they reached the age of about thirty. At that age they got smacked with the "Ugly Stick" and looked a good ten to fifteen years older than they really were.

Doc took the little boy's temperature and said mildly, "Get a Dust-Off."

Miller went outside the thatched hut in which Doc was working, and went over to Doc's jeep. He switched the radio on and turned to Dust-Off's frequency.

"Calling any Dust-Off, calling any Dust-Off, this is Hawk One-Seven calling any Dust-Off."

An Unexpected Reward

Almost immediately a voice blared over the speaker, "This is Dust-Off Three-Niner. What do you need, Hawk One-Seven, over?"

"This is Hawk One-Seven. We need Dust-Off's services. I have one Vietnamese critical with pneumonia. My location is the village on the Red Ball Express, three miles north of Hawk Hill, over."

"Roger, Hawk One-Seven, I read you. I'm north of your position; my ETA is seven minutes, over."

"Roger, Dust-Off, I'll have smoke ready for you, out."

Johnston came over to see what the commotion was all about, and thus heard the radio transmission.

"Let's clear a landing area for the helicopter," Miller yelled.

"Hey, Mouthpiece," Johnston yelled to one of the interpreters. "Tell these people to stand back. A helicopter is going to land here." Johnston pointed to the general area where a fair-sized group of villagers had gathered.

The Vietnamese interpreter yelled a few phrases in Vietnamese and the crowd moved back a little. That was all Johnston and Miller needed. Through sign language and a lot of English cussing, they managed to clear an area large enough to land the aircraft. (You have to remember that all GIs were bilingual—they spoke broken English and could cuss fluently.)

Mouthpiece was called back to Doc, who had to stop seeing patients until this child was taken care of. Doc instructed the interpreter, "Tell Papa-San, Baby-San is very sick. He may die. I send Baby-San to hospi-

The Tragedy of Vietnam, Again

tal in Chu Lai. Doctors in hospital may be able to save Baby-San. You tell him that," Doc ordered.

As the interpreter told the old man, the old man became worried and tears came to his eyes.

"Tell Papa San, he's going to hospital with Baby San," Doc added.

The old man received this news with gratitude. We could hear the engine of a helicopter off in the distance. Miller was on the radio, about to pop a smoke canister as Johnston chased children out of the clearing.

The old man went over to some of the village elders and spoke to them for a few moments. The noise from the helicopter was very loud, as Johnston was directing the pilot to bring the plane down in the center of the clearing. There was no problem keeping people away. Everyone was pressed back as far as they could get, without giving up any vantage point, because they didn't want to miss a thing.

The helicopter landed and Doc carried the child out to the Dust-Off. There was a field medical card attached to the boy's wrist; the tag told the hospital what was wrong with the child, who the child was and where he came from. Doc walked up to the doorway and handed his small patient to the medic inside. The old man had to be led up to the helicopter; he was a very brave person, because he was terrified of getting on board.

As soon as Papa San was seated, the plane took off straight up, blasting everyone below and then headed

An Unexpected Reward

toward Chu Lai. It looked as if Dust-Off was fully loaded with wounded enemy soldiers. There were two armed guards on board keeping a very close watch over those passengers. It looked like these prisoners were in no great shape to put up one last stand.

Doc went back to treating patients. Miller and Kline closed up the wash rack, since every child in the village had been washed; they also had run out of soap.

Most of the medics were treating patients with more serious problems. Some patients had cuts and bruises that looked very much like barbed wire cuts, or small fragmentation wounds. No big deal was made about these wounds, no questions were asked; they just treated the problem.

Miller and Kline probed for foreign materials in a military-aged male, then cleaned the wound and gave him a tetanus shot, applied ointment and put a clean dressing over the wound and gave him a strong penicillin shot. The only thing we refused to do is give any medication to a patient to bring home. The patient either received through injection or ate it in front of us, or they got nothing. This was so our supplies did not go to the Viet Cong or NVA.

About three o'clock, we ran out of supplies and had treated 210 patients. It had been Sergeant Deljudice's job to keep track of the number of patients and what their complaints were. We loaded up the vehicles and said good-bye to the villagers. Doc told Mouthpiece to

The Tragedy of Vietnam, Again

tell the villagers that we'd return in about ten days for a follow-up visit.

I climbed on top of Bravo-Band-Aid with the other Bravo Troop Medics. We were the first track out on the Highway One. Just as we pulled out onto the road, with children jumping and yelling good-bye, there was a loud, sickening explosion not very far away. It sounded like a mortar round at first, but Clancy knew what it was; he'd heard too many explosions before.

Bravo-Band-Aid tore off down Highway One, toward Hawk Hill. We went about an eighth of a mile and came upon a small bridge that used to have a culvert that went under the road. It was now just a gaping hole, and off to one side, in the rice paddy was an Army jeep lying on its side.

Three American soldiers lay like rag dolls near the jeep. It was difficult to tell what their conditions might be, from where we were, but none of them looked like they were in very good shape. Clancy, Kimmy Hobbs, and Steven Nussbaumer were off the APC as it came to a stop, with aid bags in hand.

Hobbs took a patient who definitely had a compound fracture of his right leg. This was not a difficult diagnosis, because the leg was at an acute angle with a bone sticking out through his pant leg. However, more importantly this patient was not breathing. Hobbs rolled his patient on his back so he could administer mouth-to-mouth resuscitation. When Hobbs stopped to catch his breath, I administered CRP. Hobbs constantly monitored the lack of vital signs and gave more mouth-to-mouth resuscitation. The only thing we couldn't do was to give up, and we prayed that the good Lord would bring this guy around.

Clancy claimed another patient who had a deep gash in his thigh, and was also unconscious, but breathing. Clancy pulled out his razor-sharp hunting knife and slit his patient's pant leg up to his waist. He yelled to Nussbaumer, at the top of his lungs, "Get me two IVs, now."

Nussbaumer ducked inside Band-Aid and popped out the back hatch carrying two bottles of Ringers plus a cutter set that contained the needle and tubing.

"Clean off his arm and plug him in, "Clancy ordered.

Nussbaumer was a new medic in Charlie Troop from California. He went about his work quickly and stuck the needle into the patient's arm.

Clancy removed the top of the other bottle and flushed the debris out of the gaping wound. Clancy was having trouble stopping the bleeding so he put a tourniquet around the patient's leg to slow down the flow of blood.

While Clancy worked on his patient, the third patient was in great pain and might have had a broken back, so he couldn't have any pain medicine. Walter Powell and George Coppage gently inspected this patient, but didn't move him for fear of doing further damage to him.

The Tragedy of Vietnam, Again

Nussbaumer helped Hobbs by placing a splint around the broken leg after he straightened the leg out somewhat and immobilized the limb.

At this stage, Doc and the rest of the crew arrived on the scene and Doc took over immediately. He made a minor modification to my CPR technique, told Clancy that his patient needed to have the tourniquet eased every few minutes, or else gangrene could set in.

Doc devoted most of his time to Walter Powell's patient, moving a backboard into position, and then tying the patient down so he was unable to move. As we all worked on patients, one of the line troops called in for an urgent Dust-Off. We were informed that Dust-Off would not be able to make the pickup for at least thirty minutes.

"That's not good enough, I want one here within ten minutes," Doc demanded.

"Hey, Doc, does it have to be Dust-Off? There's a chopper coming down Highway One, toward us right now. He's over there," a soldier shouted.

"I don't give a damn what it is, I just want to get these patients to Chu Lai, as soon as possible," Doc grunted.

Hobbs sat upright and exclaimed for all to hear, "Man, this guys breathing on his own;" I stopped my CPR. We had done everything we could for those patients. The ABCs had been performed: clear the airway, stop the bleeding, and control for shock.

An Unexpected Reward

A helicopter gunship had seen our smoke grenade and came in and landed on the other side of Band-Aid. We off-loaded boxes of ammo, so two patients could lie on the floor of the aircraft; there was only room enough for one litter. A litter was dragged out of Band-Aid and the patient with the possible broken back was placed on it. Another litter was set up so we could carry the other wounded patients to the aircraft.

We carried the two patients who didn't have a possible broken back, dragged them off the litter by their shirt collar, and slid them across the helicopter's floor, so they were out of the way. The helicopter just became their litter. The back patient was carried and loaded, litter and all. Doc sent Hobbs and Clancy along on the helicopter to tend to the tourniquet and the watch over the other two patients. As soon as Hobbs was on board, the pilot gunned his engine and the gunship was off the ground, speeding across the land.

"Miller, call Control and tell them at the Second Surge to be on the lookout for three patients," Doc ordered. We then policed up the area, gathering the personal belongings of the patients, plus the ammo we had off-loaded from the helicopter. Everything was loaded into a Bravo track. Also, the jeep was righted and hooked to another track's tow hook and dragged back to our base camp.

Since the Med-Cap had been classified as an official operational patrol belonging to the third platoon of Bravo Troop, that platoon leader was required to fill out all the operational reports about the accident, much to Doc's and my pleasure. We returned to the aid station feeling very sober after the events of the afternoon.

"Miller, call the Second Surge to see if you can get in touch with Clancy," I asked.

"Yes, sir," Miller replied as he went to hassle with the phone system, trying to call Chu Lai.

Johnston and Kline cleaned out the medical chests and restocked them. Doc, in the meantime, was seeing a patient who had been waiting most of the afternoon, and wasn't in the best of moods.

"Stewart, take the names and line numbers of the men in the jeep accident to the TOC, so their unit at LZ Baldy knows what happened, and where they are," I ordered.

"Lieutenant Noble, Clancy says all three are all right and are at the Second Surgical. Clancy says he and Hobbs will catch the mail chopper back, sir," Miller yelled out.

"Stewart, pass that on along with the message to the TOC."

I went back outside the aid station and watched huge, ugly black clouds hang over the mountains to the west. *"We're going to get soaked tonight",* I thought. The humidity was thick and oppressive; water droplets collected on the fine hairs on my face and back of my neck.

As the sun slithered out of sight, behind one of the thunderheads, a spectacular display of sunlight and

An Unexpected Reward

shadows was revealed. The black thunderhead reached way up into the sky, as the billowing formation undulated with its outline in a brilliant orange, as if the clouds had halos.

"What are you looking at?" a voice behind me asked.

"Oh, hi, Colonel Lawrence, I'm just looking at those clouds. I think we're going to get wet tonight, sir."

"I agree with you; those clouds are sure pretty, aren't they. Is Doc in the aid station?"

"No, Doc stepped out for a few minutes, sir."

"I just dropped by to say you, Doc, and your boys did a good job today."

"Thank you, sir."

"Have you got any word back on those mine casualties?"

"Yes sir, Clancy called to say they all made it to Chu Lai and all patients are under care right now. Clancy and Hobbs are going to ride the mail chopper back to The Hill."

"That bird is due in about twenty minutes. There's one other thing I want to tell you. We have received feedback that the mine was meant for one of your vehicles. Evidently, the VC told all the villagers not to go to be treated; when VC saw the turnout, they felt they had to do something. Some little bastard sat in the rice paddy waiting. We think they mistook that jeep for Doc's."

"Sir, these people are sick."

The Tragedy of Vietnam, Again

"Let's say they play by a different set of rules than we do. Because of what happened today, I want to add more security for the next Med-Cap. I want you to go back to that village; we made a hell of a lot of Brownie points there today. I'll tell Doc when I see him, but pass my thanks on to your boys."

"Yes, sir, I will."

The colonel turned and headed back to the squadron's command center. I walked back to the aid station, feeling good inside and relayed the CO's comments to all the medics in the aid station and to Doc when he returned.

Overnight Visitors

We went back to the same village, about three miles north on Highway One, ten days later and conducted a repeat of what had happened the last time. All the jobs were rotated around so no medic felt cheated. The security had been beefed up and a track sat right next to the repaired culvert, at the bridge.

That day produced close to three hundred patients and better than two hundred and fifty needed some sort of medical help; the others had come to get candy, or to look at the Americans.

We had a wonderful experience at the end of this Med-Cap. A boy of about eleven or twelve years old came up to Doc and pointed to his chin. It was one of the grossest-looking things I'd ever seen; he had a growth about the size of an orange hanging under his chin that jiggled. Doc felt the lump and then looked at his watch; it was getting late.

"This boy needs to go to Chu Lai," Doc announced. "He's not urgent and it's too late to call in a helicopter. Where's the interpreter?"

"I here, Doc" Chicken man answered. Chicken man was Alpha Troop's interpreter.

The Tragedy of Vietnam, Again

"Tell this boy's mother and father we're going to take him with us. He's going to go to the hospital. He'll be away from home for two, maybe three weeks." Doc explained.

The interpreter spoke to the boy and the boy pointed to a man off to one side, who looked about forty to forty-five years of age. The man stepped forward and was told what Doc said. It was very touching; the man put his arm around his son and gave him a hug. He then took off his well-worn plastic rain cape and put it around the boy's shoulders. The father then reached into his tattered short pants and pulls out a one-dong note, worth about twelve cents, and handed it to the boy, just in case he needed some money.

The father spoke to the boy and the boy answered. Then the child ran over to a group of women and he kissed one middle-aged woman good-bye. The boy quickly went over to Doc's jeep, which was ready to pull out. The boy climbed onto the backseat, and as the jeep drove off, all the villagers waved good-bye.

We drove directly back to the aid station, for the sun had set and it was getting very dark outside. Stewart ran down to the chow hall and ate quickly. He then smuggled a plate of food out of the dinning hall, and brought it back to the aid station for the boy. We had to keep his presence quiet, because no Vietnamese civilian was allowed in the base camp after dark.

While Stewart was obtaining supper for our guest, I got ready for supper myself. I went over to the small stainless sink and washed my hands, and then immediately turned off the water faucet. As I turned my back to dry my hands, I heard the water running, then it stopped, then it was running, and then it stopped.

Water was carried by hand to fill the wing tank outside, so water was not to be wasted. I turned around to see what the problem was, and to my surprise there was the boy trying to figure out how the water came out of the faucet.

Miller turned on a light to read by and the next thing he knew the light had been turned out. The little boy again was investigating. It suddenly dawned upon us, this child had never seen any of the conveniences that we all took for granted.

Kline started the Coleman gas stove to make popcorn, and the stove intrigued our guest. The boy reminded me of the monkey Curious George, in the children's books. Just like Curious George, our boy had to investigate the stove and in doing so he let out all the pressure. As soon as the popcorn started to pop, our guest had to remove the top to see what was going on inside and popcorn went all over the place. The little boy liked making popcorn, but did not care to eat it.

We put him on a litter in the corner of the aid station, and very early the next morning he was put on the supply helicopter and was sent to Chu Lai. Doc called one of his doctor friends to have the boy met and taken to the hospital.

The Tragedy of Vietnam, Again

Two days later. Doc got a phone call from his friend, who informed Doc the boy did not have cancer, that he had a cyst and that it had been removed; he'd be released from the hospital in three days' time.

The little boy returned to our unit by helicopter and we drove him immediately back to his village. It was really rewarding when we turned off Highway One and into the small hamlet. Most of the village was already on hand to witness the homecoming. (Their early warning system was put to use and it impressed us greatly.) The boy jumped out of the jeep and ran over to his mother and gave her a big hug. After he greeted his mother, one of the elders of the village took the boy by the hand and put him on top of the hood of Doc's jeep. Then the elder took hold of the bandage covering the boy's throat and tore it half off. The village elders all inspected the scar to make sure the American doctor had done a good job. Once they were satisfied, the old man who removed the bandage replaced it and let the boy get down so he could run off.

About a week after the return of this boy, the crew that went out every morning to sweep the road clean of mines was greeted by a delegation from this village. The road crew was informed through sign language that all the mines were uncovered. An old crusty American sergeant just couldn't believe what he saw as the villagers led him out onto the road and, sure enough, every mine was exposed.

Overnight Visitors

Slowly, we uncovered the background to this story. On our first visit to the village, the elder we talked with was not the village chief; he was maybe the second elder of the village. The old man with the half-dead baby was the chief of the village, and the boy was his grandchild.

The village chief told Lieutenant Venn, "Your doctor saved my grandson, and he has cured my village of many sicknesses and he never asked for anything. Your doctor takes care of us; we take care of you." These village people took it upon themselves to uncover all the mines laid in our section of Highway One every morning from that day onward, until I left Vietnam eight months later.

Locals dole out rice allotment to local people.

The Tragedy of Vietnam, Again

Receiving his allotment amount

Overnight Visitors

Catching every bit of spilled rice

Surprise, Surprise

It was 11:30 p.m.; Bravo-Band-Aid pulled up in front of the aid station, on Hawk Hill. Bravo Troop's orders for the day had been to recon an area known as Cigar Island. It was an island that was long and skinny, which really was part of the shoreline, it was so close. The inlet of standing water on the backside was about a foot or two deep at low tide and maybe five feet at high tide.

Bravo Troop's orders were not to go out of their way to look for trouble, but to wander in and observe for signs of the enemy and make notations of the terrain, because within two weeks' time the squadron was going to hold a massive search and destroy mission. Cigar Island was not only a rest area, but was also a hotbed of activity for not only the Viet Cong, but also for the North Vietnamese army.

Bravo dropped in a little too suddenly on that particular day; they ran into a small force of VC before they could hide. As a result, a firefight broke out immediately and, in the process, three villagers were caught in the crossfire and were slightly wounded.

The Tragedy of Vietnam, Again

Fording the inlet over to cigar Island.

Tracking in the beach on Cigar Island.

Overnight Visitors

As I went out into the pitch-black night, Bravo medics unloaded their wounded charges. I shined my flashlight on a figure approaching; it was Emanuel Rodrigo, the driver of Band-Aid, and he was carrying a small girl in his arms.

"Sorry to keep you up so late, sir, but we have some presents for you," Emanuel said, laughing as he passed, bringing the child into the aid station.

I switched the flashlight back onto Band-Aid as another child was carefully lowered over the side of the APC. Two other medics, Pasiv and Logan walked a very sleepy boy into the aid station. As they passed by, Logan laughingly said, "You're up kind of late, aren't you, sir?"

I went back down the ramp to see what I could do to help, because the line medics had to get back to Bravo Troop to get Band-Aid and themselves ready in case they had to go out at a moment's notice.

Miller had the duty again, so it was his responsibility to inform Doc that the expected patients had finally arrived.

"I'm not asleep, I'm only resting my eyes," Doc protested loudly. After a moment, Doc stumbled out of his room, rubbing his eyes, grumbling something about why Bravo Troop couldn't keep better hours. This was much to the glee of Bravo Troop's medics.

Emanuel had the first child, a girl about eight years old, lying on a litter. He had lifted up a very dirty and

The Tragedy of Vietnam, Again

well-worn shirt, and was cutting off a field dressing wrapped around her middle. Once the bandage was removed, two bullet wounds were exposed, one hit her left lower rib cage and the other had grazed her halfway up her rib cage. She also had a fragmentation wound about the size of a dime on her right upper arm. She was very lucky, for all wounds were superficial and with proper care would heal nicely.

As this was going on, the sleepy little boy, who was about twelve years old, had become very much alive. He explored the aid station, looking at this and peeking at that. Of course he had to touch everything and without being told what it was, he started to stuff his face full of old popcorn.

"Smoky," the generator mechanic, lived with the medics, by order from the colonel, because all the squadron's generators were located right behind the aid station. In the event something went wrong, Smoky was literally right next door and could get the units up and running. Otherwise he'd be on the far side of Headquarters Troop, on the other side of the compound.

Smoky had learned a great deal of first aid just by living with us, especially the art of giving shots. Smokey's specialty was giving shots to the prostitutes at the end of our access road. These girls did not like getting any type of shot. Smoky had perfected the art of chasing these girls across a rice paddy, tackling one and giving her a shot all at the same time. Doc didn't

Surprise, Surprise

Platoon Leader getting organized

NVA/VC Ambush to the left with Alpha Troop on the right.

The Tragedy of Vietnam, Again

care how they got their shots, just so long as they got them.

Seeing a good opportunity to play doctor, Smoky took the boy's shirt off and removed a field dressing that covered his back. The boy was very lucky, like the little girl, for the frag had not penetrated. A chunk of his back about the size of an egg had been torn out.

The little boy was very temperamental about the whole affair and put up a mild protest. Smoky was disgusted with the boy's clothing, which smelled as if he had rolled in a dead animal. He made the boy take off all his clothes and marched him naked outside with soap, water, and a scrub brush.

Miller had taken over caring for the little girl and on Doc's orders removed all her clothing. He put her in a large tub of warm water that had a good slug of surgical soap in it.

Emanuel returned with two line troops carrying a litter with a Mama San on it. She was about thirty-five years old, but looked about fifty. The newest patient was moaning and groaning as if tomorrow would never come.

Logan said, "Hey, Doc, watch out, she really stinks something terribly." Both Emanuel and Pasiv confirmed Logan's statement, and as she passed Miller, he caught a good whiff and he immediately gagged.

"What's wrong with her?" Doc asked.

"Oh, she got shot in the crotch," Pasiv exclaimed.

Surprise, Surprise

I turned on the large floor fan and put it on high. As a near gale force wind was produced, I pointed it at Mama San. This took care of the smell problem, for all one had to do was stand with the wind to your back, and you smelled nothing; God help anyone who was downwind from her.

Doc moved over and took over Mama San, for she was hurt the worst of all, but was still very lucky. The bullet penetrated the inside of her left thigh and exited near her left hip. There was no nerve, artery, or bone damage. It was a nice, clean gunshot wound, and in few weeks she'd be as good as new.

I took leave and went outside to one of our connex storage containers. I returned with two boxes of children's clothing. Doc's church, back in his hometown, had asked for donations of clothing and we received close to ten huge boxes full; each box was packed according to age, size, and sex.

Smoky came back with the boy and did he shine. I thought Smoky must have gotten into the shower with the kid, by looking at his uniform. The young boy was cold and wanted to put his dirty clothes back on. Smoky had trouble explaining to the boy that he was going to get new clothes. At least up until when the boxes were opened, then the expression on the boy's face told us that he not only understood, but fully approved of the idea.

Smoky took the box marked, "Boys ten years old," and started sifting through it carefully, trying to find something that would fit a twelve-year-old Vietnamese boy. There were up to thirty pairs of pants and an equal number of shirts. The boy spotted a pair of blue shorts with a brass belt buckle and he scooped them out. Much to our surprise, they fit. Smoky tried to find a shirt that would fit and came up with a Hawaiian type shirt that was an excellent fit.

As this re-clothing took place, Miller's little girl was taking everything in and had a good idea that she would get the same treatment. As soon as all of her wounds were treated, she walked timidly to the box marked girls to see what she might find. This girl was tiny, maybe the size of an American five-year-old. She eyed a pair of fire-engine red slacks and a white frilly blouse that fit more or less.

"She can grow into them," Doc commented from across the aid station.

Doc had cleaned Mama San's wounds, as he oversaw the re-clothing. Poor old Mama San must have thought this would be her last night on earth, as she moaned, but Doc was going to make sure these children were fitted out properly. I thought this event may have brought Doc back home for a short while, because Doc had three children of his own.

As Doc finished up with Mama San, three MPs came noisily into the aid station, all looking very sleepy. Sergeant Bulloch, a huge black man about the size of a linebacker on a professional football team, asked, "Where're the prisoners, Doc?"

Surprise, Surprise

Doc pointed to Mama San and the two children, "What the hell, they're kids," Sarge exclaimed.

"You're correct, they are children," Doc answered with a smirk.

"What the 'F' am I to do with them?" the big MP demanded.

"I don't know, maybe find a place for them to sleep," Doc suggested with a smile.

"Shit, Doc, I'm not running a hotel, I run a jail!"

One of the junior MPs said, "That old Mama San ain't going no place, and the children don't look like a great threat. Why not put them in the chapel; it's not being used right now."

Sergeant Bullock scowled at the MP and then stated, "All right, the chapel it is. He crossed the room and took the boy and girl by their hand. "The two of you carry Mama San," he instructed the other MPs as he walked out of the aid station.

"Sarge, I want to see all three tomorrow morning, right after sick call," Doc called out.

I felt sorry for our three patients. It must have been a terrifying experience for all three; to be caught in a crossfire and be wounded by the enemy, at noontime. Then be snatched by the bad guys (us) and stuck inside some steel machine that made a lot of noise, it smelled, and was uncomfortable, to be bounced around and driven off to God only knew where. After many hours of riding, they were cold, scared, and hungry, to be brought into an enemy base camp, where the very first

The Tragedy of Vietnam, Again

thing they did was to strip them naked, and give them a bath. Then some guy came along sticking a metal rod into their wounds, looking for pieces of metal, then he gave each one a large shot of something, and then they were finally bandaged up. I thought I would be very scared if that had happened to me.

What happened the next day was very interesting. The little boy was caught next to the POW stockade wire, giving orders to some of the military-aged men and women prisoners from Cigar Island. The MPs grabbed the boy and dragged him unceremoniously back to the S-5, Lieutenant Venn, and Sergeant Deljudice, who were in charge of keeping track of these children until we were ready to return them to their homes.

The question was who was this little boy? Why were military-aged people taking orders from this child? He was also extremely mean to the little girl; he completely dominated her. She could do nothing, accept nothing, and eat nothing without his prior approval. All candy given to the little girl, he took away.

Staff Sergeant Deljudice felt he should drop the children off at the aid station; it looked as if the MPs might have disrupted the little boy's dressings when he was dragged away from the stockade. Deljudice had other pressing business so told the medics, "I'll be back in a while."

The little boy took off his shirt and dropped it on the floor, as he jumped up onto the litter. One of the

Surprise, Surprise

medics removed the dressing and made sure no damage had been done. Kline picked up the shirt and said, "Man, this shirt is filthy; the chapel is not that dirty." As he held the shirt up, a book of matches and a piece of paper fell out of the pocket. Kline picked up the paper and opened it up. Surprise, surprise, it was a detailed drawing showing the stockade layout, the location of the aid station and the command bunker area. Doc decided he didn't like this little boy! The map convinced us that the child was up to no good. I sent a medic to get one of the interpreters and Sergeant Deljudice immediately.

Both arrived at the same time and we explained our feelings and showed them the map and matches. Sargeant Deljudice said, "You know, I've had a funny feeling about this kid from the very beginning."

We all agreed the boy needed to go directly to the stockade. Doc and Sergeant Deljudice both agreed the little girl should not go to jail. Sarge felt he could work on her and show her that the Americans were not bad people, and we really didn't eat prisoners.

Orders came down from the squadron's commander that we were to hold those children for at least two weeks, or until the sweep operation was over. We'd put them on a helicopter and fly them back to their village right after the firefight, if any. Colonel Lawrence was concerned that the children may have seen or heard something that could compromise the mission. He didn't want to take any chances.

The Tragedy of Vietnam, Again

The little girl had it made; people went out of their way to be nice to her. Someone came up with a doll, another person gave her a Vietnamese hat; she rode around all day long with SSG Deljudice in his jeep, as if she were a princess. The little boy spent the next week in the stockade all by himself, for all the other prisoners from his village had been transferred to Division before he was put in jail.

Doc and SSG (Staff Sargeant) Deljudice felt it might be smart to let the boy out of the stockade after one week of incarceration, but to keep a very close eye on him and his activities. It was interesting to see the change in that little boy. He showed great remorse for what he had done, and showed great respect toward the little girl and did not boss her at all; Doc had been Number Ten (very bad), but was now Number One (the very best). What we hoped to gain with the little boy was when he went back to his village; he might be able to be honest with himself. We knew he'd never like Americans, but when the NVA and VC came in and talked, the little boy knew what was being said was not the truth.

Our unit learned a good lesson: you couldn't be too careful about whom your enemy was; it just might be that cute little boy, about twelve years old.

Surprise, Surprise

The Battle of Tam Ky

All was quiet on Hawk Hill on that lazy September day; one platoon from each troop was out in the field following their operational orders, looking for the enemy. The rest of the troops were back in their respective motor pools pulling maintenance, checking fuel levels, ammo, weapons and a million other little things to make sure that their tracks were in good operational condition for the next time they went to the field.

Spec 4 Bob Johnston was now the senior medic in Alpha Troop. He was busy checking the medical supplies. Any needed items would be picked up at the aid station.

SP4 Robinson was bitching about being Band-Aid's driver and was determined the next new medic was going to take over the driving duties. Robinson, as driver, was responsible for the vehicle, so he was hanging upside down in the engine compartment, checking the transmission oil level.

"Hey, Robinson, make sure to strap the five-gallon can of thirty weight oil on the back of the track," Johnston ordered.

The Tragedy of Vietnam, Again

"Yeah, yeah, I'll get it," Robinson answered angrily.

PFC Patten was busy learning how to replace a worn track block, which didn't pass the morning's inspection. This was hard grunt work and all new people got to do it; this taught them how to fix a broken track in case one should be thrown in the field. Alpha-Band-Aid was operated solely by medics, thus it was in the medics' best interest to be able to perform repairs as quickly as possible, under hostile conditions.

Each platoon medic was busy working in his platoon. First thing every morning the platoon medic held his platoon's sick call and took care of all minor complaints. If the field medic was unable to handle a situation, then that patient was brought over to the aid station so Doc could take a look. If Doc couldn't solve the problem at the aid station, then the patient was sent to Division to one of the large hospitals. It was amazing the number of complaints that showed up if one of the troops thought it might be going to the field.

There were three basic sick calls a day. There was the early morning call from 6:00-6:45 a.m., another from 8:00–9:30 a.m., and a third from 5:30 to about 7:00 p.m. The first call took care of all the troops just before they went to the field. The second call was the regular sick call for all who were not going to the field, and the third was to take care of anyone who missed the first two sick calls, also for anyone who got hurt or became sick while in the field. (The aid station never

The Battle of Tam Ky

shut down; we took patients at any time, if there was a need.)

I walked past the row of vehicles in Alpha Troop Motor Pool as I made my way back to the aid station.

Fifty-eight days and a wake up then I'm out of here and back to the real world, flashed through my mind. *No more fake potatoes, horrible Kool-Aid, wonder meat, and melted ice cream. No more having a light coat of dust over everything, including my food, thanks to the choppers passing overhead. I can't wait to get back to home cooked food.* I passed the large maintenance tent that was full of holes, and then started down the hill toward the aid station.

The aid station looked good; all one could see were the three window tunnels, made out of large half sections of culvert material that was covered like the roof with multiple layers of sandbags. Large heavy canvas blackout curtains lay open, at the end of each culvert, ready to be dropped down before darkness set in.

Just as I rounded the latrine, I noticed one of the platoons returning from the field. Clouds of dust rose high into the air as the tanks and tracks raced each other to see who could reach the fuel rack first. This was a ritual every time any unit came in from the field.

As I entered the aid station I heard someone call out. "Hey, Miller, don't forget it's your turn to light the shower," as Kline set up the volleyball net for the nightly game.

"Yeah, I know it," Miller replied.

The Tragedy of Vietnam, Again

I sat down at the desk in the rear of the aid station to catch up on long overdue paperwork.

Johnston had come over from Alpha Troop to socialize with the aid station crew. He was taking a verbal beating from some of the other medics about his extreme skinniness. One day, just for fun, Doc and I had Johnston weighed just as he was, coming in from the field. He had on his normal combat gear, which consisted of jungle boots with jungle fatigues, a T-shirt, pistol belt with five clips of ammo, and a .45-caliber Colt pistol. We did not weigh his steel pot, flak jacket, or his aid bag. The total weight was 138 pounds. Bob was a good-natured person and took jokes about his physique well. He countered any verbal attack by stating, "I'd much rather have my physique in a rainstorm or in a good firefight; all I have to do is turn sideways and there's nothing for anyone to see, or to hit!"

Bob had been drafted into the Army from Minnesota, after he had run out of money and couldn't continue with college. He had been working his way through school in a band and, as Bob admitted, it was a great way to meet "chicks," but the band really wasn't that good. He didn't know what he wanted to do, so he enlisted for the draft, only if he could become a medic. Bob found out that Uncle Sam was more than willing to go along with his wishes and threw in a bonus, Vietnam. Johnston didn't care where he was sent, just so long as he got an honorable discharge at the end of his tour. Then, he'd qualify for the GI Bill

The Battle of Tam Ky

and his money problem for college would be partially solved.

I went outside to check up around the aid station before darkness set in. Dan Miller had the shower fire going, as a raging flame leapt out of the ammo casing sticking out of the fifty-five gallon barrel full of water on top of the shower. I scanned the base camp to see if all passed my inspection. The "head shed" or TOC area, on top of the hill, seemed all quiet. One or two people drifted about getting ready for nightly guard duty.

The platoon that came in from the field while I returned from the chow hall was clustered around the fuel dump, like a bunch of ducklings flocked around their mother.

The dust that the tracks had thrown into the air, had settled and the near mountains to the west were in deep purple. The sky, in back of the mountains, was a brilliant orange; it hurt your eyes to look directly at the sunset even though the sun was hidden behind the mountains. The entire base camp appeared as if it were afire, for everything had a brilliant orange glow about it. The temperature had started to cool off and the evening breeze picked up. I noticed a truck over in the Headquarters troop area bouncing around the perimeter wire, dropping off the night guards at each bunker position.

The Tragedy of Vietnam, Again

Alpha Troop maintenance was trying to get as much work as possible done in the motor pool before darkness set in. Even though Bravo and Charlie troops were hidden from view, I knew the same scene was being played out in each of these areas; I then returned to the aid station.

As I sat down at the small desk, I heard a track approach the aid station and stop in front of the aid station. Two GIs stomped down the ramp and asked, "Doc in?"

"No, he's playing volleyball. What's the problem?" Miller asked.

"Ah, I stepped on a nail while in the field this afternoon; I want Doc to check it out," one of the GIs stated.

"OK, what's your name and what troop are you in?"

The patient looked at Miller as if he were nuts.

"I need to pull your medical file, also sign in the log." Miller laughed as he pointed to the sign-in register. Miller turned to the other man and asked, "What's wrong with you?"

"Nothing, absolutely nothing, I'm just his driver. I won't let you people touch me, not after you dug that frag out. Man, that hurt more coming out than it did going in."

"Blossom, Steven, Alpha Troop," the first soldier answered.

"Sit on the bench and take off your boot and sock," Miller ordered. He then pulled the medical record and laid it on the counter. Dan filled a basin with water and started the Coleman stove to heat the water. He examined the foot and saw that the wound was more of a laceration than a puncture wound.

"When was the last time you had a tetanus shot?"

Blossom laughed nervously and replied, "I don't know, what does my medical record say?"

Dan looked at the medical record and said, "It was two and a half years ago at Fort Hood. If the world needs an enema they will hook the hose up to Fort Hood," Miller stated, as he removed the basin from the stove.

"Don't put your foot in there yet, let it cool some." Miller then poured a good slug of surgical soap into the hot water.

Dan was curious about where Alpha Troop had gone, so he asked, "Where did you go today?"

"We went over to Cigar Island; didn't see anything though," the driver answered.

"Yeah, I know what you mean. Where did Bravo Troop go, do you know?" Dan asked, hoping to find out where his old troop went.

"I'm not sure, but I think they went south of Tam Ky; you used to be their senior medic, weren't you?" Blossom asked.

"Yes, I use to be, but now I'm back here," Dan smiled.

The Tragedy of Vietnam, Again

"You lucky stiff," the driver said. "Man, would I like nothing better than to cool my heels back here in the aid station."

"Well, as far as I'm concerned you can have the medic's job. I'd puke my guts out if I had to do some of the stuff you guys do. My stomach just wouldn't take it," Steve Blossom stated.

"I think we have the best medics in Alpha Troop," the driver said.

"Yeah, but that runt in the second platoon, I wouldn't let that jerk touch a gook," Blossom groaned.

I felt all the medics were exceptional. After all, I had heard the commanders of Alpha, Bravo, and Charlie troops get into an argument, in the Officers' Club, as to who had the best medics. The more they argued, the better the medics became.

Dan soaked the foot for about a half hour and then cleaned it carefully. He put a bandage over the wound and gave Blossom a tetanus booster shot, just to be on the safe side. "I want you to come back tomorrow to make sure no infection is setting in; be here about eight thirty," Miller instructed.

That night, after the volleyball game, we settled down to our nightly routine. One of the medics made popcorn, Doc broke out the pill-dispensing cups and one bottle of champagne; beer and pop were in the refrigerator for after the champagne. Doc felt, "What the hell, this is Vietnam and let's give it a bit of class." That was why we had Champagne once a week.

The Battle of Tam Ky

One had to understand that once Doc got through his medical residency, he went into a private practice. After a few years, he bought out his senior mentor and built up his own private practice and brought in other doctors who had already done their military service. Doc hadn't been ducking military service; it appeared that Uncle Sam had forgotten about him until he was six months from being too old to go into the military.

The Selective Service put him on a fast track, and Doc was sent to Germany for a three-year tour, which meant no Vietnam. Doc hated Germany and the arrogance of the military medical machine in Germany; he hated it so much, he volunteered to go to Vietnam, just so he could get out of that place. Doc joked he was the highest paid captain in the United States military, because his partners agreed that they'd keep Doc whole, pay wise, while he was in the Army. He told us once that between the Army and his private practice he was making well over one hundred thousand dollars a year and he could afford the cases of champagne to give Vietnam a little bit of class.

During the evening's slack period, some of us used this time to write letters, discuss what went on that day, or make notes in journals or dairies. If anyone wanted to learn some more medicine, this was an excellent time for Doc to turn teacher. The next day started right up where yesterday had left off. One platoon from each troop went to the field looking for the enemy. Everybody

The Tragedy of Vietnam, Again

else was back in the base camp working on bunkers or pulling maintenance on vehicles. Today was a very hot day; no wind, no clouds and a very bright sun beat down, baking everything not covered.

About noontime, word shot throughout our base camp that Lt. Tom Genz, Alpha Two-Six, the second platoon of Alpha Troop, was in DEEP trouble. All troops, Alpha, Bravo, and Charlie, were put on a fifteen-minute alert. Headquarters Troop, along with an infused infantry unit would have to protect and defend the entirety of Hawk Hill.

All three Band-Aids worked fast and furiously, loading extra water cans, mounting weapons, loading personal gear such as extra clothes, C rations, beer, and pop, and then moved the track from in front of the medics' bunkers to their respective motor pools for one quick last minute inspection.

The motor pool was a mass of confusion. People shouted orders, made last- minute adjustments and everyone wondered what was going on. We all knew something big was coming up, for we could see the jets dropping their bombs and smoke rising up into the air about five miles to our south.

There was a sick feeling in the pit of everyone's stomach and all instincts told everyone, *don't go,* but you had to. You had to go, because you'd get in trouble if you didn't. You'd also disgrace yourself and your honor among your friends and family. There was a tremendous push-pull conflict going on within every-

The Battle of Tam Ky

one—you couldn't let your buddies down, you couldn't chicken out, but you didn't want to go out and get shot at!

On the medic tracks, the men were hoping and praying nobody would get hurt. The medics didn't want to expose themselves, but they would. Most of the line troops tried to cover up their nervousness by acting as calmly as possible. All medics gave a quick check of personal equipment, for about the fourth time: helmet, flak jacket, weapon, ammo, etc.

Johnston radioed over to the aid station and asked if he could have an extra man. He was short one, because McRoy, who was supposed to be back from R&R, had not returned yet.

Since there was nobody available at the aid station, Doc said, "Chris, grab your helmet and flak jacket and help out Alpha-Band-Aid. I'll replace you as soon as we can get someone out there.

I had no time to think; I just reacted, grabbed my gear, and ran up the hill to Alpha Troop's maintenance. I found Alpha-Band-Aid and climbed on board.

Johnston was grinning away, with his thumb sticking up in the air, as I slid in behind the right .60-caliber machine gun. "Right on, sir, right on," Johnston said, still grinning.

Johnston was about to give one more radio check, when Alpha Troop's CO, Alpha-Six, gave the order to saddle up. "March order will be Alpha One-Six in the lead, followed by the Green Element. Alpha

The Tragedy of Vietnam, Again

Three-Six will bring up the rear. Move out, Alpha One-Six. Band-Aid you pull in behind me."

Alpha Troop led the squadron, with Bravo behind us, and Charlie Troop brought up the rear; it took us about an hour to reach Alpha Two-Six's location, because it wasn't a straight route. Alpha Two-Six had backed off to the east from the contact point, just out of reach of the RPGs, and was acting as a blocking force until the rest of the squadron arrived.

Two artillery batteries pounded away to the north and south of Tam Ky; that was when the Marine and Air Force jets were not overhead dropping high explosive bombs, or making strafing runs. In between, the squadron's helicopter gunships made mini-gun and rocket runs on enemy-held positions. The US forces were holding the enemy in position until the ground forces arrived to take over the battle.

Alpha Two-Six and his platoon were very lucky. They stumbled onto two to three thousand members of the Second North Vietnamese regular army, who were getting ready to attack the city of Tam Ky.

As we passed the second platoon of Alpha Troop, we all took a verbal assault, such as "Better late than never," and "What took you so long, girls?" We followed Alpha-Six to where we were to form the line of attack. What was very demoralizing, as we advanced forward, was that all the South Vietnamese army passed us, but going in the opposite direction. We waited for approximately ten minutes as smoke grenades were fired to

The Battle of Tam Ky

allow the squadron commander a better view of where his units were deployed in relation to each other and to the enemy positions. The command helicopter had a better view of the enemy's positions, because he could see over a large area of ground and see the enemy better than the line troops.

Word was given for all vehicles to move out at idle speed, about three miles per hour and to recon by fire. With these words, all troops opened fire with their .50- and .60-caliber submachine guns. We didn't have to worry about innocent civilians, because there were none; there were only rice paddies, dense underbrush, trees, and a whole lot of enemy troops. There were no villages, no grazing animals, and no signs of any kind of living accommodations.

The noise was fierce, for Bravo and Charlie troops were doing the same as Alpha. The noise was so loud that my ears hurt terribly. We had among all three troops eighty .50-caliber machine guns and approximately one hundred and thirty .60-caliber machine guns, and twenty-five .90 millimeter canons all firing at the same time in an area about ten to twelve football fields in length.

All three troops strafed the area directly in front of them. A huge cloud of spent gunpowder filled the air and hung over us, because there was no wind to blow it away. We proceeded across the rice paddy and busted through the dense wool on the far side, and then climbed up into a potato patch. The NVA were coming

The Tragedy of Vietnam, Again

out of their spider holes and tunnels, and they were in among us; we were taking sniper fire from all sides, as bullets whizzed by from 360 degrees. We heard two loud explosions simultaneously; Band-Aid sprung into action.

"Alpha-Six, this is Alpha One-Five, I have two hit victors (vehicles); Alpha One-Six has been hit, I'm taking over," the radio announced.

"Alpha-Six, this is Band-Aid, I'm on my way."

"Alpha One-Five, Alpha-Six, Band-Aid is on the way. Watch out for him."

We broke from our position and traversed behind the line as fast as we could to where the stricken tank and armored personnel carrier sat. Michael Esmond, a platoon medic, was dragging the wounded out of the burning vehicles and was making a fast triage, looking for the most seriously wounded. He had all the wounded huddled behind the thick aluminum hull for cover.

As soon as Band-Aid arrived on the scene, some of the regular line troops jumped onboard Band-Aid to man her guns to provide additional protection for the medics as we treated the wounded. The medic driver stayed with Band-Aid in case it needed to be moved. (Doc and I asked the squadron commander to put a regular line troop on Band-Aid to drive, thus freeing up one additional medic in each troop, but our suggestion always fell upon deaf ears.)

Within minutes, a second armored vehicle was hit by an RPG and caught fire. Once again, Esmond

The Battle of Tam Ky

and others moved forward on foot to pull the wounded to the safety of a nearby dike. The firefight was horrendous as enemy machine-gun fire racked the APCs. All the tracks standing guard over the downed APCs strafed the entire area with suppressive fire.

Band-Aid's crew set up quickly behind one of the downed vehicles to perform limited emergency first aid. One of the wounded I knew was lying on his back, not moving. Lambdin carefully rolled Big Red over and cut off his blood-soaked shirt. A piece of flesh, on his back, about the size of a small dinner plate was gone. His ribs and spine were showing. One rib was definitely fractured. Johnston grabbed some sterile water and flushed the wound the best he could. Patten had two large field dressings ready and wrapped them carefully with a six-inch ACE bandage. Johnston plugged in an IV and gave instructions to two line troops to carry Big Red's litter over behind Band-Aid.

Charles and Patten looked after the rest of the tank's crew, while Johnston and I ran over to the stricken APC. Alpha One-Six had multiple fragmentation wounds of the right leg, his groin area, and lower abdomen. We quickly wrapped all his wounds the best we could and got him ready to be med-evacuated out of the area.

Alpha One-Six was brought back to Band-Aid, next to Big Red and the rest of the tank's crew, waiting for a Dust-Off. I went to one of the wounded, whose left hand had been shattered; his little finger was where his

The Tragedy of Vietnam, Again

thumb used to be. Once he was bandaged up, to protect his shattered hand from further damage, I gave him a shot of morphine and told him to go over by Band-Aid and wait.

There was an unconscious soldier who appeared to have no wounds so we put him on a litter and again had him carried over to the holding area.

The last patient had multiple fragmentation wounds to both legs. Johnston and I worked as quickly as we could, but Alpha-Six ordered us out of the area. He had noticed that Alpha One-Six's track had a good fire burning and there was a forty-pound shape charge on board. There were also other high explosives, and we didn't want it to blow up in our face.

Johnston and I grabbed the wounded man and carried him back and put him with the others, when one of the wounded soldiers asked, "Where's Dave?"

Mike Esmond, the platoon medic, and Charles were not happy because there was one man missing from the armored personnel carrier. They ran as fast as they could back to the burning track, just as a round cooked off (exploded) inside. Mike Esmond threw open the back door and found what he was looking for. He grabbed Dave by the back of his shirt and dragged him up and out of the back hatch. A litter was raced to the patient, and he was dumped upon it and removed at remarkable speed, under terrible conditions.

It wasn't like the movies where there was a dramatic explosion just as the hero reaches safety. This track burned for about twenty minutes, and then one of the tanks swung its turret around and pumped two rounds of high explosive into the burning hulk. This blew everything in and on the track sky high and the enemy had very little to salvage.

Robinson called for a Dust-Off, but for some reason Dust-Off couldn't make the pickup. We all knew why, so our commanding officer, LTC Lawrence, came in with his command helicopter and took the most critical patients. We were about to put all the ambulatory patients inside Band-Aid, but a Black Cat helicopter had seen the action and heard our radio call for help. The pilot keyed his radio and said, "Hey, you guys down there, this is Black Cat Seven-Niner, I understand you need a Dust-Off. I'm in the area and can make that pickup for you, if you want some help."

Robinson keyed Band-Aid's radio and answered, "That's affirmative, I'll pop smoke and you identify the color."

"That's a Roger on the ground," Black Cat answered. Robinson took out a yellow smoke bomb and let it fly.

The Black Cat pilot came back with, "Holy shit, will you look at that! I see purple smoke and I see yellow smoke; now which one is you and which one is Chuck, over?"

"We're yellow, out," Robinson answered.

About two minutes later, a Huey gunship came in low and fast. The pilot cranked the helicopter up on its side, changed the pitch of his rotor blades, and did

The Tragedy of Vietnam, Again

a Dust-Off-style landing, like on a dime. All the ambulatory patients piled into the aircraft as fast as they could and landed on top of each other. The pilot was a huge warrant officer who was smiling out the window; he gave us thumbs up and was immediately off. As he sped over the trees, we could see tracers fly by him, and then he suddenly shot straight up into the air to get out of the range of the small arms.

Just as soon as the patients were all evacuated out of the area, Johnston brought Band-Aid back on line, to be ready for the next call. Alpha Troop had worked their way maybe one hundred yards from where Alpha One-Six was hit. The sniper fire was still very intense. Orders were given to dismount half of the crew from each track, and to look for spider holes and bunkers.

Johnston and I dismounted and promptly found a small bunker with four dead NVA soldiers in it. Johnston started pulling the dead out to see what they had on them in the way of documents, weapons, and any good souvenirs was an excellent way to get killed. We found five RPG rockets, no documents, some food, two NVA belt buckles, and one shot-up helmet.

I became very nervous being there. Band-Aid had moved forward, as had the rest of the troop, and there were a lot of single rifle shots to be heard. I had the feeling that bullets were landing close by, and when small branches started to break and leaves fell to the ground, I knew Chuck had zeroed in on us. Johnston and I dropped to the ground and started doing a low crawl. You didn't need training in this; it just came

The Battle of Tam Ky

naturally in a situation like this. We could see dirt kick up near by, as we made exceptional speed slithering across the ground on our bellies. We made our way around some underbrush and came upon an APC that was stuck on top of a stump. It was like a stuck turtle; all it could do was spin around in a circle. That wasn't good and I thought, *this is Loony Tunes.*

Johnston and I lay down beside this track for cover, after we told them we were there. We were very thankful that the enemy were really lousy marksmen. We let the track crew on top of the APC be on the lookout, as we tried to gather our thoughts. Within a few minutes another track came by and pushed the stuck one off the stump. Johnston and I crawled inside the freed APC and much to my relief; they took us back to Band-Aid.

Band-Aid was sitting in the middle of a potato patch, beside a depilated grass shack. We were still taking a lot of sniper fire. A new sergeant to our unit got two other men to follow him. The sergeant jumped off the back of his track and raced toward a large dike to our rear. He went about fifteen yards and then flopped down onto the sandy soil. As soon as he hit the dirt, the other two GIs ran like hell, as the sergeant fired his M-16 on full automatic.

These two ran past the sergeant and crashed to the dirt at the base of the dike. The three of them started poking around, looking for peepholes. One of the men found something about the size of a rat hole, so he pulled the pin on a hand grenade and shoved it through

The Tragedy of Vietnam, Again

the hole. As he did this, he rolled off to one side and hugged the dirt. This was repeated several times at different spots along the dike. As they worked their way near the tumbled-down shack, I saw two men in white shirts running away. I didn't know who they were. I knew they weren't NVA, and then it dawned on me that they were VC. I pounded Johnston on his helmet and pointed at the two. They were running as fast as they possibly could with drawn pistols. They were about thirty to forty yards away, as Bob spun his .50-caliber around and squeezed off six or seven rounds. Both men were lifted up into the air and catapulted horizontally about ten feet through the air and then landed in a disorganized heap upon the ground. One of the VC enemy soldiers had his leg wrapped around his neck, as both lay very dead.

"Nice shooting, Band-Aid. That's two Dinks we won't have to worry about."

I didn't know who was singing our praises, but it had to be one of the tracks nearby.

(I must interject here; medics were allowed to carry weapons to defend themselves, their patients, and their supplies, and if people shot at medics, the medics were allowed to shoot back. My medics also felt there was a preventive medicine aspect to the dilemma. If you kill the SOB before he could shoot one of our troops, then the medics would not have to treat one of our soldiers, because they wouldn't be wounded.)

A Sergeant Whitmore was brought over to Band-Aid with a bullet crease to his head. He was a bloody

The Battle of Tam Ky

mess, a little dizzy; what we didn't know was that he was perfectly all right. No sooner had we dusted off the sergeant than we got Sergeant Smith. He was a mess with multiple fragmentation wounds to his face. Blood was pouring out of him! I wasn't sure if the amount of blood was due to his wounds, or because of his blood pressure; he was one mad dude.

Johnston called for an urgent Dust-Off and once again they could not make the pickup. We told them that it was all right, to just get here as soon as they could. About twenty minutes later, Dust-Off called us back and asked if we could wait for another thirty minutes. Fortunately, a Minute Man slick (an unarmed helicopter from the Minute Man unit) heard our radio conversation and made the pickup for us. When this helicopter came in, I thought it was going to crash. The pilot hit the aircraft's tail on a dike as it landed. No damage done, I guessed; because he flew the wounded off to Chu Lai.

By this time it was getting late and darkness was setting in fast. The squadron had to move out of the area, far enough back so the enemy couldn't attack us at night, but close enough so we could attack them first thing in the morning. The troops withdrew, firing as we backed out and crossed the original rice paddy.

By 9:00 p.m. all troops made a night logger on top of a knoll, in the middle of a huge rice paddy. It was about two miles away from where the action had taken place. Band-Aid was one of the last vehicles to get back, in case we were needed along the way. As we drew into

The Tragedy of Vietnam, Again

the large circle of vehicles, Robinson steered our track between two tanks. Swatter, the mobile bridge, pulled in behind us so we had excellent protection on three sides. The results of our encounter on the first day were 227 NVA/VC killed, while we lost two.

17 year old Medic Edmonds

The Battle of Tam Ky

Medic David Hanes with dark glasses getting a Bronze Star Medal

The Tragedy of Vietnam, Again

Larry Gaydon making lunch.

Ron Kline

Medics Schmidt and Reed

The Battle of Tam Ky

Medic Mike Esmond getting a Silver Star.

Medic Larson making coffee

The Tragedy of Vietnam, Again

(L to R) Dan Miller, Gary Lambdin, Walter Powell, and Eliso Garduno

Early on August 25th, two Chinook helicopters flew into the center of our logger, at 5:00 a.m. We were all up and eating our breakfast of franks and beans, or whatever we could find in our boxes of rations. Most of the men ate some crackers and made coffee. Two Chinooks flew in, carrying ammo, weapon replacements, and fuel for the vehicles.

After the supplies had been rationed out, all three troops moved out to engage the enemy once again. Our objective was to attack a suspected enemy battalion headquarters. It took approximately an hour and a half to reach the objective. Alpha Troop ended up more or less in the same position as we had been the day before. Charlie Troop was to our right and Bravo Troop was to our left.

The Battle of Tam Ky

We were all on the line as Alpha Troop worked its way up and over a small hill covered with heavy undergrowth. We all stopped about ten meters away from the edge of the dense underbrush. Hawk-Six made some minor adjustments to the line from his vantage point in his helicopter above, and then gave the order to advance. Alpha-Six ordered again, "Recon by fire." As soon as we started to move, the tank directly next to Band-Aid, was hit by two RPG rockets, wounding all on board. Two medics were on the scene immediately; we were only thirty feet away.

The enemy small-arms fire was unbelievably intense. The wounded were worked back up a small hill and over its crest for protection. The temperature was becoming extremely hot. We quickly set up an LZ for Dust-Off. From somewhere, we picked up two heat exhaustion cases. When the helicopter arrived, we got rid of all five patients.

The entire advance was held up in order to allow Dust-Off to do its thing. It took about a half hour all total; however you would never know we had stopped anything. The intensity of fighting was extreme. The NVA was throwing everything they had at us, and we in return were giving them everything we had to give. There was so much action going on, you had no clue as to what was really happening.

Every time we tried to advance, the enemy fire was so fierce we had to stand back. Alpha-Six called for help and some of the squadron's helicopter gunships

The Tragedy of Vietnam, Again

went to work with their mini-guns and rockets. When the helicopters were not making runs, the tanks were blasting away with canister (canister turned the tank's 90 mm main cannon—the inside bore was the length of a king-sized cigarette—into a giant shotgun that shot out thousands of pellets in wide patterns, killing anything and everything in its way) and Willy Pete rounds (white phosphorus) that burned white hot were also being fired fast and furiously.

After about a half hour of this punishment, Alpha-Six ordered the troop to advance. We slowly moved across the paddy and into the wool on the other side. Band-Aid was being called by various tracks to pick up men who didn't feel well; they were very light-headed. It took no time to realize that the heat was taking its toll. Heat exhaustion, fatigue, hunger, and lack of sleep were all working against us.

Johnston called Alpha-Six and informed him to order the troops to drink liquids or else he wasn't going to have people to fight the war. Alpha-Six passed the word on immediately, but it did Band-Aid little good; the damage had been done. By this time, we had seven heat exhaustion cases and two of them were unconscious. I had to reassign Patten to one of the platoons, and Robinson claimed he was a heat exhaustion case himself, and he evacuated himself with the other patients, over the strong objections of Johnston. Robinson looked and acted perfectly all right to me and this was a split-second decision on his part; the end

The Battle of Tam Ky

result was Band-Aid was now left with just Johnston and me.

I took over the driving duties of Band-Aid; Johnston remained the track commander, because he knew the field operations much better than I did. We picked up two infantry grunts to man our .60-caliber machine guns.

We tried to set up an LZ for Dust-Off to come in and get the five ambulatory patients, huddling in the hollow for protection. As we waited for Dust-Off, it sounded as if our entire squadron and all the NVA had opened up 360 degrees, all the way around our position. It seemed that all the rounds were incoming. The NVA had us surrounded and were trying to put an end to this engagement, once and for all.

We quickly put all the patients in the back of Band-Aid, and we charged through the underbrush, going as fast as we could, smashing over small trees to our rear, firing all weapons as we went. We broke through the enemy positions and continued across a rice paddy and up a small hill, about five hundred yards, where LTC Lawrence dropped in with the command helicopter to take the wounded, because he needed to refuel his aircraft.

As Johnston and I carried one very fat and extraordinarily heavy sergeant, who was unconscious due to heat exhaustion, Colonel Lawrence suddenly opened fire with his .60-caliber submachine gun, and fired

The Tragedy of Vietnam, Again

over the belly of our patient. The bullets came so close to Johnston's arm that great red welts appeared on it; Johnston wasn't happy with the colonel—that was just a little too close for comfort.

After the command helicopter departed, I turned Band-Aid around and headed back toward the action, but took an oblique course, as we didn't want to retrace our tracks. The only problem was we didn't know where the troop was. We worked our way back, trying to stay as much in the brush as possible. As we were about to cross a rice paddy, all of a sudden the track slipped over on a severe angle. I tried to keep the APC moving, and hoped we'd come up and out of the ditch. What I couldn't see was that the ditch got worse and I laid the track almost on her side.

Needless to say we were in one hell of a jam, lying on our side, surrounded by the enemy, in the largest firefight the squadron had seen for a very long time. Johnston screamed for help into the radio. In the meantime, I ordered the infantry to set up the .60-calibers, one in front and the other to the rear to give us some sort of protection.

Ten very long minutes passed before two tracks found us. They hooked cables to Band-Aid and pulled as I gunned the engine and managed to work our way out of the ditch. Once out I followed the other two tracks back to the troop.

The Battle of Tam Ky

APC- Track going into the 'Wool".

The 25th of August was a very sad day for the medical platoon, because we were informed that one of our medics in Charlie Troop had been killed. Spec. 4 Steven O. Nussbaumer, from Hayward, California, had dismounted to help the infantry company that was helping our squadron in the field. The infantry had three wounded men who were pinned down in an open area; the infantry medics weren't going in to help them. Nussbaumer and a buddy of his from Charlie

The Tragedy of Vietnam, Again

Troop, a Sargeant Soveland, raced out into the opening and grabbed one of the wounded and raced back to safety. They returned and grabbed the second injured soldier, but Sergeant Soveland was cut down, by machine gun fire, and was killed instantly. Nussbaumer made it back to safety with his patient. Then, for some reason, he went back for the third patient, and as the machine gun opened fire, Nussbaumer threw his body in front of the wounded man and shielded him from the hail of bullets.

Specialist Fourth Class Steven O. Nussbaumer was put in for the Congressional Medal of Honor by the infantry company that was assisting the 1/1 Cav on this particular day and whom Nussbaumer went to aid. As we heard, unofficially, "because of misconduct by certain officers within the 1/1Cav dealing with awards and decorations, and because of Army politics," Nussbaumer was never awarded the Medal of Honor; he received the Distinguished Service Cross instead.

Steven Nussbaumer and Sergeant Soveland gave up their lives so three fellow soldiers might live; it was the same as if they had jumped upon a live enemy hand grenade to save their fellow soldiers. It's disgusting what some people would do for a colored piece of ribbon that represented the highest decoration for bravery our country has, especially in the First Squadron, First Cavalry—"First Regiment of Dragoons."

These men, in particular Steven O. Nussbaumer should have his files reopened and be awarded what he deserved—the Congressional Medal of Honor! It also might be possible for the Army, or United States government, to take away a certain 1/1 Armor Cavalry's Congressional Medal of Honor award that was authorized with very questionable witness statements, a long time ago. I doubt if the then president of the United States would be pleased with this medal if he knew the full story behind the supposed heroic actions of this one individual. The members of the 1/1, during the review process for this award, never thought the medal would ever be authorized because of the events that took place, and more importantly who the witnesses were. Everyone was very concerned regarding the unit's XO, Major Bangstrom (not his real name), who shipped one clerk out of the unit and into the infantry for disobeying an order; he refused to sign the witness statement, because he was not a witness.

During the Battle of Tam Ky, which lasted for four days, 548 North Vietnamese soldiers lost their lives and we had no knowledge of how many of the North's soldiers were wounded. The American losses were ten soldiers killed, one Kit Carson Scout killed, and eighty-one men wounded and evacuated out of the battle. None of the heat exhaustion cases counted as wounded.

We made our way back to Hawk Hill. The Aid Station was very saddened at having lost Steve. We were tired and when we reached The Hill, only the

The Tragedy of Vietnam, Again

bare minimum was done to Band-Aid, because major work needed to be performed. The infantrymen who fired our guns did a good job, but by the time we said good-bye, they had shot up every bit of ammo, shot off the exhaust pipe, and put a few rounds through the radiator. This was going to be Headquarters' maintenance problem, for we were all going to sleep for about twenty-four hours straight.

Colonel Lawrence came over the next day to see how the medical platoon was faring, and Johnston gave the colonel holy hell about his firing skills, as he showed the colonel the red welts still on his right arm.

"But you didn't see what was coming up the hill behind you, did you, Johnston?" the CO asked.

"No sir."

"There was a group of NVA soldiers hot on your tail, and they were after Band-Aid; I don't see how any of you on Band-Aid ever survived; I was sure all of you were goners. You have no idea as to what you broke through when you came out, and how you managed to survive and get back is beyond me."

Suddenly, the welts on Johnston's arm didn't seem quite so terrible.

One of the funnier things to happen in Vietnam occurred a few weeks later. I was called by the TOC to report to the helipad to go to Tam Ky to receive an award from the Vietnamese government, for what we did during the battle of Tam Ky. There were seven or eight officers gathered including LTC Lawrence, MAJ

Filbert, MAJ Logan, all the troop commanders and myself.

Major Logan was the S-3 or tactical operations officer, but Master Sergeant Duhs had Logan's fatigues on. The Vietnamese government had a rule that you had to be present in order to receive your award, and no exceptions were allowed. Since Major Logan was out of country on R&R, his operations sergeant was standing in for him. At one point a Vietnamese officer came up to our small group and asked where we graduated from college. One person answered West Point class of '62, another answered West Point class of '64, I answered Parsons College class of '64, and Duhs, alias MAJ Logan, answered, "GED, Class of '52." It was everything we could do not to break out laughing and fortunately, the awards ceremony started shortly thereafter, where the vice president of Vietnam gave us our awards in person.

(GED - General Educational Development certificate)

Fear

It was very early October and evening started to arrive earlier. The aid station was alive with activity on that particular afternoon, because Bravo Troop was in heavy contact to our west. Doc was busy working on a member from Bravo Troop who had ugly fragmentation wounds to the back of his legs and his butt; each wound was a gaping hole of raw flesh. Kelly was sewing up the wounds as soon as Doc was through debriding them. Johnston took down the necessary information on the field medical record log, so that complete medical records were maintained.

Kline and I waited at the helipad with one of the FLAs, because more wounded were coming to Hawk Hill. The sun was setting behind the hills to the west and again the western sky had turned to a bright orange.

Kline stopped drawing his flower designs in the dust, on the hood of the jeep, with his matchbook cover; as we heard the whap, whap, whap of a helicopter's rotor blades. We squinted, as we looked toward the bright sunset; we couldn't see the aircraft, it was hidden in the dark silhouette of the hills. Within a minute, a Huey gunship set down on top of the "H" marked on the ground indicating, "This is the helipad."

A violent dust storm was created, as the helicopter passed overhead, and the prop wash again sandblasted us. Two members of Bravo troop got out and came over to where we were. One was slightly wounded in the arm and the other was a tall skinny blond-headed guy who was crying uncontrollably. The crying soldier shivered as if he was very cold, even though the temperature must have been close to ninety degrees.

Kline ordered, "Get into the jeep!" and we drove them back to the aid station.

Johnston checked the wounded man in and filled out the necessary paperwork and retrieved his medical records.

"What's the matter with these two?" Doc asked Kline.

"One has a frag to his arm, and I don't know what the matter is with the other; all he does is cry." Kline answered.

"Hey, you, come here and let me see your arm," Doc said to the new frag patient, as he pulled some more metal out of the ass of the patient on the litter. The new arrival had the bloody bandage cut off his wounded arm. He went over to Doc and held out his arm.

Fear

Doc looked it over closely and then said, "Kline, wash up and then wash his arm. You and Johnston can take care of him, but let me see what you're doing."

"Chris, take him outside and see what his problem is." I tapped the crying patient's shoulder, pointed for him to go outside, and followed him up the ramp. There were two folding chairs in front of the aid station, so I told him, "Sit down."

"Are you hurt?"

He shook his head no.

"Are you in any pain?"

Again the patient shook his head no. The only thing he did was weep constantly, but I did manage to get his first name, Bill.

After about five minutes, Johnston popped his head out of the aid station and asked, "How's it going?"

I shrugged my shoulders and replied, "He's not wounded and he's not in any pain."

Johnston ducked back down the ramp way. I tried to engage the patient in a conversation but it was very one-sided. Johnston popped back into view; he reminded me of a chipmunk sticking his head out of a hole.

"Doc wants to see him now," Johnston stated.

"OK, Bill, let's go see Doc," I said and I stood up. Bill got up and we both walked back inside the aid station. Doc had finished his debriding task and Kelly was taking the last couple of stitches in the right cheek of the butt of the frag patient lying on the litter.

"Now, what seems to be the matter with you?" Doc asked in a very friendly tone. "What's your name, son?" Doc continued almost in a pastoral voice. The patient buried his face in his hands and started to sob.

"Bill," I quietly interjected.

"OK, Bill, I'll tell you what; you're going to spend the night here in the aid station. Johnston, set up a litter in the corner and get a pillow and blanket from the other bunker. Bill, I'm going to give you a small shot that's going to help you sleep and when you wake up, we'll have a talk, is that all right?"

Bill nodded his head in agreement, and then Stewart took Bill to the facilities, while Doc made up a syringe of "sleepy time."

The patient with the arm wound was sent back to Bravo Troop, while the patient with his back side all sewed up was moved over to the EM bunker for the next three nights.

"Hey, Doc, I don't want this guy to wake up in the middle of the night," Kline protested. "I've got the duty tonight, you know!"

"Don't worry, he won't," Doc said with a grin. "He'll wake up sometime about noontime tomorrow, all right?"

"That's just fine with me," Kline replied with a smile.

"I want all of you people to treat this patient as if nothing happened. Treat him as if he's one of us, this is very important," Doc stated.

Fear

Just then Stewart and Bill returned and Doc explained to Bill that he was giving him a shot that would relax him and he should go to sleep in about ten to fifteen minutes. After the shot was given, Johnston told him to lie down and within three minutes he was out cold. I went over and put a blanket over him, and the aid station slipped back to its normal operations; Bill was a nonentity.

Photo C. Noble leaning against the aid Station's sink with Aunt Kay's eye chart in background.

The Tragedy of Vietnam, Again

Photo Doc Albers in Aid Station

Dan Miller helps Doc Albers in Aid Station.

Fear

The next day I was alone in the aid station at about two o'clock in the afternoon. Everyone else had gone out on a med cap, when Bill decided it was time to get up. He jumped up in total bewilderment as to where he was.

"Where am I?" he stammered.

He scared the living hell out of me, for I had completely forgotten about him and certainly did not expect him to jump the way he did.

"How are you doing, and did you have a good sleep; to answer your question, you're in the aid station."

"Oh yes, yes, I remember," he muttered. "I've got to get back to my unit," he exclaimed.

"Well, you're not going anywhere until we say you can go, OK?" I said as positively as possible.

I hope I won't have any problems with you, I thought.

"But I'll get in trouble; I've got to get back, sir."

"You're not in any trouble now, and you're not going to get in trouble," I stated. "Are you hungry?"

"No, I'm not hungry, but I'm thirsty and I need to go outside," Bill replied.

"You'll find the facilities over there and you'll come right back to the aid station when you're through, that's an order." I said it in a more authoritarian voice. I sure as hell didn't want this guy to take off on me.

The Tragedy of Vietnam, Again

When Bill returned I gave him an Orange Crush and then asked, "Bill, can you please tell me what the matter is, so we can help you?"

"I'm sorry, I'm so very sorry for yesterday, but I just couldn't help it."

"It's all right; don't worry about that. This is why we're here, to help people in any way we can. Now what's your problem, let us help you."

"Well, well, sir, I don't know how to say this, but I'm scared of the dark and I hate going into the field at night. I've been scared of the dark ever since I was a little boy. When we go out to the field and I have to pull ambush duty with two other people, and as far as being able to see, it's as if I have a black bag over my head. Then, the noises, the leaves, the peepers and the crickets chirping all around me; then, suddenly, in one area there's dead silence. I know something is out there, and then my mind plays tricks with me. Sir, I'm so scared I can't move; sometimes I wet my pants. I start to think about all the things that are bad in Vietnam, like that krait, that ugly black and gray snake that was brought over to the aid station about a month ago. Well, it came from Bravo Troop and, as Doc said, if that snake had bit anyone that person would die, sir," Bill was talking fast and I couldn't stop him if I were to try.

"Then I start to think, I hear panthers sneaking up, all ready to take a bite out of me. Do you remember that guy over in Headquarters Troop who shot that

Fear

panther that got tangled up in the wire? Do you remember, sir?"

"Yes, I do remember that incident."

"Sir, I'm a good soldier; I've never been in trouble, but I'm scared shitless." Bill sighed heavily. "I guess I'm in for it now."

"No, you're not in for it now. You see, you're under our medical care right now, and what Doc says medically goes and nobody, not even the colonel, can countermand medical orders unless it's another medical doctor of a higher rank. So, as I have said you're not in any trouble. When Doc comes back I want you to tell him what you just told me, is that all right?"

"Yes, sir, I will do that."

"You know, Bill, you remind me of myself. There's nothing to be ashamed about being scared; everybody is scared over here, and anyone who says they're not scared is lying. Not very long ago I was very scared when I was in 'Fat City,' and I can say I have never been that scared in my life. This was when over two hundred and fifty NVA were positioned to attack us and I had to pull AOD. I had to issue the order for a 'mad minute' and all hell broke loose. I was sent back down the hill, to the aid station, to be ready to treat the wounded. That was when I really got scared, just waiting and my mind played games with me, so don't think you're alone."

When Doc returned, it was dusk and Bill told his story ending with, "But I want to go back to my unit."

The Tragedy of Vietnam, Again

Bravo Troop was still out in the field, so Doc told our patient, "I don't want any overzealous sergeant sending you back to the field until I can talk with Captain Lewis. I want you to stay at the aid station another night, and that's an order," Doc explained.

Bill smiled at this order and put up no argument.

Later that night, Doc said, "Bill, you know you'll have to go back to the field, but I'm going to put some strict restrictions on what you'll do in the field; do you understand?"

"I trust you, Doc, and I'll do whatever you tell me to do."

The next morning Bravo Troop came in from the field. Doc waited until the troop was all settled down and Captain Lewis had had time to clean up and get comfortable.

Doc announced, "Chris, get our patient, we're going to Bravo Troop to pay a visit. Kline, go over and tell Bill to meet us at the jeep."

We briefly discussed Doc's plan of action. Bill was very nervous as he climbed onto the rear seat. Doc got into the passenger seat, and I drove us over to Bravo Troop. The drive took no more than five minutes. When we pulled up in front of the Orderly Room, Bill's platoon sargeant was just leaving.

"Well, well, well, will you look at what has decided to come back?" the platoon sergeant sarcastically exclaimed, as he spied Bill on the back seat. He stopped and reentered the Orderly Room.

Fear

"Bill, you stay here and don't talk with anyone; that's an order," Doc stated. "We will tell you when to come in, do you understand?"

"Yes, Doc, I understand."

"Come on, Chris, you go first, you know Lewis better than I."

As we entered the Orderly Room, the platoon sergeant had a leering look on his face, as if to say, we were going to have some fun as soon as we get our hands on that piece of crap outside.

I didn't say a word, but walked through the Orderly Room and into Captain Lewis's quarters. "Wayne, how was it out there?"

"Oh, hi, Chris, and how are you, Doc?" Wayne Lewis replied.

Doc answered, "Wayne, we need to talk about one of your boys. I would like your sergeant to hear what I have to say, if that's all right with you?"

"No, no problem; hey, Sarge, come here," Wayne Lewis called out.

Bill's platoon sargeant came into the rear quarters in a very military manner. I wasn't sure if he was trying to put us on or what.

"Yes sir, you want to see me, sir?" he snapped out, as he came to attention and saluted Captain Lewis.

Wayne Lewis ignored the sergeant and said, "We're all ears, Doc, what's on your mind?"

"As you know, we have been in charge of one of your people for the past two days; you and I have a

The Tragedy of Vietnam, Again

problem on our hands. I want to ask you some questions if I may. Have you ever had any trouble with PFC Bill Smith before?"

"No, not until Smith turned chickenshit on me two days ago," the CO replied.

"That's what I want to talk about; he didn't turn chicken on you at all…"

"Oh, come on, Doc, everyone would like to get out of the field; if that's all they have to do, then I've a huge problem," Wayne Lewis interrupted.

"The problem with Smith," Doc continued, "is that he's terrified of the dark. He has had this problem ever since he was a little boy. He's a good soldier, by your own admission, with the exception of this one breakdown. He wants to come back to Bravo Troop, and he's willing to go back to the field, but he's scared as to what's going to happen to him." Both the sergeant and the captain listened carefully to what Doc was saying.

"So, what am I supposed to do with him? I can't trust him not to crack up again," Captain Lewis stated.

"Oh, I think you can use him and I don't think you'll have any trouble. You're going to have to recognize that he has a problem, and you're willing to work with him. I suggest medically that you handle him as if nothing has happened. Let it be known that anyone who gets on his case is in for a world of crap from you and the sergeant here. When Smith goes to the field, make sure someone is always near him, and when it's his turn to pull guard duty, have him pull radio watch. The red light on the radio will give just enough light so you won't have any problem. If you do not agree to this, I'll pull Smith out of this unit and will have him reassigned to some unit down in Chu Lai. I don't want anyone screwing with this kid; have I made myself clear?" Doc demanded, as he looked both directly in their eyes.

I had observed everything in case Doc needed a witness later on.

Wayne Lewis looked at his sergeant, "Any problem, Sarge?"

"No, sir, I can't foresee any trouble, and I'll pass the word quietly to back off and say nothing about this incident."

What a two-face, this is the guy who was going to eat someone up because he had turned chicken on them, I thought.

"Chris, go out and bring Bill in here," Doc ordered. "Sarge, you go do what you're going to do."

I went out to the jeep and found Bill talking with another member of Bravo Troop.

"Smith, come with me, please," I ordered.

Bill got out of the jeep and he was terribly scared. As we walked up the short walkway to the building, Bill whispered, "Are they mad?"

Just then the sergeant walked out and said, "I've got to check on the maintenance tent."

The Tragedy of Vietnam, Again

I put my hand on Bill's shoulder and whispered, "Don't worry, Doc has it all arranged and it's a good deal."

When we walked into Captain Lewis's quarters, Bill's CO said, 'Welcome back to the unit, Smith. Doc has been telling me he wants some changes made as far as your duties in the field. If this is all right with you, you'll ride my track from now on, as a .60 gunner, and you had better be good with a radio, because you'll pull all your guard duty as my radio operator. Is this agreeable with you?" Wayne Lewis asked.

A flood of relief showed on Bill's face. "Sir, thank you and I promise you'll have no problems with me." Tears flooded his eyes, as he thanked Doc and me.

We saw Bill from time to time in the aid station but never again as a patient.

Quang Ngai

It was a beautiful September day, just a perfect New England type of summer day, nice clean air, with a bright blue sky as one or two puff clouds floated slowly overhead. The temperature was in the high eighties.

Doc and Kline were finishing up sick call when the field phone rang. The voice on the other end asked me to please come to the TOC for a meeting. As I left the aid station, the morning activities caught my attention. Johnston was washing the three jeeps, while Stewart repaired a few broken sandbags in our garage.

The garage was nothing more than a three-foot high sandbag wall that encapsulated three sides of each vehicle. This was to prevent shrapnel from harming the more vital parts of the vehicles such as tires, radiators, engine, etc. The open end was nothing more than a potluck affair, for the rear of each vehicle would either be shredded or the frags would miss; it was like a game of chicken.

A large oil tanker truck was spraying diesel oil all over the dirt roads on Hawk Hill, to help keep the dust down. With so many tracked vehicles running about, the dirt was ground to a very fine powder and was a

The Tragedy of Vietnam, Again

constant problem. Whenever anything passed over the road, or even when the wind blew, everything downwind was completely engulfed.

As I reached the TOC area, a detail of "Dead Heads" (people who had screwed up and were on report) were raking dirt and oiling the entryway with two gallon watering cans. I entered the TOC and was surprised to see all the troop commanders, their executive officers and most of the senior NCOs sitting down. I slipped into a chair and waited. All the operation maps had heavy black security drapes covering them. There was small talk about why we had been called together, but no one had the correct answer.

LTC Lawrence finally entered the TOC with his executive officer Major Filbert. Also, the squadron's operations, supply and intelligence officers slipped into the back row of the room. LTC Lawrence walked to the front of the room and he said, "May I have your attention." We all stopped talking immediately.

"Before we get going I want to ask a question. Who here does not know where the city of Quang Ngai is, raise your hand."

I raised my hand, because I had no clue where Quang Ngai was. I did feel a little foolish, because I was the only person to raise my hand.

"Well, at least we have one honest person here," Major Filbert said with a grin.

Quang Ngai

"Where's Quang Ngai?" Colonel Lawrence asked Lieutenant Jackson, the XO of Alpha Troop, Tom was a recent graduate from West Point.

"Quang Ngai is south of Chu Lai, sir."

"How far south, what type of terrain is there, and how is it different from our operating area?" The colonel asked the gathered group.

Nobody could answer the questions.

"You see, nobody really knows where this place is, except that it's somewhere south of us," the Colonel stated. "The city of Quang Ngai is having a lot of trouble with the NVA and Viet Cong. It's a situation similar to what Tam Ky had, awhile ago. It's felt that they need some extra fire power, so General Gettys wants the squadron to be put on alert."

Major Filbert produced a map and LTC Lawrence took a pointer and pointed to a spot on the map south of Chu Lai. "Quang Ngai is approximately seventy-five miles south of Hawk Hill. The squadron is to be prepared to move out by fourteen hundred hours today (2:00 p.m.). Each of you knows what has to be done. The colonel and his staff went through the logistics as far as resupply, operations support, local scouts, infantry support to help fight on the ground, etc."

I was instructed that the mobile aid station would be brought to Quang Ngai and needed to go over to Headquarters Troop Maintenance to be gone over thoroughly. This was a wise decision on someone's part, because the mobile aid station had really not been driven for seven or eight months. We were instructed to bring enough medical supplies to handle all our needs for an extended stay. Doc was to remain at Hawk Hill and I was to operate in the field. If we needed, Doc would be flown in once everything was established.

"Anyone whose vehicle breaks down, because of faulty maintenance while going to Quang Ngai will be given an Article Fifteen (a mild but automatic military disciplinary action). I don't need the squadron spread all over the countryside. Also, do not discuss our destination with your men. I don't need that information to precede us. Just tell the men that we're on alert to move out at a moment's notice," LTC Lawrence explained.

We got up and as I walked out, Captain Donaldson, the new commander of Headquarters Troop said, "Chris, bring the aid station over to maintenance. I don't want you guys breaking down, because if you do, it will be my ass that gets chewed."

I laughed and thought, *and mine as well.* I assured him that the mobile aid station would be brought right over.

As I walked into the aid station, Kline was cleaning some medical instruments at the sink, before they went into the autoclave to be sterilized. Miller was taking an inventory of the shelves, Johnston was cleaning the floor, and Doc was making notes in some medical records at the small desk in the rear of the aid station.

Quang Ngai

I informed Doc as to what was going on, except for the destination.

The medics were all ears. Doc was quite happy at not having to go to the field. Colonel Cousland made Doc go out once on a recon patrol. Dick Albers thought that was a huge waste of time and was counterproductive. What if he had been hurt or gotten killed? Doc was too valuable a person to have joyriding around the countryside. This was not to say that Doc was chicken, because he wasn't, not by any stretch of the imagination. Doc was correct, it was a waste of time; however the colonel was also correct. Doc should know what his troops had to go through every day, out in the field. As I said, Doc was happy to let us bring the gear down to Quang Ngai and set everything up.

Doc stopped writing and told Johnston and Kline to take the mobile aid station over to maintenance. Both Johnston and Kline knew their way around tracks, because they had spent a lot of time in the field. I knew that they'd go over that vehicle very carefully.

Miller and Kelly went over the medical chests and made sure everything was on board. Stewart filled the water cans and put them off to one side next to the aid station.

"Chris, you might want to check out some weapons, just in case," Doc said.

I went over the Headquarters' Supply and checked out a .60-cal machine gun and eight boxes of ammo. This was in the event we were overrun, or ran into

The Tragedy of Vietnam, Again

a situation where we had to defend ourselves. I also picked up eight body bags in case anyone should get himself killed. These bags were kept out of sight and were brought out only when required.

The entire Hill was abuzz with activity. I drove one of the jeeps over to Charlie Troop and the medics had stripped all their weapons down to individual pieces. They were cleaning each and every piece carefully. Charlie-Band-Aid was in Charlie Maintenance being gone over from front to back, and bottom to top. Everything was checked. A mean-looking sergeant was pouring water into the bottom of the track to see if the bilge pump worked. Charlie-Band-Aid almost sank when it tried to ford a small river a few weeks ago; this time the pump worked just fine.

Kimmy Hobbs was in the medics' bunker going over the medical supplies, making a list of everything that Charlie Medics would need. "Lieutenant, do you have any extra litters, at the aid station?"

"We have maybe fifteen; you may take no more than three. That will leave three for the aid station and the rest go with us so we can resupply the medics in the field." I had to try to keep everybody happy, knowing these litters were for the medics to sleep on.

I stopped off at Bravo and Alpha troops and talked with the medics there. They were all deeply engrossed in getting ready for our trip south. I passed on messages and acted as a courier between troops as supplies were being swapped around. All the line medics

Quang Ngai

thought it was "cool" that the Mobile Aid Station was going into the field with them.

Later that morning, after each medic track was cleared to go to the field, they came to the aid station to restock their medical chests. Doc insisted that each Band-Aid carry as much drinking water as possible. All too often a platoon would drink out of a "clean well." The next thing the aid station knew one platoon was nonoperational as they were doubled over with severe stomach cramps and unbelievable diarrhea.

By noon we were ready to roll. The mobile aid station was packed. Johnston and Kline had also brought along their own private arsenal of weapons including two M-16s, one M-79 grenade launcher, and enough ammo to supply a small army.

We overlooked only one thing and that was getting beer and soft drinks. By the time we went to Headquarters supply, all the good refreshment supplies were gone. We did manage to come up with half a case of Orange Crush and one case of rusty cans of Old Milwaukee Beer. Supposedly this beer came off a ship that hit a mine in some South Vietnamese harbor and sank. At least the cans looked as if this story might be true and for some reason the beer was flat, which convinced us the story had to be true.

The military saying of "Hurry up and wait," is true as we waited until four thirty that afternoon before word came down for the squadron to move out. There was a lot of commotion, radios blared, and vehicles all

The Tragedy of Vietnam, Again

over the Hill started their engines. Alpha Troop was to lead, then came LTC Lawrence's command and communication track, the Mobile Aid Station, two flame tracks, the squadron's mobile bridge (called Swatter), 1 VTR (vehicle tank retrieval), and one seven-thousand-gallon tanker truck full of diesel fuel. All of these vehicles belonged to Headquarters Troop. Bravo Troop fell in behind the squadron's vehicles, and Charlie Troop brought up the rear.

I was impressed, because it took all of twenty minutes to have all vehicles formed up and on our way out the access road. The column consisted of ninety armored personnel carriers, twenty-seven M-48 tanks, and all the previously mentioned vehicles. The total number of vehicles was one hundred eighteen. The fire power of this column was impressive. We had two hundred and forty six .60-caliber machine guns, one hundred and ten .50-caliber machine guns, twenty-seven 90 millimeter cannons, plus nine mortar tracks. We also had sixteen helicopter gunships and eight slicks that would join the fight just as soon as we could find the enemy. Blue Ghost, our helicopter company, was based at Chu Lai's airport rather than on Hawk Hill for safety reasons.

It was a beautiful drive down Highway One. The sun was dipping down in the west and long shadows were starting to fall across the golden fields of rice. Farmers, children, water buffalo all lined the roadside, and I'm for sure the enemy as well; all watched as we passed in review.

Quang Ngai

Highway One, near Hawk Hill

Small Hamlet along Highway One.

The Tragedy of Vietnam, Again

As we drove through the various villages and hamlets, the ritual of casting off the rejected food took place. By the time we reached where Fat City was, we were getting hungry. It was about five thirty or quarter to six, so Johnston decided to try to cook supper on top of the mobile aid station, while we continued to drive down the road. He told Kline to drive carefully, not to go over any potholes and not to jam on the brakes. This cooking operation was fairly successful; the coffee and hot chocolate were hot, and the C rations were slightly warm. It was impossible to drink anything without spilling it.

We reached Chu Lai about six thirty to quarter of seven and a lone military jeep blocked our way, parked in the southbound lane, or on the western side of the road. The sergeant then started to write vehicle violation tickets for each vehicle. We were driving tracked vehicles on an asphalt road, which was against Division rules. LTC Lawrence landed his helicopter in the road, about twenty feet from the sergeant. I guessed this MP thought it might not be too cool to mess with the lieutenant colonel who had just dropped out of the sky, and who was in charge of one hell of a long armored column. He backed his jeep up and allowed the lead tank to pass, while giving it a very stern look.

As soon as the column had to stop for the MP, all vehicles switched their radios over to the squadron's frequency. As a result, everybody knew exactly what this lone MP had done, and as a result personnel on ev-

Quang Ngai

ery vehicle gave the overly efficient MP their own salute as they passed by. This MP had to stay and receive this punishment from all one hundred and eighteen vehicles, because he had parked his jeep on the wrong side of the road and he could not cross over until the last vehicle passed.

Shortly thereafter, the good Lord took care of us for being disrespectful toward that poor lone MP; because a huge black cloud passed by and did it pour. It rained for about twenty minutes or just long enough for all of us to get thoroughly soaked. It was as black as ink outside. We couldn't see where we were going and the wind picked up, so everybody just froze.

All the glamour and glory of our massive road march evaporated. The CO and his staff were probably all back on Hawk Hill, having a nice hot meal of fake food, in dry clothes, saying, "Boy I'm glad to be here rather than being somewhere out on Highway One."

I huddled in a deck chair behind the exhaust stack, trying to get some warmth. We rumbled on till early morning, having to stop at dozens of checkpoints, that didn't know we were coming. Each checkpoint meant a delay of about fifteen to twenty minutes or until proper authority could be given to allow us to proceed.

About 3 a.m., we rolled into Quang Ngai and we set up a staging area. It was so dark we couldn't see anything. The mobile aid station was to park next to a building, and since we weren't part of the squadron's perimeter, we wouldn't have to pull any guard duty.

The Tragedy of Vietnam, Again

Johnston, Kline, Miller, and I all grabbed litters and fell asleep immediately inside the buttoned-up mobile aid station.

We awoke with a start when we heard airplane engines starting up. We then heard a public-address system announce the departure of Air America's flight from Quang Ngai to Da Nang. We all woke at the same moment and wondered what was going on and where were we. Kline slipped into the driver's compartment and lowered the back ramp.

I looked out and saw we were next to a taxiway that ran along one side of the airport, and the terminal building and hangers were on the other side of this taxiway. All the APCs were in a herringbone defensive arrangement down one side of the taxiway. All the command tracks, including the mobile aid station, were off to one side, next to a hanger. Within a few minutes of waking up, the seven-thousand-gallon truck started to refuel all the vehicles.

Quang Ngai

Main street in Quang Ngai

Since we weren't scheduled to go anywhere immediately, Miller started to boil some water for breakfast. Kline flew our Red Cross flag from the antenna, so if anyone wanted to come to sick call they would know which command track we were. This Red Cross flag was not flashed around; we had been told the NVA had a bounty on the head of all medics they killed.

After fifteen minutes, breakfast was served, steaming LRRP rations, hot chicken and rice. Kline and Johnston gave Headquarters Troop Supply some "bull story" as to how we had to feed the patients in the field. Anyways, we were going to eat fairly well. Breakfast was topped off with some fruit cocktail and hot coffee.

Since these command tracks didn't open up the way a regular line track did, we brought along four

The Tragedy of Vietnam, Again

folding deck chairs, which we set up at the bottom of the ramp. We must have been the envy of many, as we sat in our chairs drinking coffee and listening to the armed forces station on a portable radio, while the rest of the squadron got ready to pull out.

Blue Ghost helicopters flew over our position and then set down on the other side of the taxiway, and the refueling of the helicopters started immediately.

While all this was going on, there was a commanders' meeting going on next to us, in the Field TOC. LTC Lawrence and his staff had been briefed by Division on their way down to Quang Ngai, and the colonel was passing this new information on to the troop commanders. As soon as this meeting was over and all the vehicles were refueled, the squadron went to work very quickly. The Blue Ghost pilots fired up their helicopters and flew off. As soon as the track's engines were semi warm, the line troop's column started to move out, in a westerly direction away from the airport.

Johnston turned our radio on so we could hear what was being said. The squadron's channel was quiet, so he switched over to Alpha Troop's channel. I walked over to the TOC and stuck my head inside the rear hatch. The colonel looked up at me and said, "Hi, how are you and your boys doing over there?"

"Fine," I answered, "I was just wondering what you want us to do, sir?"

"You stick with the TOC element. We'll be moving in an hour or two. We want to see what's happening out there first," the CO answered, as he nodded in a westerly direction.

"Do you have your radio on, Lieutenant?" the command sergeant major asked.

"It's on, but the medics are listening to the line troop's frequencies; you people are fairly quiet."

"That's OK," the CO said with a smile, "You're close enough so we can call to you when you need to change the radio frequency; your boys are concerned."

I walked back to the aid station and noticed the airport was a very busy place. Passenger planes were coming and leaving all the time. Large numbers of people were greeting aircraft, or people waited to board a flight. The airport's loudspeaker blared information about every ten to fifteen minutes. It reminded me of what the "real world" was like. I had not seen so much civilian activity in a long time. Hawk Hill was a quiet place except for when we were ducking mortars, bullets, and/or rockets.

The lowered back ramp allowed a slight breeze to flow inside. I sat down on the ramp and asked, "What's happening, Johnston?"

"Not much, they're still getting into position, but Blue Ghost reports seeing a lot of NVA running around."

"Charlie Troop thinks they will be on line in about twenty-five minutes," Kline said. We all listened to a lot of radio static, because there wasn't much conversation going on.

The Tragedy of Vietnam, Again

I fired up a piece of C-4 to heat water for coffee and leave enough water so people could shave in it, not that any of us really needed to shave more than once a week.

After a while, a prisoner showed up from nowhere. He had been wounded slightly. His hands were swollen and had turned an ugly purple from been tied too tightly behind his back; he also wore a blindfold. The first thing that Miller did was cut his hands free to let the circulation return to his swollen hands. Then Johnston removed the blindfold. His Vietnamese guard was not happy about this, but didn't say a word; probably because he didn't know any English.

The prisoner had a flesh wound in his upper arm. Since we were bored and had nothing to do, this prisoner had never seen such service. We also didn't like the looks of his guard. The wound was thoroughly cleaned, medicated, and wrapped. We felt he probably would not see any further medical attention, so Johnston gave him a huge shot of penicillin in his butt; Miller gave the prisoner a tetanus shot in the arm; Kline took two high-powered codeine tablets and gave them to the prisoner with a drink of water.

"What are you doing, why are you giving him those codeine tablets?" Miller demanded.

"I think he needs to take a trip, they're just going to beat the holy hell out him," Kline answered. "Look at that guard; he can't wait to get his hands on him again."

"Let's tape his hands behind his back, and then if the guards leave the tape alone, he'll at least have some circulation," Johnston suggested.

As soon as his hands were taped, the guard grabbed the prisoner and shoved him out of the aid station.

The prisoner said something in Vietnamese and bowed his head toward us, as he was kicked by the guard.

"That's why I gave him those pills," Kline said, "I just hate how cruel the Orientals can be, and whatever they do to him, it won't hurt as much."

"The Koreans are the worst when they go on a search and destroy mission or just sweep an area. They kill everything, men, women, children, chicken, water buffalos, you name it and they'll kill it. That way the Koreans know the enemy didn't get away," Johnston said. Johnston knew, because the unit he came from was right next to a Korean division.

"Well, I feel that I did my Boy Scout deed for the day in helping that prisoner. I hope they don't kill him," Kline said more to himself.

The Tragedy of Vietnam, Again

Treating the enemy, getting a shot.

Shortly after the prisoner was taken away, one of the communication sergeants walked over to where we were and said, "Switch to the squadron's frequency; we're getting ready to move out."

Miller switched the channel and gave a communications check. The radio answered, "Is that you, 'Big Band-Aid'?"

"That's affirmative, we're ready whenever you are," Miller answered.

"Well, I guess we just got a new call sign," Johnston said with a laugh

"It looks that way, but what a stupid name, Big Band-Aid," Kline answered in total disgust.

LTC Lawrence had taken off in his helicopter while we were treating the prisoner. None of us saw him go, so Major Logan, the Operations Officer was in charge of the TOC element. The major had located a rise that overlooked the operational area where the line troops were positioned. According to Blue Ghost, this hill had no enemy activity near it, and a large raised grave area occupied the very top.

The command tracks fired up their engines and left in single file; Band-Aid took up the rear position. As we left the taxiway, our radio told us to be on the alert, because we were the only armed vehicle. It also dawned on me that Kline, Miller, and Johnston were the only enlisted people in our little group who had been in the field. All the other Headquarters people had never been to the field that I knew of. I had been to the field about six times before; Major Logan always flew in and out of the field, so this was a new experience for him as well. This trip could prove to be very interesting.

The terrain was different than what we had been used to. The land was rolling hills covered with small trees. We had no problem running over the trees, as we blazed our way along. It looked as if maybe the countryside had been sprayed with Agent Orange, because the leaves were sparse on the trees. It kind of looked like New England in late fall. The earth had a light brown color, not like the reddish-colored soil around

Hill 29. We moved around a low hill and then cut due south for about two clicks.

When we moved up and over a ridge, I could see jet fighters flying close support and dropping five-hundred-pound bombs. We heard the bombs explode, as well as the machine gun fire. It sounded like a good firefight was in progress. On the other side of this low ridge there was a valley and in the center was a long, low hill.

Major Logan's track cut across the rice paddy and up the spine of the hill to its very top, where he established the TOC. I was told to set up the aid station beside the large raised grave area. Major Logan's track and the communication track were about fifty feet away from us. The view was a very picturesque setting, except there was a large-scale battle going on in the middle of it.

Quang Ngai

Mobile Aid Station set up in Quang Ngai, back ground, 7,000 fuel tanker

We lowered the back ramp and set up the tent that was attached to the rear of the vehicle. We unloaded supplies from inside and we set up two litter stands with litters. Medical chests were set up off to one side. The back ramp was kept free so we could raise it quickly if need be.

We did not fly any red cross, but Kline put out two white metal signs in the shape of an arrow pointing to our location that read "Aid Station," in red paint. Starlight scopes would pick these arrows up in the dead of night.

We didn't see many people that first day, because our people didn't get hurt. The enemy, according to the radio, lost fifty-five dead. I guessed there were a lot of NVA wounded. A lot of bullets were flying around

The Tragedy of Vietnam, Again

that entire day. Late in the afternoon, how it ever got there I'll never know, but the seven-thousand-gallon fuel truck showed up completely refilled, and was told to park inside a cut at the eastern end of the hill, which made all of us at the aid station very happy. We all had visions about what that truck would look like, if it were mortared. Major Logan told the driver that nobody was to be anywhere near that truck once it becomes dark; it was felt the enemy would go after it after darkness fell.

About an hour after the sun had set, the troops came in from the field and set up a night defense around the hill. Bravo-Band-Aid pulled up to the aid station to see how we were doing. It was dark but not total darkness. We were making supper by flashlight inside the tent. When Clancy saw we had LRRP rations he went wild.

"Where did you get those LRRP meals, sir?" Clancy pointed toward the open case of meals; fortunately, the other case was hidden out of sight.

I burst out laughing at the expression on Clancy's face and shrugged my shoulders, then gestured toward Johnston and Kline.

Clancy put the strong arm on the three medics; Clancy was determined to get some of the meals. High negotiations began instantaneously. Miller, Johnston, and Kline all knew what they were doing. I sat and watched and would act as a referee if necessary. The end result was that Bravo-Band-Aid had four cases of good beer and two cases of soft drinks. It was determined that one case of beer was worth ten LRRP meals (one meal fed two people). This left one case of beer for three people, because Miller only drank soft drinks.

That evening we were told to post a guard on top of the mobile aid station. On these command tracks it was difficult to stand guard, because there was only the driver's compartment in the front of the vehicle and a small escape hatch on the top deck. From the driver's compartment you could only see directly in front of the APC, and you had to be at least twelve feet tall just to see out of the top hatch. As a result, we set up a folding chair next to the open hatch on the top deck.

It was felt that the best way to defend the aid station, if attacked, was with one M-16 in the driver's compartment and another firing from the escape hatch with a pile of medical chests to stand upon. The 60-caliber machine gun would be fired from the graveyard to cover both Band-Aid and the TOC area.

I went over to the TOC and told Major Logan of our plan and he agreed with it. I wanted the TOC people to know where we were, because we didn't need any grenades chucked our way.

I asked the medics how they wanted to pull guard duty; they could have a shift of an hour and a half each but be woken up twice, or pull two and a half hours each and be woken up only once. They all agreed that being woken up once was best. Since I was democratic

The Tragedy of Vietnam, Again

in my thinking, we drew straws as to when each of us pulled guard duty. I pulled the 0200 to 0530 to the glee of the others.

Once the back ramp was raised and locked in place, we arranged the inside of that metal box as comfortably as possible. We put litters side by side and I fell asleep very quickly.

I was aware of a rocking motion, as I sailed my boat back home. There was a good breeze with a chop across the water. I was fetching the windward mark, when I heard, "For Christ's sake, are you dead! Wake up, Lieutenant." Miller was trying to be quiet, and not to wake the others. I rolled over and slowly registered that I wasn't not on the water, but in Vietnam. I put a hand out in the pitch blackness, and touched Miller to let him know I was awake. I slowly pulled myself together, gathered my flak jacket, steel pot, my poncho liner, and then climbed up and out of the top hatch.

It was blacker than black, all the way around. I could see nothing. "Is anything going on?" I asked Miller.

"No, it's all quiet, sir," Miller answered as he slid down the hatch and replaced me on my litter. It was lonely sitting up there all by myself, but I had a sense of great responsibility. All my sleeping men had put their trust and lives in my hands. A flare burst into light about two miles off to the northwest. It had to have been fired from an artillery battery far away, because I didn't hear any cannon fire. As that flare died out, another magically appeared. I found out later

Quang Ngai

Division was giving us artificial light so our starlight scopes would work. By placing the flares two miles away our night vision would not be affected.

You thought about all sorts of things while looking into blackness. It gave me the willies knowing that there were people out there crawling around, who would just love to kill me.

I was very happy to see the eastern sky start to lighten up. It reminded me of when my friends and I from high school spent the night out on the beach, so we could see the sunrise. We were all so tired and cold; we couldn't wait to get home and go to sleep. I felt the same right then; I was cold, hungry, and very tired.

So far the trip to Quang Ngai was not very eventful for us, but was very busy for the rest of the troops. The enemy was there; he was all around us and I had a feeling that today might be busier than yesterday.

At five o'clock it was still dark outside. All the line troop engines started up and the tracks disappeared into the countryside to our west; another day had started. Within twenty-five minutes of leaving our hill, our troops were engaging the enemy. Tracers were flying in all directions. It seemed most were coming directly at us, but going over our heads.

We disconnected the tent from the rear of the vehicle and then repositioned the aid station slightly so we were pointing directly at the bullets. This gave us better protection to our rear by moving the APC. There was no action to our rear and we were also protected

The Tragedy of Vietnam, Again

by the TOC vehicles, as well as that large graveyard to our eastern side. We lowered the back ramp so if we took wounded we wouldn't have to jump in and out of the back hatch. Running up and down the ramp was a lot easier while carrying litters, and if the situation changed for the worse, then the ramp would be closed.

Within twenty minutes we started receiving wounded. The first patient we got had minor injuries. The more seriously wounded patients were flown directly to the Second Surgical Hospital in Chu Lai. About noontime we received a North Vietnamese soldier who wasn't really wounded; he had a deep red welt along his left calf. All he had for clothing was a tattered pair of shorts that didn't fit at all; they were way too large for him. He had no other clothing, no shoes, shirt, or other possessions. We also received, at the same time, three American GIs who were also slightly wounded. Since nobody was going to die on us, the Americans came first. We put the prisoner on a litter and Kline told him through sign language that if he tried to get off that litter, Kline would kill him. Our NVA patient understood exactly what was meant. We put his litter inside the APC, off to one side and out of the way.

We treated the wounded Americans, yet kept a close eye on our prisoner. As we finished with the Americans, we received more wounded Americans. As a result, we didn't get to our prisoner for quite some time. While our NVA friend was watching and waiting, he realized that we weren't going to kill him and he became more relaxed. Finally Miller and I went to the prisoner and worked on his leg. We cleaned it and put some ointment over the welt and covered it with a gauze patch, so the wound would not get irritated.

We told him through sign language to stay put, which he indicated he understood. He asked, through sign language, if he could have a drink. We nodded and Miller poured him a cup of water. He then asked if he could have something to eat, so Miller opened up some of our C rations and gave him a tropical bar and some peanut butter crackers. Miller told the prisoner that he could pour himself more water if he liked. Again, this was all done through sign language; by the time they got through this exchange both the prisoner and Miller were smiling at each other.

We were alerted by radio that more wounded prisoners were being sent to us from the field. Their ETA was about thirty minutes. I went over to the TOC and asked Major Logan if we could have an interpreter to assist us with these wounded; sign language wasn't going to work.

Major Logan went to the radio, changed frequency and requested one mouthpiece be flown to the TOC location immediately. It was really nice having someone nearby who had some real pull.

The Tragedy of Vietnam, Again

Treating the enemy.

Our ARVN (Army Republic of Vietnam) interpreter arrived about the same time as the wounded NVA prisoners. What we didn't know was that some intelligence group from Division wanted information out of these prisoners and they had sent another interpreter and an American captain along to interrogate them.

These patients were a lot worse off than our friend on the litter. Our mouthpiece was asking questions so we could fill out field medical cards and obtain a medical history for each patient. The captain and his sidekick were basically thugs; they terrorized the patients. The captain ordered us to hold off all treatment until he told us we could start. He wanted to get information; as his ARVN partner asked questions, this US captain bent a prisoner's leg up and then repeatedly tapped the patient's knee cap on the same spot with the barrel of his .45 pistol. After about six minutes of this torture, the captain picked up the leg with the badly broken ankle and started to move the broken foot; I stopped him short.

"If you want to be court-martialed keep it up, because I'm just about to press charges. If you wish to ask these prisoners questions you may do so, but you will not touch any of them. If you have a problem, then you may register your complaint right over there with Major Logan." I pointed to the TOC. I was mad, my medics were mad and this captain knew we were pissed, and that he had overstepped his authority.

The AVRN interpreter, who had come with the captain, continued questioning the patients. As this process went on, our first NVA patient beckoned to me. He was more or less out of sight from the other NVA prisoners, but our prisoner could see them.

I went over and asked in English, "What's the matter?"

He shook his head no, and then pointed to the patient who was being interrogated; our friend then pointed his finger up into the air. I called for our mouthpiece to see what he was trying to tell us.

Evidently, our friend hated the NVA army and the war. All his friends were killed within the first forty minutes of yesterday's action. What he was trying to tell us, was that the prisoner with the broken ankle was not a corporal, as he claimed, but was in fact an NVA major. There was another prisoner who wasn't telling the truth; this patient also claimed to be a corporal, but was in fact is a sargeant major. I felt it was wise to shield our friend from the others. I placed a medical chest so the other prisoners could not see inside the track. If our friend were found out, he'd be dead.

Our friend's name was Hung Ney; he was seventeen years old and was a North Vietnamese army cook. He was the sole survivor of his company after the first forty minutes of fighting, on the first day; Hung wanted no more war and he told us his story:

Hung Ney was drafted at age fifteen to join the North Vietnamese Army. He had been required, like all of the North Vietnamese children, to be a member of the Communist youth group before entering the army

Hung had never liked the Communist government. His family farmed and before Ho Chi Minh took power, his father and mother could take their produce to market and sell directly to the people. They made money and had a nice place to live, and could afford to buy nice things. After the Communists came, they were forced to sell their products to the government-run cooperative; then there were no profits.

Personally, Hung did not like the Communist party, but could not express his feelings for fear of punishment and reprisals. If one talked out against the Communist policies, that person would be arrested immediately and sent to a re-education center for a period of time.

Hung said, "The people in North Vietnam are told of great victories in the South. After my unit and I infiltrated, I saw that this is not true. The North Vietnamese government had lied to the people and the people only know what the government tells them.

"If I refuse to fight, my family will be harassed by the government. The government tells us no news from home so the morale of the NVA troops in South Vietnam will not be hurt. People in North Vietnam do not like the Army draft, because we have to stay in the army until the war is over. Our officers do not really trust us and we're constantly being watched. There're some good officers and there're some bad ones. That major is not a good officer and that's why I told you who he is. The same is true for that sargeant; they are very cruel people.

The Tragedy of Vietnam, Again

"I'm a cook for my company; I cook mostly rice and canned pork. Sometimes I go fishing and try to catch supper, but I'm not a very good fisherman. I have to clean the pots and pans. Each soldier has his own mess kit, which he has to wash.

"After supper, we all have to sit around talking and listening to the political officer. We do not like it, because he tells us how good we're doing and how badly the Americans have done. The political officer never comes with us on combat missions. He never sees us under the conditions we are in now. He is on the other side of those mountains hiding in a cave. No, we don't listen to what's said. We sing songs and tell jokes when we're with our friends. We try to keep each other's spirits up.

"If we did not have local South Vietnamese people to help us, we couldn't operate in the South. We have very well-trained soldiers, and we have a lot of good weapons. We will win the war, even if it takes one hundred years. The Americans have to have everything immediately. If you cannot win the war quickly, then you won't fight; we can wait and that's why the North will win."

I wondered who was whose prisoner, but Hung had a valid point. I was intrigued listening to this guy. I told our interpreter to keep asking him questions; I said, "I'm interested in hearing about their medical program."

Quang Ngai

"We have very good doctors. Each company has several aid men and each battalion has one doctor and other aid men. Those who are seriously wounded are sent back to North Vietnam. These patients are kept in special hospitals in North Vietnam. There are many patients in these hospitals.

"Most of us have malaria, even though we take pills that are supposed to prevent us from catching it. All seventy-five men in my company had malaria. We also have to take a vitamin pill daily.

"The political officer tells us that the Americans will torture and kill us if we're captured, but I don't care. I'm tired of fighting and seeing all my friends die. I don't know what will happen to me."

Our interpreter asked Hung Ney "Would you like to become a 'Kit Carson Scout' for the Americans? You can go to school and learn how you can help South Vietnam."

Hung Ney shook his head no and said, "I don't want to fight anymore. No more killing, no more hurting people. I want to go home and be with my family."

We kept Hung Ney with us until one of the last helicopters that night. I went over to the TOC and told Major Logan about Hung Ney and how he had helped in the aid station. Major Logan notified Division that we were sending them a special prisoner who had been very helpful in identifying NVA officers and senior NCOs. We requested that this prisoner not be put near the other prisoners from Quang Naig. We didn't think the other prisoners knew that Hung had been in the aid station, but we wanted to be on the safe side.

I was impressed with Hung Ney. I had this image of a brutal, ruthless enemy who liked killing babies and old people in order to make a point, which I'd seen the remains of with my own eyes. I was not prepared to meet an NVA soldier who was very much like any soldier, in any army around the world.

The next morning, about eight thirty, a helicopter landed between the aid station and the TOC, and a Navy lieutenant and an Army E-5 sergeant jumped out. Much to my surprise I recognized the sergeant; he was Nicholas Dawson and came from my hometown.

I yelled to him over the noise of the helicopter, "Hey, Nick, what are you doing here?"

He looked at me and ran over. "Well, I'll be, fancy meeting you here. I knew you were somewhere around here," he said as we shook hands.

"What's up, why are you here?" I asked.

"I got shanghaied; I went to school with…" Nick said, as he jerked his thumb toward the Navy lieutenant. The lieutenant appeared to be annoyed that his partner had left him. "He requested that I be his Army liaison. He's a spotter for the Navy ships in case your troops need some backup fire power; he's a huge pain in the ass with an enormous ego."

"How long are you to be with him?"

"I don't know, probably a day or two."

"Look, so far all the troops spend the night right here on this hill. Come over tonight and we'll give you a meal," I quickly said, as it became apparent the Navy spotter was becoming upset. I went out from the aid station's tent and introduced myself; the Navy lieutenant was surprised to see that I was an officer.

"I apologize for waylaying your sargeant; we come from the same hometown."

This individual was all business and he introduced himself, in a patronizing Bostonian accent. "John Southwell," he uttered. "We have to report in. It's been nice meeting you." He turned and headed toward the TOC; Nick shrugged his shoulders, rolled his eyes, and then followed the lieutenant.

The two disappeared into the command track. After about a half hour, Major Logan, the lieutenant and Nick Dawson boarded a helicopter. As the aircraft rose, Nick was facing toward us. He made a motion as if to eat and then stuck his thumb up in the air. I stuck my thumb up and gave the OK sign as the helicopter rushed off toward the west.

We received four injured GIs that afternoon. We treated them and kept them with us until their units came back from the field. Our beer supply vanished with four extra beer drinkers. Even the lousy beer was drunk. Johnston was in a foul mood over no more beer and complained bitterly about being forced to drink stale orange crush.

The Tragedy of Vietnam, Again

There was nothing going on, so Miller and Kline went over to the TOC to listen to the radios to find out what was going on. I was exhausted so I found a litter and went to sleep with instructions to wake me if anything should happen.

About seven o'clock that evening, the troops returned to our hill and set up a night logger. It was the same routine as the night before. At seven thirty, Nick Dawson climbed up the hill to the aid station and asked if he could spend the night with us.

Kline pointed to the litter stand and said, "That's yours so long as a patient doesn't need it."

We boiled a large pot of water and fixed some LRRP meals. Nick and I split a curry and rice packet. Over the meal, Nick filled us in about what had happened in the field that day. There were some large bunkers that LT Southwell radioed in to his battleship, and she lobbed in some shells. We were approximately three to four miles away from the coast and the ship was probably a good ten to twelve miles off shore.

Nick said, "It's very impressive as to how accurate the Navy is; in no time at all those bunkers were blown to smithereens."

Later that night, a track came up the hill to the aid station, its diesel engine really straining, as if it wasn't going to make it up all the way up the hill. It was pitch-black outside and we had only one small light inside the aid station that barely lit up the inside of the track, much less the tent area. The track stopped and a voice

Quang Ngai

called out, "Hey, Doc, we understand you need some beer." We heard two thuds on the ground and then the sound of the straining engine, as the track went off in the darkness.

Johnston and Kline quickly retrieved the beer and put this good beer into our blood box. Nick Dawson could not believe that GIs would just give away two cases of beer. We didn't even know who gave us the beer, so we could thank them. It was embarrassing because the line troops really did like the medics and appreciated what we did for them; this was their way of saying thanks.

That night Nick pulled guard with me, but I rotated all the time slots by one. Since I'd had the worst time slot the previous night, I got the first or the best time slot that night. If we were still in the field tomorrow I'd then take the second time slot.

Nick and I sat on top of the aid station and he explained that he just couldn't stand John Southwell. "I've known him since the time we went to the same junior high school; we were both in the same class. I bumped into Southwell in Chu Lai the other day when he was transferred off the *New Jersey* and reported to my unit for TDY (temporary duty assignment). Southwell requested that I be assigned to him, because we know each other and get along well. My colonel agreed, so now I have to follow this idiot."

"Why do you dislike him so much?"

"Well, it all started during our last year in the ninth grade. I hurt myself playing football, and could not

The Tragedy of Vietnam, Again

participate in any sports. Leo, the old janitor, asked me if I would help him for a moment, so Leo and I went into a janitorial supply closet that's off the eighth and ninth-grade locker room. Leo kept the door open, but did not turn on the light, as we could see the supplies. We both also had a full view of the locker room.

"We hear a boy race into the locker room, and as he slid to a stop we can see him. He looked one way and then quickly in the opposite direction and seeing nobody, he then quickly went through every locker relieving them of all money. This boy then changed into his athletic clothes and ran out onto the athletic field; from that day on I have no respect for John Southwell.

"To add insult to injury, what Southwell made me do today, in my opinion is just as dishonest as stealing everyone's money. There was a lull in the action and he ordered me to take pictures of him inspecting captured weapons, walking through a rice paddy as if he's leading a patrol in combat, and standing behind a .60-caliber machine gun pretending he's a gunner fighting in heavy action.

"After I had taken a full roll of thirty-six exposures, Southwell had the gall to say, 'This is great stuff. I may not get another chance to get really good pictures.'

"So, I ask him, 'what do you mean, these are really good pictures?'"

"'One never knows what will happen in the future. If I were to run for a political office these pictures are

Quang Ngai

just pure gold.' That's what that slime ball grinned back at me."

The next day Nick and the phony Navy lieutenant went back to Chu Lai. The line troops went back out to recon the valley; the enemy had totally disappeared over night; completely gone! By noontime, Major Logan told us to pack up the aid station, because we were rolling out in twenty minutes.

We fell in behind Major Logan's track and wound our way back to the airport, where we met the rest of the squadron.

Major Logan got in one of the Blue Ghost helicopters and took off. The squadron made much better time going back, because it was bright daylight and we could see where we were going. The only point of contention was when we had to pass over an old metal bridge rated for ten tons. I guessed we had passed over this same bridge when we came down and it was all right then. However, when two tanks got too close to one another, the combined weight of eighty to ninety tons was too much for that old bridge. The military brass in Saigon were not upset, they were totally pissed off, because this was the only way to cross this major river and now a new bridge had to be built immediately. Highway One had just been shut down, thanks to the 1/1 Cav.

The Tragedy of Vietnam, Again

Broken bridge after the Quyang Ngai operations

We approached Chu Lai and the main entrance came into view about three in the afternoon. LTC Lawrence ordered the lead tank to take a right turn and proceed down the road until we reached the ocean. The 1/1 Cav were the guests of Major General Gettys, the commanding general of the Americal Division, and we were to receive a twenty-four-hour emergency stand down on the beach to perform *emergency repairs* to our 'vehicles'.

Half of the column made the right-hand turn when five or six MP jeeps descended upon us like flies on discarded organic matter. They were very upset, because our tracked vehicles were once again driving on their new asphalt road. LTC Lawrence ordered all ve-

Quang Ngai

hicles to accept the traffic tickets, and all tickets were to be turned over to Major Logan.

Once on the beach we formed one huge logger, just below the Americal Combat Center Compound. Most everyone stripped "au natural" and went skinny dipping; nobody had taken a bath for about four days and everyone stunk. About five o'clock, three Blue Ghost helicopters landed with all the mail from Hawk Hill.

Dinner was real steaks from Australia, cooked over grills on the beach, washed down with plenty of good, cold beer, thanks to the general. After supper had been devoured, we all went to the Combat Center to see an Australian show. General Gettys talked to the troops, LTC Lawrence said a few words, and Major Logan gave all the traffic tickets to General Gettys amid cheers from the men, and then thing got a little bit out of hand. Someone set off some star cluster shells, which in turn set fire to the Combat Center, but nobody really cared at that point in time.

The next morning, after an early swim and a hot breakfast, we left Chu Lai via a back road; we didn't want to get the pea-brained MPs upset again. We arrived on Hill 29 about 11 a.m.; all vehicles had to be cared for.

We were glad to be back. Doc and Kelly were happy to see us. It was lonely for them with everyone gone. Doc told me the next day that he was proud of us. The Colonel had told him that his boys "did a great job in

The Tragedy of Vietnam, Again

Quang Ngai." I didn't know about "the great" part, but we had a good time and did our job.

Conscientious Objector

At the very end of September we were desperate at the aid station, as heavy action flared west of Tam Ky. We had just lost four Charlie medics all at once when one RPG hit a Dust-Off as they were loading wounded onboard. All three troops were short of medics, but having four go down all at once, in one troop, put too much of a strain on the unit; we were forced to take drastic measures.

I put an emergency call into the Division surgeon general's office and asked to speak to Colonel Anderson.

"This is Colonel Anderson speaking."

"Sir, this is Captain Noble speaking, 1/1 Cav (I had been promoted two weeks prior). Four of my medics from Charlie Troop are being airlifted to Chu Lai, on a Dust-Off, as we speak. I need medics, sir. I've been short medics for the past three months, I have nobody to move into Charlie Troop. I need replacements immediately or else I can't render the proper medical care to the unit. Can you help us, sir?"

The Tragedy of Vietnam, Again

"I have nobody here right now, but I'm to receive six new medics tomorrow. I'll assign you what I can, but all the units are presently short of medics."

"I need all of these men, but I'll take whatever you can give me, sir"

He laughed, "I'll see what I can do, and they'll be up tomorrow on the noon chopper."

"Thank you, Colonel Anderson, I appreciate it, sir."

"So, what's the verdict?" Doc asked.

"I don't know. We'll find out tomorrow. He's getting a new batch tomorrow and will send up whatever he can spare."

Emanuel Rodrigo had been the driver for Charlie Troop ever since he was transferred over from Bravo Troop. I hesitated to make him the senior medic, because he was part of "Project 100,000" and was under the protective custody of Division. If Emanuel got into trouble, we were not allowed to touch him, I had to call a major in Chu Lai, and he'd handle the case.

(Project 100,000 was where the military admitted 100,000 people who were not the brightest of all people; they were unable to pass the military entrance test. This was the test where you were shown a paint bucket and you had to match which of the four items went with the paint bucket, like the paint brush. As I understood, this Project 100,000 was a test to see if really stupid people could function in the military.)

I sent Kline immediately out to Charlie Troop, to act as senior medic. I also sent one medic from Bravo and one from Alpha Troop until I could get these new bodies out to Charlie Troop. I felt terrible about sending Kline out, and not being able to give these new men an orientation before going out in the field.

Fortunately, Colonel Lawrence realized we had a personnel shortage problem, because Doc told him, and orders were issued immediately that Charlie Troop was to assign a driver to Charlie Band-Aid. This released some of the pressure, so I pulled Kline back to the aid station, because he had only four weeks left in Vietnam, and I'd be damned if he was going to get killed at the end of his tour. As a result, I made Emanuel the acting senior medic.

Division sent me four medics on the noon helicopter, and three bounced off and were ready to go, so they were the ones I reassigned immediately to Charlie Troop.

The fourth man, I had a slight problem with. I wasn't sure what he was. His skin wasn't black; it was more of a very light yellowy-orange color. His eyes were unique; I'd never seen eyes like his before. His irises were a yellowish color, similar to a cat's eyes; his hair was jet black. What really stood out about this individual was the fact that he was constantly crying and read the Bible.

"What's your name?" I asked.

"Tapping, sir."

The Tragedy of Vietnam, Again

"Why are you crying, Tapping?"

"I'm not supposed to be here, sir."

"What do you mean you're not supposed to be here?"

"I'm a CO (conscientious objector), and I'm not to be here, sir."

"Tapping, the only place, in the military for COs is with the medics. You'll never have to carry a weapon, never handle ammunition, and will never have to kill anything. Now what's your problem?" I asked in as nonthreatening a voice as possible.

"I'm not supposed to be in a unit like this."

"I don't understand, what do you mean, can you explain?"

"This is a combat unit, and I'm not supposed to be here, sir."

"I have three COs in the unit right now, and as a CO you'll go to the field as a medic and you will pull guard duty, but on a radio, not behind a weapon."

This was not what Mr. Tapping wanted to hear as a flood of tears engulfed him. I had a good idea about what his problem was, and that was the same concern every person in the unit had; they didn't want to go out and have someone taking pot shots at them.

"May I see the chaplain?" Tapping sobbed.

"Get in my jeep and I'll bring you to the chaplain right now, but he's going to tell you the same thing that I just told you."

Tapping did not get any better after his visit, because the chaplain explained that no conscientious objector could ever be the chaplain's assistant, because the assistant had to carry a weapon to protect the chaplain, and he already had an assistant.

I brought Tapping back to the aid station and realized that this poor private was not only totally useless to me, but to himself and to the United States Army. He was also a coward. I wondered why, in the good Lord's name, was this guy was ever brought into the military, much less how he got through basic training.

"Tapping, I agree with you that the Army has made a mistake, we can't use you in this unit. I want you to go back to Chu Lai and you're to report back to the Division surgeon general's office; you tell them that I ordered you to do so, all right?"

"How will I get there, sir?"

"A helicopter is going to leave from here in about ten minutes, and you'll go back in it, do you understand? I'll call Chu Lai and they'll be expecting you at the Division surgeon general's office; you do remember how to get there?"

"Yes, sir, I remember.

"Good, get your stuff and bring it over to the helipad, and good luck."

"Yes sir."

And that was the last of Mr. Tapping.

Once this misfit was out of hearing range, I called Division. "Colonel Anderson, this is Captain Noble. I

The Tragedy of Vietnam, Again

want to thank you, sir, for the medics you sent me, I really appreciate it, sir; especially Tapping, sir."

He burst out laughing. "I didn't know what to do with him, so he's a bonus for getting the other three."

"Sir, I can't use him, there is no way he will ever fit in with this unit. I've sent him back, sir."

"You what, you have sent him back? What the hell am I going to do with him?" the Colonel demanded.

I was tired and didn't want to play games, so I blurted out, "Sir, I don't care what happens to Tapping, he can count pills for all I care, but we just can't use him, not in this unit, sir."

"How's everything up there, do you need anything?"

"So long as I don't get my men killed or wounded too badly, we can get by, sir."

"You're doing a good job, keep it up and keep me posted. I'll have someone pick up Tapping."

"Thank you, sir, and I'll keep you posted."

Division had a difficult job, because all the line units needed medics constantly and there were not enough to go around. I knew the Division surgeon general had pulled out all the stops, so I could get these three. I found out later that Colonel Anderson took my suggestion and assigned Tapping to the Division pharmacy, to count pills.

Most conscientious objectors were a pain in the butt, because they thought that by getting themselves classified as a conscientious objector, it would keep them from going out in harm's way, but this wasn't true. Conscientious objectors were required to go to the field just like any other soldier, but they did so without any weapons and they never had to fire a weapon. This did not mean that a CO was not going to get shot or possibly even killed.

Most of the men who arrived as a COs came back to me within a month's time into their tour and asked if they could have a weapon. This really made things very difficult, especially for me. As a result, I went out of my way to make it as difficult as possible for them to get a weapon.

This individual had to prove to me, that in fact he really did want to drop his conscientious objector status. I then made him write me a letter for his file, telling me why he wished to drop his CO status. He then had to wait two to three days to think over his decision before I'd agree to it. If I did agree, he then had to take firearms training with the supply sergeant until he was proficient with a firearm.

This paper trail saved the unit after one soldier's family went to their congressman and complained that we forced their son to carry a weapon. The letter the soldier wrote to me requesting a weapon, plus his personal cover letter answering this congressional inquiry, set the record straight. He further informed this congressman, "… in fact the military went out of their way to have me not drop my Conscious Objector

The Tragedy of Vietnam, Again

status, but I insisted; my parents just don't understand how it is over here in Vietnam."

There was one conscientious objector in Bravo Troop who never asked for a weapon; however, a strange event took place. Bravo-Band-Aid was sitting in front of the medics' bunker across from the Orderly Room. The only person on Band-Aid was my CO who was supposedly cleaning out the medical box.

The Bear, Master Sergeant Grant, was sitting in the Orderly Room working at his desk; it was quiet just like the Bear liked it, no problems.

Suddenly, a single shot rang out and a bullet crashed through the Orderly Room's wall and sent Webster's Dictionary flying across the room. The Bear was not happy, as the bullet started with the letter "A" and stopped on the word "Spanish."

The Bear dashed out of his office to catch the culprit, but found only my CO shaking in his boots, who denied he had had anything to do with this serious violation. The Bear called me up to say, "Captain, your f-ing conscientious objector just shot up my Orderly Room and killed my dictionary."

"You've got to be kidding me, Sarge."

"No, I'm not kidding you, but he's a hell of a lot more scared than I am mad, and I think he's learned a good lessons to keep his f-ing fingers off things he knows nothing about."

The Bear and I had an understanding, especially after the Radford incident. He had been pleased when

Sargeant Williams described the punishment I dished out to Radford, and for how long it lasted. Radford didn't really mind his punishment either; it was a lot better than going to jail.

One of the greatest events I witnessed was watching Emanuel Rodrigo take to the three new medics in Charlie Troop; he acted just like a mother hen taking to her chicks. These new men were shown everything, and Emanuel made sure they understood exactly what had to be done and why.

I forgot that he was a member of the Project 100,000 and let the situation remain as it had developed. Doc felt that the medics who were injured should not go back to the field, because they all had ruptured eardrums. We sent one to Chu Lai as our liaison and the others came to the aid station.

Court martial

Private Steven Jones was a driver for Division Medical Supply, and his job was to bring medical supplies out to the field units all along Highway One. One day Private Jones requested that he be allowed to transfer into the 1/1's medical platoon, so he could put into practice what the military had taught him, and not be just a delivery boy. It just so happened I was always in need of medics, so I asked the Division surgeon general if this transfer could take place.

Jones showed up about two weeks later when we were still in Fat City. Private Jones was a pleasant-looking person whose father was a high-ranking officer in the US Air Force. There was no hint that trouble might appear down the road for the unit, the squadron, or the Army. Jones fit into the unit nicely and was an excellent medic, who volunteered to go to the field. I assigned him to Bravo Troop because they were short a medic. This was great for me, because it was a lot better to have a person who wanted to go to the field, rather than have one who dreaded it.

Jones became the platoon medic for the Third Platoon. Everyone seemed happy, Jones fit in well,

The Tragedy of Vietnam, Again

his California style was laid back, and he flowed with events as they happened. More importantly, he functioned well in the field and the line troops liked him.

People did notice that when Jones was in the field he would go off poking around in the underbrush, under stacks of wood and check out all the nooks and crannies. He also carried two empty sandbags, one inside the other that could be tied shut with a secure tie string, if need be. Whenever he was asked about these bags he replied, "Oh, you never know what you might find out here."

Under Jones's bunk, in Bravo's Third Platoon, he kept a large wooden artillery shell box that could hold two large artillery rounds. This box was about five feet long by eighteen inches wide and about ten inches high. Jones had drilled holes through the sides of this box and affixed screening over the hole from the inside. The hinged top had a heavy-duty hasp and padlock keeping it tightly shut. Jones had the key around his neck constantly.

When Jones was asked about the box he replied, "Oh, it's to keep things in when I find something." Again he went no further about what these "things" might have been. Since Jones had not caused any trouble, and he fit in well with the rest of the troop and was functioning as well as all the other medics, people overlooked his idiosyncrasies.

One day while the Third Platoon was in the field, Jones was off on one of his search missions when he spotted what he was looking for. Jones moved extremely quickly, with tremendous agility, and within a flash his prize was firmly secured around his waist in the double-lined sandbags.

Nobody had seen Jones catch whatever it was and Jones was not telling anyone. The prize was placed out of sight with the rest of his medical supplies. This routine went on for maybe two to three months before he was noticed. One of the men in his platoon asked, "What you got in the bag?"

"Oh, it's a bug I want to show Doc, I don't know what it is."

This answer satisfied this soldier's curiosity; he couldn't care less about bugs, just so long as they stayed away from him.

When Jones was back in base camp he asked me if he could have some traps to catch mice. He thought there were mice around the Third Platoon.

I thought, *this guy is really a conscientious medic, I like that.* Nobody else had volunteered to go out and catch mice in their platoon, so I lent him two traps.

After about two to three months of not hearing or seeing Jones, one of the line troopers from Bravo Troop came to me and asked, "Excuse me sir, but I don't know if I should say anything—may I have a word with you, sir, in private, please?"

I wondered what this was all about, so we went outside and sat in one of the jeeps.

"What's on your mind?"

The Tragedy of Vietnam, Again

"Well, sir, some of the men in the Third Platoon are scared of your medic Jones."

I looked at the soldier, a little surprised, "Why are people scared of Jones?"

"Well, sir, Jones has been catching poisonous snakes out in the field, and he's mailing them back home to California. We don't like snakes coming into camp, much less into our bunker, sir."

"What! I know nothing about this, but I'll look into this matter immediately; thank you for passing this information on."

We parted company and I told Doc what I had just been told. We decided that if in fact Jones was catching poisonous snakes, then this habit would stop immediately. We had some Chinese snake antivenom in the aid station, but we didn't have a clue about how to administer the medicine. All the instructions were written in Chinese and nobody in all of Division knew how to read Chinese.

I drove over to Bravo Troop, to the Third Platoon. I found Jones on his bunk and I asked him straight out, "Jones, are you catching poisonous snakes and are you sending them back home? Is this true?"

Jones looked at me and said, "Yes, I'm a professional snake handler and I'm supplying a business I partially own."

"What do you do with these snakes back home, sell them?"

"No, sir, we sell their venom and we raise other snakes from them," Jones answered.

Court martial

"Are you aware that the men around you do not feel comfortable, and don't like these snakes so close to them?"

"Yes, sir, I'm aware of that."

"Do you have any snakes on hand at the moment?"

"No, sir, we have not been to the field for a while and I sent the last shipment back last week."

"Good, because I'm giving you an order to stop this business as of now; do you understand?"

"But, sir, it's perfectly safe; I know what I'm doing," Jones protested.

"Jones, if the colonel knew what you're doing he would probably court-martial you for endangering the lives of your fellow soldiers. Also, I doubt if the US military or the US Postal Service knows what you're shipping back to the United States. How many snakes have you shipped back so far?"

"Seventeen," Jones said, as he hung his head.

"Jones, are you going to stop as of now?"

"Yes sir."

"I'm sorry I have to put an end to your business, but you have to see this from the military side as to why this has to stop." Jones nodded his head in agreement, and I left him to his thoughts.

On my drive back to the aid station I thought, *Jones had taken the news a lot better than I had expected.* What I didn't know was that there was

The Tragedy of Vietnam, Again

to be a change in Jones's attitude from that day forward.

Everything Jones had lived for, while in Bravo Troop, up to this point was catching snakes and sending them back home. He knew he could not go out and sneak catching them, because his own platoon turned him in. Jones also knew that it was against military regulations to catch deadly snakes and send them home through the United States Postal Service. He also had been ordered to stop; there was no way he could continue.

The change in Jones happened slowly; his laid-back manner became tense. He didn't take as good care of himself, as he had in the past. I got the feeling that Jones was only going through the motions of being a line medic. Doc noticed a lot of patients from Bravo's Third Platoon were showing up at the aid station, with very minor problems, rather than being treated in their own platoon.

About three weeks after Jones and I had our discussion, the Third Platoon went out to the field. It was one of these very hot days where after two to three hours of bouncing around in an APC, everyone's body was not only covered with sweat, but each and every muscle was weak and hurt. Your head pounded, you stunk, you were dirty, hungry, and not in a very good mood. After eight hours of bouncing around, on the return to Hawk Hill, the track Jones was riding on went out of control and ran off the road. The vehicle crashed into a bamboo hut. The men didn't know why the driver ran off the road and if they did, they weren't saying anything. The driver said only, "I don't know, it just slipped off the (dry) road."

The only casualty was to the hut, which had a gaping hole in one side, and Jones. Jones had been riding on the back deck, on the accident side. As the vehicle went into the hut, a splinter about two inches long and one and a half inches wide was jammed into his inside thigh, up near Jones's crotch; to put it in simple words, this splinter was in a fairly tender spot.

The driver put the APC in reverse and backed up onto Highway One. Since this accident was only a half mile from our access road, the platoon continued down the road. Jones was brought directly to the aid station. As Doc looked him over, Jones seemed almost elated. Jones had figured that this injury was going to send him back home. He had only four months left in the Army, and he'd be able to play with his snakes after that.

As Jones lay on the litter under the powerful Navy search light, Johnston started cutting off Jones's pants. When he finished, Doc cleaned the wounded area; it was really ugly looking. A good chunk of wood was flush with the skin. A bluish tallow white ring of flesh surrounded the wound. Because the splinter was squeezing the surrounding tissue extremely tightly, there was no bleeding.

The Tragedy of Vietnam, Again

Doc washed his hands carefully and started feeling the wounded area. "Does this hurt?"

Jones shook his head no and asked, "Are you sending me to Chu Lai?"

"No, I can take care of you right here," Doc answered in a reassuring tone.

I watched Jones's face and saw that this was not the answer Jones was looking for.

Doc gave Jones a shot of painkiller and proceeded to cut the chunk of wood out of his leg. "Well, Jones, would you like save this splinter? You can mount it on a piece of wood; it's very impressive," Doc stated.

"No, throw it away," Jones replied, looking at the chunk of bamboo. The hole in Jones's crotch was also very impressive. Doc flushed the wound, applied medication and wrapped it so the leg could drain. Jones was given a tetanus shot and a huge dose of penicillin to ward off infection.

Stewart came into the aid station with a pair of crutches we had stored in one of our connex boxes. Doc gave Jones an excuse from going to the field, but told him he could still take sick call for the men in the Third Platoon. Stewart drove Jones back to Bravo Troop in the jeep.

Doc and I caught the end of supper, which was wonder meat in a cream sauce, beans that tasted of the tin can, and again dehydrated potatoes.

Jones came over to the aid station the next morning complaining that he was in great pain. I was sure he

Court martial

was in some pain, but medics were known to be terrible patients; they complained about everything. Jones's leg had stiffened up. Doc took a look and had Jones put hot soaks around the wound for about forty-five minutes. Then Doc cleaned the area again, medicated it, and then rewrapped the wound with a drain.

While this was going on Jones informed Doc, "This is a serious wound and it's going to take a long time to heal."

Doc said dryly, "Your leg will be healed within two weeks, and it will be almost as good as new, and in three weeks you'll be able to go back out to the field." I thought Jones might have gone into shock with these words by the expression on his face.

About a week later, word came to the aid station that Jones was causing trouble in Bravo Troop. He wasn't cooperating with the rest of the medical platoon; he talked negatively about anything and everything. When Doc and I finally received complaints from just about everyone, Doc suggested that Jones be sent on a second R&R to settle him down. Jones had been an excellent soldier with the exception of his snake-catching activities, and if there was a problem, we didn't want to exacerbate the situation.

I went to Bravo Troop and pulled Jones off to one side and informed him, "Doc is fed up with your attitude. We realize that you're injured and the unit has made allowances for that. We feel it's to everyone's best interest if you go on a second R&R for medical reasons only, but you'll remain in the field for approximately three weeks after the R&R. We'll pull you back, like we do with all the medics, to the aid station when you have six weeks remaining in the country; will you go along with this offer?"

Jones smiled and said, "Yes, I'll go along with it!"

"There's only one condition and that is your attitude has to become a lot more positive, do you agree to this?"

Jones agreed and was thrilled to go; he departed six days later for Hong Kong with promises of becoming a productive member of the medical platoon. While Jones was gone everything ran smoothly; the Third Platoon was covered by the rest of the medics in Bravo Troop.

The squadron was looking for the enemy each and every day; one platoon from each troop went out in circular sweep patterns to see if the enemy could be found. About a week after Jones left on R&R, Bravo Troop engaged the enemy west of Tam Ky.

The firefight the first day resulted in two of Bravo Troop's medics getting wounded. Doc and I scampered around, playing musical chairs with medics. I pulled Hale out of the aid station to go back to the field for a day or two, even though he was close to going home, and I also pulled one medic from Charlie Troop. Jones was due back the next day and Division had promised us replacement medics within a week.

Court martial

The next day Bravo Troop was still engaged with the enemy and there was no sign of Jones. Our medical liaison called to tell us that he had seen Jones in Chu Lai, but he was laying low.

"Go find Jones and tell him he's to return to the hill on the next helicopter today; he can be court-martialed right now for not following his R&R orders to return immediately to the unit."

When the six o'clock chopper arrived, there was no Jones; I was really upset. I called Chu Lai and told our liaison, "Go find Jones and if necessary physically put him on board the first helicopter to Hill 29." Alpha and Charlie troops were both on their way out to assist Bravo Troop, and we needed all medics available to render assistance to the wounded.

About noon, I was working alone in the aid station doing paperwork when Jones showed up with a smirk across his face. As he entered the aid station he said, "Sir, I'm not going to the field!"

"What, what did you just say?"

"I'm not going to the field, that's what I just said!"

"Jones, I need you in the field, your troop needs you in the field and your fellow soldiers need you in the field. We're short medics, so don't fool around."

"Sir, I refuse to go to the field," Jones said once again.

"Look, Jones, do you know what you're saying?"

The Tragedy of Vietnam, Again

"Yes, sir, I refuse to go to the field," he answered with a smirk again across his face and with defiance in his voice.

"Jones, don't say a single word, but you come with me." We got into the jeep and drove over to the Orderly Room of Headquarters Troop.

"Sergeant Williams, may I look at your copy of the Uniform Code of Military Justice?"

The Master Sergeant looked at me and then retrieved the book. I quickly looked up Disobeying a Lawful Order, Cowardice in the Face of the Enemy, and Failure to Render Aid to One's Fellow Comrade.

"Jones, if you do not obey my lawful order you'll be charged under all of these sections, do you understand? Sergeant Williams, may we borrow this book for the evening?"

"That's fine, Captain; may I ask what the matter is, sir?

"Not right now, but if Jones doesn't see the light of day by tomorrow morning, then you'll be informed, Sarge.

"This is very serious. I can put two and two together, Captain."

"I know, but I don't want to screw him up, if I can help it."

"No, I think you're doing the correct thing, but this can't be allowed to go on for very long. I hope you know what you're doing, young man, because if you don't do what is correct, you'll be in a lot of trouble."

Court martial

Jones just stood there with his head hanging low, as he stared at the floor.

"Thank you, Sergeant Williams, and I'll keep you posted." Jones and I departed the Orderly Room.

Doc returned from lunch, so I filled him in about what had happened. Doc looked at Jones and said, "Jones, you're to be on the next helicopter going to your unit, and if for some reason you're unable to do that, then report here to the aid station."

"Jones, I suggest you look over the Code of Justice and look up the punishment for each of the three charges that will be brought against you; this is your decision, so be very careful," I stated.

The last helicopter departed Hawk Hill at six o'clock that evening, and at six thirty Jones sauntered into the aid station to return the book.

Doc looked at him in disbelief, "Do you realize that you're going to get a court-martial?"

"I don't care, my brother-in-law is a civil liberties lawyer and he says it's better to be court-martialed, than to be a dead hero!"

"Well, the choice is yours, Jones, and I hope that you understand what might happen to you. Remember your brother-in-law is not going to feel the effects of his advice; you are," Doc stated.

"That's all right, Doc, I'm prepared to be court-martialed, at least I won't get killed."

"All right, I'll give you one last chance to change your mind. You go back to Bravo Troop on the first he-

The Tragedy of Vietnam, Again

licopter tomorrow. If for any reason you cannot make that aircraft, you're to report back here, to the aid station, immediately. Do you understand this order?"

Jones did not say a word. He just turned and started to open the door to leave.

"Jones, think of what will happen to you and what effects this will have upon your future. The choice is yours," Doc added. Then Jones walked out into the evening's dusk.

"What can we do?" I asked.

"Nothing, he has been ill advised by his family and he'll not listen to any of us. I feel sorry for him," Doc answered.

So far Doc and I had kept our problem between ourselves. The other medics knew something was going on, but had no clue what, because no one had heard what Jones had said. The aid station fell into its nightly routine. That night I went up on top of the aid station to sleep, where I could think and feel at peace. I came to the conclusion that Jones had had more than his fair share of chances to change his mind. He took advantage of Doc and me when he accepted the second R&R, which was not right, but Doc thought it would help Jones's mental health. I went to sleep thinking, *Jones has made his bed and now he'll have to accept the consequences of his actions.*

The next morning, Jones walked into the aid station with his disgusting smirk across his face. "Get in the jeep, Jones, right now," I ordered before Jones could say one word.

I drove Jones over to Headquarters Troop along with the borrowed book on military justice. *It's going to be a hot day,* I thought as dust bellowed behind the jeep. The trip to the Orderly Room was very quick.

Once we arrived I ordered, "Jones, come with me!" It was interesting. I thought, *I really don't care what happens to him now. I'm no longer a nice guy. We've tried but to no avail; Jones is a nonentity who's nothing but scum under our feet.*

Sergeant Williams looked up and knew we had trouble. "Master Sergeant, I would like to press charges against Jones, and the charges are: Disobeying a Lawful Order, Cowardice in the Face of the Enemy, and Failing to Render Aid to his Fellow Comrades."

Captain Donaldson came out from his office behind the Orderly Room.

"Jones, stand at attention," I snapped. Jones shuffled from a slouch to a more erect stance.

"What can I do for you, Chris?"

"Captain Donaldson, I'd like to press charges against this man. He refuses to go to the field, sir."

"He refuses to go to the field!" the captain stated. "Is this true, BOY?" he fired right into Jones's face with a glare that could kill. "You stand at attention when I talk to you, do you understand?" Captain Donaldson screamed. Charles Donaldson had graduated from West Point four years earlier, and he was giving Jones what all plebes learn about very quickly, the wrath of one's supe-

The Tragedy of Vietnam, Again

rior. Jones showed fear on his face. "Well, BOY, what's your answer? Are you going to the field or not! If you don't go, then I'll hang your f-ing ass, do you understand, boy!"

Jones was trying to answer the captain, but was having trouble.

Sergeant Williams said in a calm voice, "Jones, you answer the captain. Are you going to go back to the field? Take your time and be very careful as to how you answer this question."

Jones drew himself up and said very slowly and clearly, "Sir, I refuse to go to the field. You may court-martial me if you would like, but I will not go to the field."

Captain Donaldson said, "Since I'm your commanding officer, I'm the one who will press charges against you, Jones. In order to make this legal, I'm ordering you to return to Bravo Troop, and you will be on the ten o'clock helicopter. If for any reason you do not make that aircraft, you will report to Sergeant Williams immediately, and he'll make the necessary arrangements for you to go to Chu Lai. While in Chu Lai you'll consider yourself under arrest and you'll not leave your quarters. Do you understand these orders?" Captain Donaldson spat out.

"Yes, sir," Jones meekly answered.

"Now get your f-ing ass out of here and you make sure you're on that helicopter," Captain Donaldson ordered.

Jones quickly turned and raced out of the Orderly Room.

Court martial

"He won't make that helicopter," I said. "His brother-in-law is a civil liberties lawyer and is the driving force behind Jones's actions. Jones showed me the letter from this guy and it says, 'It's better to be alive with a court-martial, than to be a dead hero.'"

"Sergeant Williams told me about this yesterday, so I've been waiting for you today. You could have brought the charges, but you have only a short time left in the country; it will be better for me to press the charges. I have eight months left in Vietnam, and it will take at least two to three months just to get the court proceeding underway."

"Well, let's wait to see if he does go back to the field," Williams stated. "If he doesn't, then we have to act quickly. The other troops will be watching this closely; if they see Jones get away with this, then we'll have a real mess on our hands."

"If Jones doesn't go to the field, then Jones will no longer belong to the medical platoon. He'll become part of Headquarters Troop and Sarge will be in charge of him," Captain Donaldson ordered.

"I feel sorry for him; I'm sorry for the trouble this is causing everyone."

"Captain, don't you feel sorry for Jones. You have gone out of your way to try and get Jones back on course, and that's a lot more than most officers would be willing to do," Sergeant Williams said.

The Tragedy of Vietnam, Again

"That's correct, don't feel sorry for him, this has nothing to do with you or Doc; it's all within Jones," Charles Donaldson added.

When I left the Orderly Room, Jones was nowhere to be seen.

I returned to the aid station and told Doc what took place at Headquarters Troop, and that Sergeant Williams and Captain Donaldson were in charge of Jones if he did not get on the helicopter. Doc and I were both pleased we'd not be the ones to press charges, because Jones was one of our boys and he was in very serious trouble.

We went about our business at the aid station, trying to forget Jones and hoped he'd change his mind and get on the helicopter. About noon, the aid station's phone rang and Kline answered it. He handed the phone to Doc who talked quietly for about thirty seconds. I watched Doc as he hung the phone up. Doc looked in my direction and said, "Jones is going to Chu Lai."

Johnston and Miller both said in unison, "Why is Jones going to Chu Lai?"

"Jones is in very serious trouble," Doc answered. "He's going to be given a general court-martial for refusing to go to the field.

Johnston said, "What!" with total shock across his face. All the medics were in shock.

"Jones told Captain Noble the other day he refused to go back to Bravo Troop. We have been trying to get him to change his mind, but failed. So Captain

Court martial

Donaldson ordered Jones to the field and Jones has refused that order," Doc explained.

"So that's what been going on," Johnston stated. "I knew something was cooking what with all the low talk and private conversations."

"What a dumb fool," Kline said. "He only has two months left in the Army."

"Well, he just might end up with a whole lot more time if he gets a court-martial," Johnston commented.

Headquarters Troop gathered up Jones, with all his gear and sent him off the Hill, all by himself on a special helicopter. Captain Donaldson informed LTC Lawrence, about what was going on.

"I don't want Jones near any line troop personnel, whatsoever," the colonel ordered.

That evening a group of about ten line medics from all three troops came to the aid station asking about Jones. "Is it true that he refuses to go to the field, and where is Jones now?" Mike Whitman asked.

"Jones is in Chu Lai, why?" Doc replied.

"Where is he in Chu Lai?" Bill Eason quietly asked.

"Why do you want to know?" Doc asked.

These medics didn't really answer this question, and then quietly left the aid station, with Johnston in tow.

"Chris, something is brewing," Doc stated with great concern.

The Tragedy of Vietnam, Again

"I agree that was a strange gathering."

Johnston returned to the aid station about ten minutes later, and whispered to me, "They're looking for Jones; they're going to kill him!"

I was shocked and asked, "Are you absolutely sure about this?"

Johnston whispered, "I'm absolutely sure, sir, they want to kill him."

"Thank you for telling me," I quietly replied. After a reasonable amount of time passed I told Doc, and then excused myself quietly to go looking for Captain Donaldson.

I found him in the Officers' Club and the topic of conversation was all about Jones. Captain Donaldson was playing poker with the colonel and the other line troop commanders. As soon as they saw me, they all started laughing and ragged me, "Do you have any other problems for Headquarters Troop?"

"Thank you for your kind concern, but actually, yes, we do have a problem."

"What's the problem?" the Colonel interrupted.

I pulled up a chair and explained about the visit from the line medics.

The colonel asked, "Who are these other medics and what did Johnston say?"

"These are really good medics!" the gathered group of commanders stated in unison, after I explained the situation.

Court martial

Colonel Lawrence asked Captain Donaldson, "Where have you stashed Jones?"

It was felt that Chu Lai was not a safe place for Jones to cool his heels. After a few moments of discussion, Captain Reed, the CO of Bravo Troop, asked the group, "Do you remember Jason Graves?"

Captain Prothero answered, "Yes, he was two years ahead of us, at the Point and went artillery, why?"

"Well, I bumped into him the last time I was in Chu Lai, and he said he has taken over a battery that's out in 'East Jesus.' He described it as the most god-forsaken place he has ever seen. It sits on top of a mountaintop that's about one hundred feet wide and two hundred feet long with near vertical slopes on all sides; the NVA and VC have them completely surrounded and the only way in or out is by helicopter," Captain Reed exclaimed with a smile.

Captain Donaldson went to the field phone and called Chu Lai to have them put the wraps around Jones and he was to stay out of sight.

Later the next day Jones was told to gather his belongings and to get on a helicopter. He was told the truth, that there was a group of medics looking for him and they'd kill him if they could. As a result, Jones was hidden until his court-martial. The helicopter took off and flew about ten minutes south of Chu Lai, and then barely into the mountains. The aircraft set down on top

The Tragedy of Vietnam, Again

of the highest mountain, on a small outcropping. That particular spot controlled two valleys, as well as part of the coastal plain.

The helicopter set down long enough so Jones could get off. The mountain top had trenches dug in around all sides, as well as from bunker to bunker. The enemy would love to overrun this location, but they couldn't, because it was too steep and it would cost them too dearly if they should try. As a result, the VC and NVA went out of their way to make life as miserable as possible. This unit was mortared at least two to three times every night; the attacks were coordinated when the enemy wanted to move supplies into or out of the valleys.

That was Jones's safe haven for the next two months. He wasn't allowed to leave; Jones survived by pulling KP every day he was there.

One of my medics called me when he returned to the United States to inform me, "Jones got his court-martial, and Captain Donaldson charged Jones with the same articles I had looked up: Cowardice in the Face of the Enemy, Failure to Render Aid to Fellow Comrades, and Disobeying a Lawful Order. The court dropped the first two charges, because they would be too difficult to prove. Jones was only charged with disobeying a lawful order. He was found guilt as charged, and was given two and a half years at Fort Leavenworth Federal Prison, and was given a dishonorable discharge from the Army."

Court martial

(There was some discussion many years later whether Jones actually went to prison. Because of his father's rank, his father might have been able to pull strings to keep junior out of prison—so much for Jones!)

How Some People Got Killed & Drugs

It was monsoon season now and the weather had changed considerably. The word monsoon meant the changing of the direction of the prevailing wind. With this change of the wind's direction, rain was brought on, or the rain was taken away.

When the rain came to the I Corps, in Vietnam, that meant a lot of rain came; heavy curtains of rain with huge drops, the size of the end of your finger. It rained so hard that sometimes you couldn't see large objects only fifteen to twenty feet away at noontime.

What surprised me was how cold it felt during the monsoon. I didn't know about the Delta Region, because I was never there. We all had to wear sweaters both day and night for approximately two and a half months. This was a miserable time, for it looked as if the heavens were about to open up at any moment, twenty-four hours a day. It rained a drizzle for about two hours, then tapered off to heavy dew, only to drizzle again. The drizzle would intensify and before you knew it, it was raining so hard a curtain of water poured down, so you couldn't see. This would last for

The Tragedy of Vietnam, Again

about fifteen to twenty minutes, then the squall died down to a drizzle once again; then the whole process started all over, again and again.

We tried to plan our activities by what the weather was doing; going to the chow hall, taking a shower, or doing anything. During these months it was terrible for morale, because your clothing and bedding never dried out, everything was damp.

The two largest fears we all had were that the water-soaked sandbags would collapse the bunker's roof, or the drainage ditch around the bunker would be damaged and the bunker would fill up with water.

The enlisted men hated pulling guard duty in weather like that. You were stuck on the perimeter with two other people to guard the base camp from intrusion during the night. The bunker was cold, wet, and cramped. You and your buddies were not only cold, damp, and tired, you were irritated at being in Vietnam, being on the bunker line, and you were tired of seeing nothing but blackness.

All these elements set up very dangerous conditions, especially if the individual was not very smart. When people became careless, then someone was going to get hurt, and then the medics, like the nursery rhyme said, would have to try to put the pieces back together again.

We all heard about the big accident that had happened early one morning in a unit down the road from us. One of our medics came in from Chu Lai with the story as to what happened. One of the bunker guards came off duty, early in the morning, with all his gear, consisting of two claymore mines, ammo for his .60-cal machine gun, his weapon, pillow, and a blanket.

It was military policy that all weapons had to be cleared of any ammo and all claymore mines needed to be disarmed. To unarm a claymore mine was as simple as unplugging a lamp from a wall socket; once unplugged the mine was totally harmless. Well, this particular soldier tossed all his gear into one of the corners of his sleeping bunker, which he shared with approximately twenty other men. Then along came another soldier, who had done everything according to the regulations, and dropped his gear on top of the first man's gear. Something hard landed on the detonation handle of the first man's claymore mine, compressing the handle, which in turn was connected to the cap, which was plugged into the mine. The word around Division was ten dead and five wounded.

Some deaths in Vietnam were so stupid that it made you really wonder about the brainpower of some people. In the same unit as the claymore mine accident, they had a soldier playing with a grenade as he was waiting in the chow line; he was twirling the grenade around his finger and the obvious happened. The pin came out and three men were killed and seven wounded.

In our unit when we had a small force in Fat City, one of our men, on a rainy night had too much to drink and he had nothing to do. This idiot decided he was go-

The Tragedy of Vietnam, Again

ing to scare his buddy by shooting one round through the air mattress, as his friend slept upon it. Well, I don't know if all would have been all right if only one bullet came out, but he forgot his M-16 was on full automatic. Before he could get his finger off the trigger, one bullet tore off the calf of his buddy, as he slept, and five other bullets hit the man sleeping on the other side of his buddy. Neither person was killed, but both were returned to the United States all screwed up, and probably would walk with a limp for the rest of their lives.

There was another case when one soldier went to visit his best friend, while they both were on guard duty one night, but they were in different bunkers. In the middle of the night his friend shot his buddy through the head, not knowing who or what he was, as his friend approached the other's bunker to socialize.

We had four or five people shoot themselves with their .45 pistol. These accidents came from playing with weapons or cleaning "unloaded" weapons. We had one person shoot himself through the foot as he tried to clear his weapon and drive an APC all at the same time.

We heard about the Marine in Da Nang who wanted a really good picture of a mortar round going off, as the NVA walked mortar rounds across the airfield. This Marine had it all planned, as to when to take the picture and still have time to duck back under cover. Well, the enemy didn't know his plan and didn't fire the critical round when this person was going to duck;

his next of kin got a really good picture of the blast that killed him.

The Chu Lai beach was beautiful, but on the wrong day it could be a killer. It had a fierce undertow and more than one person went for a very long swim, all underwater.

Another big cause of deaths was vehicles. We came upon a two-and-a-half-ton truck with eight people riding in the back and two in the cab. This truck was going like hell down Highway One; if you were doing thirty miles per hour, you were speeding. That truck was doing close to fifty miles per hour, and the men in the back were having a hard time hanging on, according to witnesses. Well, this truck hit a bridge abutment, flipped over and the truck burst into flames. All the men were either trapped underneath the bed, or in the cab, and all burned to death.

A jeep with MPs was returning to their base camp from picking up their beer ration. They came up behind a convoy, and the MPs had to eat a thick curtain of dust. It was so dense one could not see more than thirty feet in front of the vehicle. Well, those idiot MPs decided that they were willing to play a game of chicken, and tried to pass the convoy. An ARVN five-ton truck was coming in the opposite direction; end result was four dead MPs, and one crushed jeep.

There was a person, whom I knew very well in our unit, who didn't do what he was told. If you weren't

The Tragedy of Vietnam, Again

trained to do something, then you don't do it. On that particular day his troop was out in the field and they were receiving potshots from a sniper. The troop's commander ordered the line troops to dismount and search for this sniper. After about fifteen minutes, this person, who I knew had not been trained to go look for a sniper, came across a funny-looking trap door in the middle of the rice paddy. He went over and picked up the cover and as he stuck his head over the edge to see what he could see, he caught half a clip of AK-47 in his face.

The most pathetic case I read about in a man's health record after I had come back from Vietnam. This patient and some of his friends had a pet monkey, and one of the soldiers gave the monkey a "Willy Pete" (white phosphorous) grenade, to see what the monkey would do. Need I go any further? One soldier and one monkey killed and five other soldiers with severe third-degree burns to their faces, trunks, arms, and hands.

I never witnessed, nor smelled any marijuana being smoked in our unit. From the medical platoon and the aid station's position we didn't have a drug problem; drugs were not being used in the field that we knew of. I witnessed only once a sergeant who was drunk in the field, but two PFC (private first class) had this sargeant completely under control. What caught my attention was when I overheard one private say, "Sarge, if I see your f—ing face outside of this track, I'll kill you, do you hear me?" and then this E-6 sergeant was shoved unceremoniously into the back of the track and the back door was secured shut.

Any and all medical equipment captured in the field was to be turned into the aid station. Over time we had approximately four or five NVA medical aid bags turned in, and each time we found a wax-covered ball about the size of a lime. This ball, I guessed was a cake of near pure heroin. As I understand it, the NVA medics peeled back some of the wax and then let his patient lick the powdery cake. This allowed his patient to go on a really good trip, for an extended period of time, as the NVA patient was carried back to North Vietnam.

These balls, I guessed were worth a lot of money in the open drug market, in the United States, but they weren't sent back, they were all still in the aid bag. If our unit had a drug problem, we would never have seen any of those waxed balls. All balls we collected were put in a gallon can and burned with diesel oil.

If one looked at the people who got into serious trouble—like with drugs, black market, etc.—they were for the most part rear-echelon personnel, who didn't have enough to keep them busy. As a result they got sidetracked with everything they shouldn't be doing. In a line unit it was just too dangerous to go around with your mind all screwed up with drugs or alcohol, as you went out looking for trouble day in and day out.

In the 1/1 Cav, race was not an issue. It couldn't be, because the stakes were way too high, and everyone

The Tragedy of Vietnam, Again

was totally dependent upon everyone else. It made no difference whether you were black, white, Hispanic, or purple; everybody was totally dependent upon each other for survival. Also, if you got someone really upset with you, there was a very easy solution to solve this problem, but it was used very sparingly; it was called "fragging."

As stated, everybody depended on everyone else. This was what Hollywood has not figured out, and people don't go about smashing each other in the face with a rifle butt; so much for Hollywood.

The Press

(This National Press segment is a description as to what was said based upon firsthand observations. Unfortunately, I don't have the individuals' names; otherwise I would use them.)

There's always good and there's always bad no matter where one goes in this world. Organizations, such as large corporations, universities, military units, or governments are only as good as the individuals who make up the institution. General Bradley once said something to the effect, "A general is only as good as his privates."

This held true with the press. On occasion reporters would show up on Hawk Hill to visit our unit. They wanted to see how it really was going; to get the firsthand information as to how the boys in "Vietnaaam" were doing. Most reporters who fell out of the sky and ended up in our lap were either freelance reporters working for small town papers, who wanted a local story about a local boy, or they were from the large national press corporations, looking for the hottest scoop.

The Tragedy of Vietnam, Again

One day I was informed by Major Filbert that part of my additional duties, in the 1/1 Cav, would be escorting reporters around the unit and that I had to make myself available to assist them in any way I could. I was to take them anywhere they would like, show them anything they would like to see within our base camp, answer all their questions fully and honestly and take them to any individual whom they might like to talk to. If need be I was to assist them in arranging transportation to their next stop. However, no reporter was to go out on any type of mission, because they were not trained to go in harm's way. The unit wasn't going to put our soldiers in danger, because of untrained people on board any of our APCs.

A freelance reporter might represent two to three hometown newspapers, because the local paper couldn't afford to send a fulltime reporter. The newspaper supplied the individual with local names, as well as the necessary press credentials to gain admittance to South Vietnam. With these press credentials, this individual could receive a travel permit for travel throughout the country; transportation was up to the reporter to arrange; however, it was to the military's advantage to assist and try not to upset the press, as much as possible.

Our unit received several visits from individuals representing small town papers throughout my stay, and each time a specific individual was being sought. These freelance reporters were usually in their early twenties and they regarded Vietnam as some sort of game or a fun park, which they wanted to see firsthand. My medics and I were asked astute questions such as, "Gee, what's it like out there? Have you guys seen a lot of action? Have you had to kill anyone yet? Hey, can I go out on a mission with one of your units? I want to see the enemy."

I explained, "Going out on Band-Aid is out of the question, because first, it's against my orders; second, you're not trained to go in harm's way; and third, there's no room for additional people on any of the tracks. Every person on each track has his own job to perform and if trouble develops, a passenger is going to be in the way and people can get hurt, like my medics. This order is not only for civilians, but for all military personnel as well. 'No passengers go to the field!'"

Usually, our freelance reporters got upset and made all sorts of accusations. They accused the unit of trying to hide something. Maybe we were committing atrocities in the field and didn't want them to report on it; what was it that the 1/1 Cav was trying to hide?

My usual answer at this point was, "If you want to visit certain people, tell me who they are. You may ask them any questions you want. I will bring you to any individual you would like to see, and then I will get lost, because I don't want to interfere with any of the answers. If you don't have any names of people, I'll let you talk to my medics, or I'll ask any soldier whom you pick out, and will ask them if it would be all

The Tragedy of Vietnam, Again

right if they talk to the press. We have nothing to hide." Usually our guests, for some reason, backed down and enjoyed a meaningful visit and got information they could use in their stories. In any case, I would arrange transportation back to Chu Lai for the reporters, if they hadn't made arrangements already.

The other type of reporter from the large news network was a completely different kettle of fish. These people knew they were better than anyone around and you didn't tell them anything; they would tell you.

One day in late summer in 1968, the command bunker called the aid station to warn me that some reporters were about five minutes out from Hawk Hill. Charlie and Bravo Troops were engaged in enemy action to the west, and the command bunker was very busy fighting a war.

As I approached the helipad, an unarmed helicopter was approaching our position. What I didn't know was the 1/1 Cav was basically the only unit in all of Vietnam, on that particular day, to be engaged with the enemy. So when the passengers got off the aircraft, it wasn't one major network but three; ABC, NBC, and the AP (Associated Press).

These people used different tactics than the freelance reporters. I guessed they called this being more professional. I greeted the group of five and asked if I might be of assistance.

The Press

The oldest looking of this group answered, as they walked toward the antennas on the TOC, "You just point us in the direction of your HQ (headquarters); we want to talk to your CO!" I was literally pushed to one side, as those three reporters and two cameramen descended upon the command bunker

Inside the nerve center, it looked like any other office anywhere, but not quite as fancy. There was a plywood floor, desks and chairs, typewriters, file cabinets, and even a coffee pot. Off the main bunker were two smaller bunkers, each with a heavy black curtain covering the doorway. One was crammed on two sides with radios. The other room had a long table with chairs around it and large local maps hung from three walls. Each map had a black cloth hanging over it, to ensure unauthorized eyes did not see something they weren't supposed to see

The squadron's command sergeant major intercepted our guests as they entered the area.

"We're the press and we want to see your commanding officer," the senior-looking man ordered.

"I'm sorry, gentlemen, but Colonel Lawrence is not available. He's coordinating the battle action, may I help you?"

"Is the executive officer here?" another reporter asked.

Before the senior ranking NCO could answer, Major Filbert said, "May I help you?" The major had been in the radio room making sure that an accurate

The Tragedy of Vietnam, Again

record of events was being taken and had heard their conversation.

The next thing Major Filbert knew, he was being bombarded with questions about the battle. "Where's the action taking place? Show us on the map. How many men are in the field, how many casualties have we taken? How many of the enemy have been killed? Where are you from, Major, how do you spell your name, where did you say you're from?"

Major Filbert answered the questions asked and he tried to accommodate the press, but he also had to run the battle and coordinate details such as emergency resupplies, emergency reinforcements of troops, etc. As soon as the major tried to turn the newsmen over to another senior NCO, the press explained that they were working for TV and wanted transportation out to the battle.

"I'm sorry, gentlemen, but all our helicopters are engaged in battle at the moment," the XO stated.

"Look, Major, we have permission from Division and that you're to make available helicopters for our use," a middle-aged reporter snapped back.

"That's out of the question, as I just told you; all our helicopters are engaged in combat."

The senior-aged reporter noticed Major Filbert's West Point ring. "You went to West Point, didn't you, Major. You should know about following orders. Why don't you call up Colonel Smith, in Division, and he'll tell you as to what your orders are, Major."

The Press

The XO knew what they were trying to do and he also knew they were full of Bull. At about this point, LTC Lawrence unexpectedly walked into Headquarters, because his helicopter needed to be refueled and to replenish the spent ammo.

Major Filbert was happy to see him and explained who these gentlemen were. LTC Lawrence was unimpressed and told the press that all available aircraft were being used. Maybe if Division had a spare helicopter, they could try to get Division to supply one. Unfortunately, all the 1/1 Cav helicopters were being used in battle and none could be spared at the moment.

At this point, the press, all three networks, turned very ugly. They threatened both the CO and XO with very bad press and accused them of trying to interfere with "freedom of the press." It was amazing how powerful these people thought they were. They went on to say that neither of these two officers would get another promotion, because of the bad press that was about to be released. They would follow up with stories about cover-ups, massacres, genocide, atrocities, and so on and so forth, if helicopters were not made available.

After this temper tantrum, the press then stormed out of the TOC, only to find they had been stranded, because the Division helicopter had departed without them, which added to the press's frustration.

In the meantime, LTC Lawrence called Division and talked with Major General Gettys, the command-

The Tragedy of Vietnam, Again

ing general of the Americal Division and the outcome of that phone call was the 1/1 Cav had to pull one helicopter from combat and make it available to those idiots.

Strict orders were given to the aircraft crew that no more than two people were to go up at any given time. Each trip was to be no longer than forty-five minutes each, and the aircraft was not to fly under two thousand feet. The pilot was to take his orders only from Major Filbert, and was not to listen to any suggestions from the press.

I hoped that what I witnessed on Hawk Hill was not the normal operating procedure for the national press.

What those so-called major network reporters produced was an embarrassment to legitimate journalism. Both LTC Lawrence's and Major Filbert's names were obscenely misspelled, and they accused the 1/1 Cav of trying to prevent the press from doing their job. Those members of the press did the world a disservice by publishing a lot of vindictive trash. Also, these gentlemen and their statements about having so much influence over the military, that neither military man would ever be promoted again. Well, Lieutenant Colonel Lawrence went on to become a lieutenant general in the United States Army.

The Politician

Politicians, as a whole, were in a class all by themselves. They usually wanted to check up on "their boys." The impression I received from these middle-aged, slightly balding men, was that they were trying to cash in politically by "being over there." The politicians were not interested in talking with junior officers, NCOs, or enlisted men; they wanted to talk only with "the top brass" about Vietnaaam, even though it was the junior officers, the NCOs and the enlisted men who were fighting the war. (One note of interest, no Vietnamese ever said they came from Vietnaaam. They refer to their country as Vietnam. It's a short, soft "a" sound. The vietnaam is the same as if one eats Italian dressing, but says they are eating Eyetalian dressing.)

We had several such visits from congressmen, and on one such visit, a congressman wanted to see one of our medics. The call was put to the aid station for Spec 4 Elisio Garduno, an excellent medic in Alpha Troop; he was to report immediately to the TOC. He needed to put on a clean uniform, polish his shoes, and be clean shaven, because some VIP wanted to see him.

I went over to Alpha Troop medics' bunker, and brought Garduno over to the TOC and told him to

The Tragedy of Vietnam, Again

report to whatever officer was with the congressman from Texas. Garduno reported as he should and the "Poll" grabbed his hand long enough so one or two good photographs could be taken by a member of the Poll's VIP party.

I was interested in who this person was, so I stood off to one side and listened as the Poll said, "Son, you're a credit to our country and to the United States Army. When I get home I'm going to call your mama and papa and tell them what a fine job you're doing. What's their telephone number, son? Do you want me to tell them anything?" This sounded as sincere as seeing Santa Claus in the local mall at Christmas time.

Once the hometown politicking was over, and the picture had been taken, Garduno was unceremoniously excused; it took no more than two minutes at most. The Poll then moved into Phase II, which was of far greater importance than meeting Garduno, and that was to get photos of Mr. Poll climbing all over tanks and armored personnel carriers, and inspecting captured enemy weapons, while the camera was burning up the film. All these pictures meant only one thing, "Hey, look at me. I've been there and I'm one of the guys with the real story, so vote for me!"

The average stay for these politicians was approximately one hour. We found this very interesting, that the politician was capable of picking up so much information in such a short amount of time with so many pictures taken to document the trip.

The Tragedy of Vietnam

The third week in November had arrived, and I was short, so very short, it was time for me to catch the helicopter to fly down to Chu Lai. I couldn't believe myself; I was depressed about leaving as the helicopter lifted up into the air. Over that year, very close bonds had developed between me and others within the unit. I didn't want to break these bonds; I knew once they were broken, they'd never be the same.

As Dan Miller said, "Vietnam has been some of the very best times of my life; it's also been some of the very worst times in my life. I'll never have friends like I have right now."

I was out processed as efficiently as I was in processed to go to Southeast Asia, only in reverse. I flew from Chu Lai to Cam Ranh Bay to catch the charter flight to Japan, and then on to Seattle, Washington. That was the end of the ride as far as the military was concerned. For me, once in Seattle I had to scrape around to find my own transportation back home. There was no fanfare, no recognition, no help to arrange for travel, and if a flight was booked full, I was then put on a standby list.

The Tragedy of Vietnam, Again

I arrived at LaGuardia Airport in a snowstorm. Not only was my internal system out of whack for dealing with cold weather, but I had only my summer short-sleeved uniform to wear, per Army orders. As I waited for my mom, shivering, a sergeant major came up to me and said, "Welcome home, Captain." He then looked at my medals and said, "That means more to me than the Medal of Honor," as he touched my Combat Medics Badge. He said "Thank you and good luck, sir." This made me feel good, and then he turned and disappeared into the crowd.

It felt good being home, but things had changed. I listened to the news from Vietnam, I wanted to hear how the 1/1 Cav was doing, but the press never reported on the Americal Division. While watching television, I could identify all the weapons that were shown and understand all the war jargon being spoken. What really disturbed me was that sometimes what was said did not necessarily coincide with what was shown. Small items like one unit was in heavy contact, but the unit's identification number on the rear of the vehicles was totally different from the unit mentioned.

I was overwhelmed with events and just being home once again. My mom wanted to give me a welcome home party, because it was a good excuse to pay people back who had been nice to her while I was in Vietnam. Most of the people I knew, but there were a few people I'd never seen before. This one lady, whose name I never did get, came up to me when I was alone

The Tragedy of Vietnam

for a moment and hissed, "How could you do what you did?"

"Excuse me; I'm afraid I don't understand what you're talking about."

"You know perfectly well. How could you kill babies, how can you live with yourself?"

I was absolutely shocked by this assault and replied in dismay, "I'm a medic; we saved lives. We didn't go about killing people for the fun of it, and my unit never killed any babies; I do know for a fact that the enemy killed babies, old men, and old women just to make a point; I saw their remains. I don't know what you're talking about." I turned and walked away from that stranger, who was standing in the living room of my own home.

It did not surprise me when I read a full column in the New York Times about a news station and how they had distorted the news in late 1968. During FCC hearings, it was brought to light that correspondents in one country were sending the news via satellite, when in fact it was no more than a superimposed image on top of training films here in the United States.

Listening to the nightly antiwar drumbeat from ABC, NBC, CBS, and hearing how the war was run so poorly; how the Americans were losing the war was wearing. We all knew what we saw in Vietnam, and we all knew what we did, but the people back home had no clue about what was going on in Vietnam. It became very obvious to me that all those phonies I wit-

The Tragedy of Vietnam, Again

nessed who paraded through Hawk Hill, the press and the politicians didn't do their jobs when they came back home; instead they had put their own spin on Vietnam for their special interests. We have a very poor press, here in the United States, and we have a bunch of self-serving people running our government.

The debate about whether being in Vietnam is legally correct was of no concern to me. I knew what I saw, and I saw how my government's politicians ran our government and micromanaged the war in Vietnam, all for their own political reasons.

(Up to this point, everything was written in 1968–1970. From this point on, I have used my Vietnam experience and related that to our current events in 2008.)

Politicians & Press – Vietnam

I went to Vietnam as a patriotic young American, whose family has had a close member fight in most every conflict this country has ever fought, starting with the French and Indian Wars, to include my own son who went to Afghanistan in 2004, and my daughter-in-law who was on orders to go to Iraq in August of 2007.

After being home for a while, I felt out of place, as I began to understand what had developed and could relate to the dynamics between the press, the politicians and the American public. It is very true that Vietnam had an enormous effect in turning me into who I am today. My priorities and my feelings regarding our government have been strengthened. I now understand how our government works. How our government lied to the American people and has done so throughout the decades.

President McKinley lied to the American people when he said the *USS Maine* was sunk in Havana's Harbor by a Spanish mine. The Captain of the *USS Maine* insisted the ship was sunk by a coal bin explosion

The Tragedy of Vietnam, Again

on board the ship, and this was proved to be the truth after an investigation into the cause of the explosion. Unfortunately, the Spanish American War was well underway when the truth was finally learned.

All governments lie; Adolph Hitler lied to the German people about how Poland had attacked Germany first and he managed to convince the German people to follow him into World War II.

Bill Hitz was one of my father's very best friends and he was a leading prosecuting attorney for the US Justice Department, in Washington. As Robert McNamara, the secretary of defense, was being interviewed on television, Bill Hitz exclaimed "That SOB can't open his mouth twice without contradicting himself. He's nothing but a liar!"

Robert McNamara was not sensitive to any kind of advice as to how the United States government could get out of Vietnam. Johnson had a small inner core of advisors who were confident in their views and analysis as to what was appropriate for the Vietnam military venture. In fact their policy was doomed to fail because it was founded upon deception of the American people and Congress. This is due in part to having set short-term goals.

McNamara managed to sell President Johnson on McNamara's steady-pressure plan, because he sold it as a plan that would not hurt Johnson's pet project, his "Great Society" welfare program.

I did not realize what was going on when I first came home. I didn't fully understand the dynamics of our government and our press until much later. I guess I had invested too much of myself into what I did while in Vietnam, and I still had another year to serve in uniform. Emotionally I was still in Vietnam with my comrades on Hawk Hill, and subconsciously I didn't want to learn the real truth; however, the truth has a way of creeping in as time passed by.

In 1964, when the war in Vietnam was not going as the administration had planned, President Johnson decided he needed more authority to raise the stakes in Vietnam. He needed more troops on the ground and he wanted to bring the war directly to North Vietnam. Johnson needed this increased authority from the United States Congress so he had the American government stage two events.

It was announced that the North Vietnamese Navy had attacked two different American destroyers on different days. The destroyer Turner Joy and the destroyer Maddox were never attacked by the North Vietnamese navy. The Gulf of Tonkin Resolution was passed by the Congress based upon a huge lie. The end result was that Johnson got to bomb North Vietnam and the American troop strength was increased to five hundred thousand soldiers stationed, on the ground, in South Vietnam.

Leading committee chairmen were playing their own games throughout the war with Vietnam, so they

The Tragedy of Vietnam, Again

could serve their special interest groups, whoever they may be. Senator Fulbright was one of the more active members who tried to make the military look bad. In making the military look bad, it was a direct reflection upon every single person who wore the uniform.

Senator Fulbright wanted to make a point, so he held a very public hearing that was a carefully orchestrated charade; it was basically a propaganda event to sell to the senator's special interests, as the senator presented John Kerry who made his carefully planned entrance into the public's grand spotlight. John Kerry was the perfect tool for Senator Fulbright. This show served the senator well, it served the antiwar movement well, it served the press well, even John Kerry was served well; everybody was served, but our country.

It was absolutely incredible that our politicians, our government leaders in Washington, D.C., could sit in their plush offices and allow thousands upon thousands of young American soldiers to be killed and wounded every month, when these politicians all knew that Vietnam was based upon nothing but lies and special interests.

Unknown to my friends and me in the 1/1 Cav while we were in Vietnam, there was a massive media disinformation program going on. It is well documented in the Vietnam history today. Most every newsperson, most every single television anchor lied through their teeth repeatedly as they showed footage and graphics from Vietnam. When we were in-country we did not know this, because we never saw any television. It was not until we came home did we start to question what we saw. But then, our press would never lie to the American public, would they?

The American soldier never lost any battle in Vietnam. The Vietnam War was lost mainly due to television, the rioting in the streets across America, and lastly Vietnam was lost in the hallowed halls of our Congress by breaking the will of the American public.

As I said, the media grossly misrepresented the events that took place in Vietnam. The Tet Offensive of 1968 was an embarrassment because of grossly distorted reporting. The media reported the Tet Offensive as a victory for North Vietnam and how it was a total defeat for the Americans and South Vietnamese military forces. The media expounded on how devastating the attacks had been, and how well coordinated the attack were throughout the entirety of South Vietnam.

The truth of the matter was the 1968 Tet Offensive was a total defeat for the North Vietnamese and Viet Cong military forces, who broke their own cease-fire truce. Within a three to four week period after that attack, the North Vietnam army and Viet Cong lost approximately forty thousand soldiers, all dead. It took the North a few years to rebuild from their devastating losses.

Another event that took center stage for the media that prompted sensational news, was when a stray mor-

The Tragedy of Vietnam, Again

tar round happened to land in an ammunition dump. This was a totally lucky shot and as a result, the local public got a fantastic pyrotechnic show. The press used the results of this shot to full advantage, around the world. This coverage demonstrated the skills and accuracy of the North Vietnamese army. The press constantly reported the news from across Vietnam as hopeless and the North was gaining ground, which was not true; the North Vietnamese never gained any ground and never won a battle in Vietnam.

The media feasted upon the riots across America and many riots were probably caused by the misinformation that the media constantly kept pumping out. The press made a lot of noise about people who burned the American flag or their draft cards in public. We also had to listen on TV to the hippies and antiwar movement sing silly chants and slogans, none of which built strength within our country. So why did our press do what they did, blatantly misrepresent the news? There can only be one or two answers to why the press acted, in my opinion, in a criminal manner. One, the media was totally incompetent, as they flagrantly and habitually distorted the news to satisfy the media's special interest groups. Secondly, they were totally inept tools, of their special interest groups, that pass on whatever copy was shoved under their noses and report the misinformation as legitimate news.

A glaring example of misinformation that was passed around the world, was the pathetic photograph of a little nine-year-old girl who was running down a Vietnam street naked after being hit with some napalm. Her name was Phan Thi Kim Phuc. The photographer blamed the Americans for that bombing and said so in the caption, when in fact it was not the Americans that dropped that napalm bomb. It was the South Vietnamese Air Force that dropped the bombs in that area and the photographer knew it, or should have found out who dropped it before he mislabeled that photograph. That one photo sold a lot of copy for the media, and the photographer was given many awards, but that caption really hurt the United States.

During the time of the Vietnam War, Walter Cronkite was a truly trusted newsperson across America. The war news was a constant stream of bad news, about those who died, the bodies coming home in flag-draped coffins, and how poorly the war was being run. This constant press beating wore upon the American people, as our media used such words as "imperialism," "colonialism," "war mongers," etc., and it took its toll on America.

A special news report was given to the American public, as the Paris Peace Talks were going on. The secretaries of state and defense asked for calm and told the world "There is a light at the end of the tunnel." Walter Cronkite took part in that special report about the Vietnam War and took it upon himself, as he said it was "unwinnable and there is no way this war can be justified any longer." With those words Cronkite

The Tragedy of Vietnam, Again

destroyed the American presidency of the day, and the US Military. Mr. Cronkite won the war for North Vietnam and the Communists. President Johnson was quoted as saying, "If I've lost Cronkite, then I've lost middle America." Because of Mr. Cronkite's statement, President Johnson shortly thereafter told the country that he would no longer seek to remain president of the United States.

Politicians & Press – Iraq

Today the citizens of our fine country have to address some major problems. There are some close similarities between Vietnam and Iraq, and we cannot just walk away from the situation in Iraq like we did in Vietnam. The United States were the one who destroyed Iraq's entire infrastructure. We are the ones who allowed the terrorists to terrorize Iraqi citizens and murder thousands upon thousands of innocent people in Iraq; all because the United States did not have a plan to stabilize Iraq once the bullets stopped flying. The United States unfortunately has an obligation to stand by Iraq, until Iraq can defend itself, whether the United States likes it or not.

The press, as was discussed, grossly distorted the news from Vietnam so they could sell their copy and please their special interest groups. The media in Iraq, for some reason, is a "no-show." Why has our press walked away from their duty to the American public to search for the truth and then report the truth, no matter how painful it may be? There seems to be a pattern to our media of not telling the truth, like the Jessica

The Tragedy of Vietnam, Again

Lynch heroic tale, or the Pat Tillman killing. Where is the truth? Where is our legitimate media?

Why does the press today report the petty news from Washington or disasters from across the country, or from around the world? We hear the excuse, "Oh, the war on terror," or words to that effect. Why don't you tell the American public that the government has put a muzzle around our press, and the government controls the news, much like the Soviet Union's media under Joseph Stalin and Mr. Brezhnev; at least this is what it appears to be. Why does the press not stand up and do their job, to report the news and stop spinning "the news" in favor of their special interest groups? The press today is trying to spin the news so their candidate will end up as our next president. It really doesn't matter what the people of the United States want; everything in this country is for special interests, by special interests.

I asked the question of a soldier who was home from Iraq for a two week leave this Easter, 2008. The question was, 'What's going on in Iraq - is the surge really working?"

Their response was not surprising to me, "You don't know much about what is going on over there (Iraq); very little is reported here."

I then called an officer friend, who just returned from a year's duty in Iraq, and asked the same question. The answer was the same as the person I met over Easter. This Major then went on to say, "The only time we ever saw the media was just after a gross terrorist attack where there was a large loss of civilian life. The media just appeared, out of nowhere, to get footage of the blood and gore, *to show around the world.*" This person concluded by saying "The American public knows very little as to what is going on in Iraq."

To change the subject slightly, we have an executive branch of government that has troubles in telling the truth. These are not simple misstatements or a slip of the tongue, from time to time. There seems to be a habitual stream of untruths coming from our president, the vice president, and many of members of the cabinet. It seems as if President Bush has a secret agenda that he does not want the America public to know about. The war in Iraq needs a lot of explaining, especially as to why we attacked Saddam Hussein; what was the real reason why the America forces attacked Iraq?

A very interesting question was raised in a book written by Mr. Paul O'Neill, after President Bush forced him out of office, as secretary of the treasury in 2002. The reason for Mr. Paul O'Neill's early resignation, as I understand, was that Mr. Bush needed a more loyal spokesperson to push for the president's massive tax giveaway program.

After the Iraq war broke out and Mr. O'Neill published his book about his time in the Bush White House. He said that George W. Bush wanted, from the very beginning of his administration, to remove Saddam Hussein from power. This would have been

The Tragedy of Vietnam, Again

almost a full year before the World Trade Center was attacked by Al-Qaeda. President George W. Bush adamantly denied this claim that he wanted to remove Saddam from power, but I think history will be able to tell the truth.

The world knows that George W. Bush and his vice president, Mr. Cheney, have problems in telling the truth; they seem to spin disinformation that happens to fit their agenda with the greatest of ease, and they attack anyone who opposes them, like Valerie Plame. Again, why did America go to war in Iraq?

Our enemy is Al-Quiada and they are in Pakistan and Afghanistan. Al-Quiada was never really in Iraq until we blew the holy hell out of the country. It seems we may also have a few hidden enemies within our government, or at least some people may not be working for the betterment of our country, but for their special interests. Many politicians, from both sides of congress, aided this administration by saying nothing when it was not in our best interest to go to war; the world had Saddam Hussein contained, he was not a threat, to us, our allies, or to our "friends in the neighborhood."

We all heard statements made by both President Bush and Mr. Cheney. President Bush stated the following in very public forum, these statements we all remember hearing:

- "Saddam Hussein had five hundred tons of sarin gas, mustard and VK nerve agents."
- "Saddam Hussein had approximately thirty thousand weapons capable of dumping chemical weapons on innocent people."
- "According to intelligence Iraq has a growing fleet of manned and unmanned aerial vehicles that could be used to disperse chemical or biological weapons across broad areas."
- "According to evidence from intelligence sources, secret communications and statements by people now in custody stating Saddam Hussein aids and protects terrorists, to include members of Al-Qaeda."
- "Our intelligence sources tell us that Saddam Hussein has attempted to purchase high-strength aluminum tubes suitable for nuclear weapon production."
- "Satellite photography reveals that Iraq is rebuilding facilities at 'sites'"
- "The British government has learned that Saddam Hussein recently sought significant quantities of uranium from Africa."
- "We know he's been absolutely devoted to trying to acquire nuclear weapons, and we believe he has, in fact, reconstituted nuclear weapons."
- "We gave him a chance to allow the inspectors in, and he wouldn't let them in."

The Tragedy of Vietnam, Again

Every one of these statements George W. Bush made in his State of the Union Speech before Congress in February 2002 has turned out to be untrue; history has already validated this point.

Mr. Bush has consistently stated when anyone criticized his handling of the war, "I listen to what my commanders on the ground do and what they say," or words to that effect. It was reported by the *Washington Post* regarding President Bush's desire to increase the troop strength in Iraq, over the objections of the commanders on the ground, the President said, "I will listen, but not necessarily defer to the present military commanders in the field. A senior aide said later that Bush would not let the military decide the matter. 'He's never left the decision to commanders,' said the aid, who spoke on condition of anonymity so Bush's comments would be the only ones on the record."

(Footnote - Washington Post Staff Writer, Thursday, December 21, 2006)

This is a reassuring revelation considering George W. Bush's outstanding record of military service during the Vietnam War.

It's frustrating to live in a situation where many restrictions have been placed on our freedoms, that the American public is entitled to enjoy under the Constitution and our Bill of Rights. These two documents, the Constitution and our Bill of Rights, are the bedrock that guides this country. Our government has ordered agencies to spy as to what books are read in our public libraries, and have our telephone calls listened to by super computers. It appears that controls have been put on the press as well, especially news from Iraq. This is not the American way of doing business; it gives the appearance of a closed, controlled state that does not trust its citizens.

In my opinion, what this administration did was not candid, nor forthright in dealing with the American people or with the world. I feel what was crafted was a campaign to topple Saddam Hussein, one that was skillfully planned and was designed to win over the American public, possibly before President Bush took office in 2000. This campaign was to win over the American people for war by tying Iraq to the War on Terror, in response to the World Trade Center attack, by Al-Qaeda, on 9/11. President Bush announced to the world that he was on a crusade—what a poor choice of words, but may have been the most truthful of all words ever spoken by George W. Bush.

This administration also painted Saddam Hussein as a co-conspirator with Osama Bin Laden in the attacks on New York City. President Bush, Vice President Cheney, and members of the cabinet all said, "We need to bring this evil dictator to justice." Saddam was never a co-conspirator as the government claimed, and Iraq was never used as a training base for Bin Laden. Saddam was obsessed with total control of his country and could not allow a person, such as Bin Laden, a base to operate from. This does not say that Saddam

The Tragedy of Vietnam, Again

Hussein should not be held accountable for his evil doings.

Unfortunately our government has given our children and probably our grandchildren an enormous debt to pay back, approximately two to three trillion dollars, (that is twelve zeros behind the two or three). President Bush and Congress gave away approximately $262 billion dollars (that is nine zeros behind the 262) to mostly the more affluent Americans.

Mr. Bush could have gone down in history as one of our better presidents, if this money had been invested into massive improvements within our country, improvements that are desperately needed today: such as developing alternative fuels for this country, improving all our roads and bridges that are currently falling down, fixing all our public school buildings that are in disrepair, and developing or improving mass transit systems for most major population centers. That amount of money could have covered the cost for most, if not all of what this nation needs today. We don't need a two to three trillion dollar debt.

The present president may have not, in my opinion, acted "to preserve, protect and defend the Constitution of the United States". Vice President Cheney, also may not have not lived up to his oath of office "...to protect the Constitution and the United States from all enemies, foreign and domestic, and that he will bear true faith and allegiance to the same..." Both of these men swore upon the Bible to protect our country, twice.

If someone made false statements to bring our nation into war against another country, and knowingly used false evidence, then our administration has a huge problem, especially if this was all done for a possible third nation. If proven, I can envision that our administration could be brought up on charges under the Constitution's Impeachment Clause for high crimes for misusing the national security intelligence data. I feel it would also be a violation under some federal anti-conspiracy statute, which would make it a federal crime to defraud the United States, or any of its agencies.

I understand that in January of 2008 the executive branch of our government was told to stop destroying electronic communications from executive branch computers. Why was the executive branch doing this? Are they trying to cover their tracks? Are they trying to destroy evidence that could be used against them, maybe after they leave office? These are questions that need to be answered.

I hope our executive branch of government will have to defend its actions in a court of law. I hope that our president does not pardon people within his administration "for any and all crimes that they may have committed," as they leave office, because if that is done, then we the people will all know that those people violated their oaths of office and have disgraced our country.

The president has a larger problem, because he can not pardon himself. The only way I could see a pardon

The Tragedy of Vietnam, Again

for this president is after he has testified under oath, and if he is found to be guilty, then the sitting president, at that time, should give "this president" a pardon only to protect the "institution of the presidency." Strings should be attached to this pardon, such as this President will never represent this government ever again, under any circumstance; that he will basically retire and never be seen again, in any public forum. It appears this administration may go down in American history as one of our worst, if not the worst administration we ever have had. Many citizens feel this administration has done more harm to our country than all our enemies put together. Our old friends around the world not only dislike the American government, but many of the American public as well. Much of Europe regards the United States today, as we regarded the former Soviet Union, not so long ago, as the "Evil Empire."

I speak not as an un-American, or as an anti-Republican, or as a Democrat who has nothing to offer, and I'm not a Liberal; I'm a very disappointed American who is fiscally responsible and who's ashamed of what is going on in our country today. I'm embarrassed as how our elected officials don't work together for the betterment of this nation as a whole, and do what is correct, rather than only work for their Special Interests.

We have a majority in our Senate and House of Representatives, Democrats, Republican and Independents, whose members have capitulated and have not done theirs job for a number of years, except to feather the members' own nests and interests. Why, why did Senator Arlen Specter suddenly decided to hold hearings about the New England Patriots "spygate" just three days before the Super Bowl was to be played? Doesn't Senator Specter have other issues much more compelling to deal with than football, or is he placating some of his special interests? If this is what he feels is urgent for our nation, then it's time for Senator Specter to leave government office. I only use Senator Specter, because this is typical of what I'm talking about regarding our politicians and how they are totally ineffective; especially the earmarks that are attached to almost all important pieces of legislation. Earmarks get these politicians reelected over and over, and we the people have to pay the financial bill.

We the people of this land need to look at our government and we the people need to make some basic changes to get our fine country back on the correct course. The tragedy of Vietnam and Iraq is that our government, whether it is Republican, Democrat, or Independent; they for the most part lie constantly and are self-serving. They do not look out for the people's best interest; they look out only for themselves and their special interests, so they can get re-elected. Our government caters to special interests that may have instigated the war in Iraq, through our backdoor. Remember Vice President Cheney repeatedly said

The Tragedy of Vietnam, Again

before the war started, "This is good for our friends in the neighborhood."

The United States should never fight another war unless we, here in North America, are attacked and we go directly after those who committed the aggressive act in such a way as to remove the guilty in a crushing defeat. This is what we did after Pearl Harbor was attacked and when the World Trade Center was attacked. Vietnam never attacked America, Iraq never attacked America. The United States did not follow through in going after Bin Laden, in Afghanistan, and as a result we still have that national security problem lurking about for seven years now; this problem needs to be addressed, by the world, sooner than later.

The choice is in the American public's hands to speak out and to vote capable people into office. You may not like the individual, but is that person qualified to run our country or be a Senator, etc? We need to elect not career politicians into public office, but the most talented people available based upon quantifiable accomplishments, not a lot of hot-aired individuals who have slick tongues and have accomplished almost nothing in their lives.

We also need a fair and honest press to make our democracy work, for this country as a whole, not for their special interest groups, no matter who they may be. The press needs to validate candidate claims as to their accomplishments, or if in fact are they truly qualified. Stop trying to manipulate our elections. Report the news; stop trying to make the news.

This holds true for government officials at all levels in local, state, and federal government—stop trying to manipulate the legislative process, distorting facts and serving special interests. What Washington needs is fresh brains and term limits; we need to flush out all the hacks, both young and old, who have out lived their usefulness.

The tragedies for the Vietnam veterans is the same for the Iraq veterans; we both went off to war basically as naïve and patriotic young people, going to defend our country. Unbeknownst to us, our government, both times, did not tell the truth in sending us off to war. The tragedy is that our nation has not learned from our mistakes in the past, and if we, as a nation don't learn from our mistakes, we will repeatedly make the same mistakes again and again; just like the expression, "History repeats it's self." This is the grossest of tragedies our government can possibly orchestrate.

* * * * *

Appendix 1

A CHRONOLOGY OF EVENTS

PRESIDENT	AVERAGE AGE OF MEDIC	DATE	EVENT
Eisenhower	12 y.o.	5/5-19/57	President Diem visits US and US pledges to help South Vietnam.
	15 y.o.	4/17/60	North Vietnam accuses US of turning South Vietnam into a base for preparation of war.
		5/1/60	American U-2 plane with pilot Frances Gary Powers shot down over Russia.
	15 y.o.	5/13/60	VP Nixon announces additional aid for South Vietnam.
		5/23/60	Adolf Eichmann captured by Israelis in Argentina.

The Tragedy of Vietnam, Again

PRESIDENT	AVERAGE AGE OF MEDIC	DATE	EVENT
		8/7/60	Cuba begins confiscation of $770 million of US properties.
	16 y. o.	1/3/61	US breaks diplomatic relations with Cuba.
Kennedy		1/20/61	JFK inaugurated.
		4/12/61	Moscow announces putting first man in orbit around earth.
		4/17/61	Cuba invaded, at Bay of Pigs, by approx. 1,200 anti-Castro exiles.
		5/5/61	First US astronaut, Alan B. Shepard, rode a rocket 116 miles around the earth's surface and traveled a total of 302 miles from launch pad to splash down.

Appendix 1

PRESIDENT	AVERAGE AGE OF MEDIC	DATE	EVENT
		5/6/61	Kennedy says US considering use of US armed forces to prevent a Communist takeover of South Vietnam.
	16 y. o.	5/16/61	VP Johnson announces in Saigon additional US military and economic aid will be given to South Vietnam.
		7/21/61	Virgil Grissom becomes second American astronaut.
		8/6/61	Soviets launch spacecraft that makes 17.5 orbits in twenty-five hours.
		8/13/61	East Germany erects Berlin Wall between East and West Berlin.

The Tragedy of Vietnam, Again

PRESIDENT	AVERAGE AGE OF MEDIC	DATE	EVENT
Kennedy	16 y. o.	10/11/61	Kennedy announces he is sending General Maxwell Taylor to South Vietnam for a survey and report.
		10/13/61	Kennedy makes speech, headlines read: "Kennedy vows to keep US Alive and Free – Neither Red nor Dead."
		10/29/61	USSR blasts a fifty-megaton hydrogen bomb, biggest man-made explosion in world history. Headlines a few days later read: "Red Fallout Contaminates Milk in U.S."

Appendix 1

PRESIDENT	AVERAGE AGE OF MEDIC	DATE	EVENT
Kennedy		11/16/61	Kennedy decides to bolster South Vietnam's military strength, but not commit US combat forces at this time.
	17 y. o.	2/20/62	John Glenn is first American to orbit Earth.
		2/24/62	Red China declares her security is threatened by "undeclared war" of US forces in South Vietnam.
		4/30/12	Secretary of Defense Robert S. McNamara makes first inspection trip to South Vietnam.
		5/31/62	Adolf Eichmann hanged in Israel.
		7/3/62	Algeria obtains independence from France.

The Tragedy of Vietnam, Again

PRESIDENT	AVERAGE AGE OF MEDIC	DATE	EVENT
		8/11/62	Cuban Missile Crisis: USSR tries to build missile base in Cuba. JFK orders Cuban blockade.
		10/1/62	James Meredith is escorted by federal marshals in order to register at University of Mississippi.
Kennedy	17 y.o.	(*)10/30/62	US troops stationed in South Vietnam equal ten thousand men.
		12/24/62	Cuban releases over one thousand prisoners from Bay of Pigs invasion attempt.
	18 y.o.	3-21/63	Pope John XXIII dies and the ritual of choosing a new pope – Pope Paul VI.

(*) The first large increase of American troops into South Vietnam

Appendix 1

PRESIDENT	AVERAGE AGE OF MEDIC	DATE	EVENT
		6/17/63	US Supreme Court bans Lord's Prayer and Bible verses in public schools.
		8/28/63	Two hundred thousand blacks and whites hold rally in Washington, D.C.
		9/2/63	The "Hot Line" installed between Washington and Moscow.
		10/2/63	Robert McNamara and General Taylor go on second trip to South Vietnam. McNamara says, "The major part of the US military task can be completed by the end of 1965."
Johnson	18 y o	11/22/63	JFK assassinated in Dallas.
		12/18-21/63	McNamara's third trip to South Vietnam.

The Tragedy of Vietnam, Again

PRESIDENT	AVERAGE AGE OF MEDIC	DATE	EVENT
Johnson	19 y o	12/31/63	US troop strength in South Vietnam at sixteen thousand.
		1/9/64	Panama suspends relations with US.
		/27/64	US Supreme Court rules that Congressional Districts must represent the population of each district as much as possible.
		3/6/64	McNamara's fourth trip to South Vietnam.
		3/14/64	Jack Ruby, convicted murderer of Lee Harvey Oswald sentenced to death by a Dallas jury.
		5/11//64	McNamara's fifth trip to South Vietnam.

Appendix 1

PRESIDENT	AVERAGE AGE OF MEDIC	DATE	EVENT
		5/20/64	Death toll to date, 132 US killed in combat in South Vietnam.
	19 y. o	5/27/64	US reports sending military planes to Laos.
		6/22/64	Three civil rights workers, Schwerner, Goodman, Chaney, murdered in Mississippi.
		6/29/64	Civil rights bill passes banning discrimination in voting, jobs, public accommodations, etc.
		(*)8/7-11/64	Congress approves the Southeast Asian Resolution, authorizing aid to Vietnam. Johnson signs bill.

(*) The Gulf of Tonkin Resolution

The Tragedy of Vietnam, Again

PRESIDENT	AVERAGE AGE OF MEDIC	DATE	EVENT
		9/27/64	President's commission on the assassination of JFK issues Warren Report conclusions.
		12/18/64	New Panama Treaty negotiated.
Johnson	20 y. o.	2/1/65	Martin Luther King and twenty-six hundred others arrested in Selma, Alabama.
		2/7/65	Johnson orders continuous bombing of North Vietnam below the twentieth parallel.
		2/21/65	Malcolm X is assassinated in NYC.
		3/8/65	First US combat troops, thirty-five hundred Marines, land in Da Nang, South Vietnam.

Appendix 1

PRESIDENT	AVERAGE AGE OF MEDIC	DATE	EVENT
		4/28/65	Fourteen thousand US Marines land in the Dominican Republic during their civil war.
		7/28/65	LBJ orders US troops increased to one hundred twenty-five thousand.
		8/11-16/65	Blacks riot for six days in Watts section of LA. Fire damage est. $170 million. Thirty-Four dead, over one thousand injured, nearly four thousand arrested.
		11/9-10/65	The blackout of eight northeastern states and parts of two provinces of Canada.
	21 y o	3/15/66	Black teenagers riot in Watts.

The Tragedy of Vietnam, Again

PRESIDENT	AVERAGE AGE OF MEDIC	DATE	EVENT
		10/24/66	LBJ attends Manila conference. Pledges to win war and rebuild Southeast Asia.
		1/1/67	Year begins with heavy fighting from DMZ to Delta in South Vietnam.
	22 y. o	1/27/67	Three Apollo astronauts—Grissom, White, and Chaffee killed in spacecraft fire during a test launch.
		6/5/67	Israeli and Arab Six Day War.
Johnson	22y.o.	6/23-25/67	Glassboro, New Jersey, summit between LBJ and Alexei Kosygin.

Appendix 1

PRESIDENT	AVERAGE AGE OF MEDIC	DATE	EVENT
		7/23/67	Racial violence in Detroit; Harlem; Rochester, New York; Birmingham Alabama; etc.
		8/31/67	Senate Preparedness Subcommittee urges to widen the air war in Vietnam.
		11/7/67	San Francisco votes against immediate Vietnam withdrawal.
		11/24/67	I have my orders to report for duty in the Republic of Vietnam.

Appendix 2

Definitions of Terms Used

AFVN	Armed Forces Vietnam radio station
AK-47	Soviet-made Kalashnikov automatic assault rifle
ALPHA	US Military phonic letter A
Ammo Dump	Location where live or expended ammunition is stored
AO	Area of operation
AOD	Administrative officer on duty
ACAV	Armored cavalry assault vehicle
APC	Modified ACAV used as a fighting vehicle with turret armor for the track commander, gun shields for the .50-caliber machine gun and two side-mounted gun shields and mounts for M60 machine guns.
APO	Army post office in San Francisco for overseas mail to Vietnam
AR	Army Regulation
Article 15	Section of the Uniform Military Code of Justice—a form of nonjudicial punishment
ARVN	South Vietnamese soldier

The Tragedy of Vietnam, Again

AWOL	Absent With Out Leave
BRAVO	US Military phonic letter B
B-52	US Air Force high altitude bomber
Boc-si	Vietnamese word for doctor
Band-Aid	Name for medics' APC
Battalion	A military unit consisting of four troops or companies equaling consisting from 300 up to 1,000 soldiers; 1/1 Cav had approximately 950 men, no women.
Battery	An artillery unit equivalent to approximately one hundred and fifty men
Bird	anytype of aircraft
Body Bag	A plastic bag used to transport the dead from the field
Boonies	A term used to describe going way out into the countryside
Bronze Star	US military decoration award for heroic and meritorious service, not involving aerial flight
BS	Bull S---
CHARLIE	US Military phonic letter C
C-4	Plastic, putty-like explosive. It burns white hot and when charged can make a violent explosion

Appendix 2

C-130	Large four-engine Air Force cargo plane
Cache	A hiding place
C+C	Command and control helicopter
Carbine	A short-barreled, lightweight automatic or semiautomatic rifle
CAV	Cavalry, the First of the First Cavalry
Chinook	CH-47 large cargo helicopter
Chop Chop	Slang for food in Vietnam
Claymore	Antipersonnel mine, when detonated propels small steel cubes in a 60-degree fan-shaped pattern to a maximum range of one hundred meters or three hundred feet
CO	Commanding officer
Cobra	AH-1G attack helicopter
Code of Conduct	Military rules for US soldiers taken prisoner by the enemy
COL	Colonel
"Commo"	Shorthand for communications
CP	Command post
C ration	Combat rations, canned meals for use in the field
CS	A riot control gas that burns the eyes and mucus membranes. It comes both in gas or crystal form

The Tragedy of Vietnam, Again

DELTA	US Military phonic letter D
DEROS	Army term meaning date of expected return from overseas
Duce-and-a-half	A two-and-a-half-ton truck
Dink	A derogatory term for an Asian
Dinky dau	To be crazy, from "diem cai dau"
Doc	Medic or corpsman
Dust Off	Medical evacuation by helicopter
ECHO	US Military phonic letter E
EM	Enlisted men
Evac'd	Medically evacuated by helicopter
First of the First	1/1 Armored Cav
FLA	Frontline Ambulance
Foxtrot	US Military phonic letter F
Frag	Fragmentation grenade
Freq	Radio frequency
Friendly fire	Accidental attack on US or allied soldiers by other US or allied soldiers
GD	God Damn
GED	General Educational Development certificate
GOLF	US Military phonic letter G
GI	Government issue
Gook	Derogatory term for an Asian
Green Berets	US Special Forces
Grunt	Infantryman
Gunship	Armed helicopter

Appendix 2

HOTEL	US Military phonic letter H
Hamlet	A small rural village
H/E	High explosive
Ho Chi Minh	The leader of North Vietnam
Hooch	A hut or simple dwelling
Hot area	under fire
Hot LZ	A landing zone under fire
HQ	Headquarters
Huey	Nickname for the UH-1 series helicopter
INDIA	US military phonic letter I
I CORPS	The northern most military region in South Vietnam
II Corps	The Central Highlands military region in South Vietnam
In-country	in Vietnam
JULIETT	US Military phonic letter J
Jungle boots	footwear that looked like a combination of combat boot and canvas sneaker used by the US military in tropical climates, where leather rots because of the dampness
Jungle fatigues	Lightweight tropical fatigues
Jungle Rot	Jock itch, easily cured by not wearing underwear in Vietnam.
KILO	US Military phonic letter K
Kick	one kilometer, or a little over one thousand yards
KP	Kitchen police or mess hall duty

The Tragedy of Vietnam, Again

LIMA	US Military phonic letter L
Line number	a unique number that identifies a particular soldier
Line Troop	Soldiers who go out looking for the enemy day in and day out
Litters	Stretchers to carry the dead and wounded
Little People	The enemy
Loach/LOH	Light observation helicopter
LRRP	Long Range Reconnaissance Patrol—an elite team usually comprised of four to seven members who go deep into the countryside to observe the enemy activities without being seen or making contact
LST	Troop landing ship
LT	Lieutenant
LTC	Lieutenant colonel
LZ	Landing zone
MIKE	US military phonic letter M
M-16	The standard US military rifle used in Vietnam
M-60	The standard lightweight machine gun used in Vietnam
Mad Minute	A weapon free fire for practice or emergency defense
Mama San	slang used by US forces for older women

Appendix 2

Med Cap	Medical Civil Action Program or Medical Civilian Aid Program
Med Evac	Medical evacuation from the field by helicopter
MFW	Mike Foxtrot Whisky—Multiple Frag Wounds
MIA	Missing in action
Mortar	A muzzle loading cannon with a short tube to lob rounds at the enemy from a short distance
MP	Military police
NOVEMBER	US military phonic letter N
Napalm	A jelly gasoline mix that burns fiercely
NCO	Non-commissioned officer (sergeant)
Number One	Slang for the Vietnamese—The Very Best
Number Ten	Slang for the Vietnamese—The Very Worst
NVA	North Vietnamese army, soldier
OCS	Officer Candidate School
OCSAR	US Military phonic letter O
PAPA	US Military phonic letter P
P-38	A tiny collapsible can opener
Papa San	Slang for older Vietnamese men
Perimeter	Outer limits to our area—beyond belongs to the enemy
PFC	Private first class

The Tragedy of Vietnam, Again

Platoon	A subdivision of a troop or company size military unit normally consisting of two or more squads.
Poncho Liner	A nylon insert to a poncho, also used as a blanket
Pop Smoke	To ignite a smoke grenade to signal and aircraft
POW	Prisoner of war
Puff the magic Dragon	also called Puff—An USAF AC-47 propeller-driven aircraft gunship, with five or more mini guns along one side of the ship. Each mini gun was capable of firing six thousand rounds a minute and was used to provide ground support.
QUEBEC	US military phonic letter Q
Quad-50	a four-barreled assembly of .50-caliber machine guns
ROMEO	US military phonic letter R
R+R	Rest and recreation
Recon	Reconnaissance
Red Ball	An enemy high-speed trail or road, a truck convoy
REMF	Rear-echelon mother f----er, the rear echelon personnel were hated by the line troops

Appendix 2

ROTC	Reserve Officer Training Program offered at various colleges and universities across the country
RPG	Rocket-propelled grenade—a Russian-made portable anti-tank launcher
SERIA	US military phonic letter S
S-1	Personnel
S-2	Intelligence
S-3	Operations
S-4	Supply
S-5	Civil affairs
Saddle Up	Put on your gear because we are ready to go
Search and Destroy	An operation in which the Americans search an area and destroy anything that the enemy might find useful
Short	A term used by everyone in Vietnam to indicate your tour of duty in Vietnam is about to end
Silver Star	US Military decoration award for gallantry in action
Six	any unit commander from company up
Smoke grenade	a grenade that releases brightly colored smoke. Used to signal helicopters
SOB	Son of a bitch

Spec 4	Specialist 4th Class—equivalent to a corporal
Spec 5	Specialist 5th Class—equivalent to a sergeant
Spider Hole	Camouflaged enemy foxhole
Starlight Scope	An image intensifier using reflected light to identify targets in the dead of night
Steel Pot	Helmet
Syrette	collapsible tube of morphine attached to a hypodermic needle. The contents of the tube were injected by squeezing it like a toothpaste tube
TANGO	US military phonic letter T
Tet	Buddhist lunar New Year. Buddha's birthday
Tet Offensive	1968, a major uprising of the Viet Cong, VC sympathizers, and the NVA characterized by a series of coordinated attacks against military installations and provincial capitals throughout South Vietnam.
TOC	Tactical Operations Center
Triage	The procedure for deciding the order in which to treat casualties, so those who can survive will survive. The most seriously

Appendix 2

	injured may not be the first to be treated.
Tunnel rat	a soldier who crawls through enemy tunnels killing any enemy and gathering any and all intelligence material.
UNIFORM	US military phonic letter U
USAF	United States Air Force
USARV	United States Army Republic of Vietnam Command
VICTOR	US military phonic letter V
VC	Viet Cong
Ville	Vietnamese village
WHISKY	US military phonic letter W
WIA	Wounded in action
Wood line	Row of trees or the start of a wooded area
"The Wool"	The edge of dense vegetation that a tank or APC could plow through.
WP, Willie Pete	White phosphorus
X-RAY	US military phonic letter X
XO	Executive officer
YANKEE	US military phonic letter Y
ZULU	US military phonic letter Z
Zippo	A flame-throwing APC, or any flame-throwing device

Appendix 3

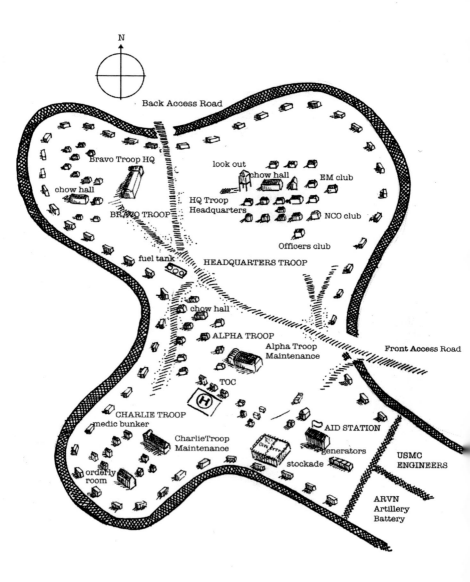

Appendix 4

1/1 Cav's Battle Map

1. Dink Valley - September, 1967
2. Cigar Island - October, 1967
3. Area Cow - October, 1967
4. Que Son Valley - November, 1967 - January, 1968
5. Pineapple Forest - December, 1967
6. Tam Ky - January, 1968
7. Pink Ville - February, 1968
8. Pineapple Forest - February, 1968
9. Western Valley - March, 1968
10. Cigar Island - March, 1968
11. Burlington Trail - April-May, 1968
12. Western Valley - May, 1968
13. Battle for Tam Ky - August, 1968

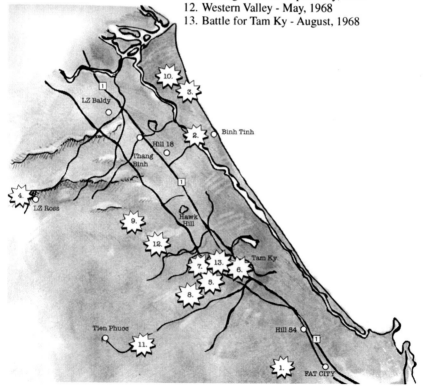

Made in the USA